American Red Cross

AMERICAN RED CROSS
W.A.T.E.R.
safety

instructor's manual

Mosby
Year Book

St. Louis Baltimore Boston Chicago London Philadelphia Sydney Toronto

Printed in the United States of America

Mosby-Year Book, Inc.
11830 Westline Industrial Drive
St. Louis, MO 63146

ISBN 0–8016–6941–3

92 93 94 95 96 B 9 8 7 6 5 4 3 2 1

ACKNOWLEDGEMENTS

The American Red Cross Swimming and Diving textbook and Water Safety Instructor's Manual were developed and produced through a joint effort of the American Red Cross and the Mosby-Year Book Publishing Company.

Members of the Development Team at American Red Cross national headquarters responsible for developing this instructor's manual included: Earl Harbert, Manager, Customer Service; Rhonda Starr, Senior Associate, Aquatics Project; Thomas J. S. Edwards, Ph.D., Kathy D. Scruggs, M.A., and Trudi VanDyke, M.S., Associates; Terry Cooper, Treecee Engler-Polgar, Patricia A. Terrell, Analysts; and Susan M. Stimpfle, M.Ed., editor. Administrative support was provided by Debra E. Clemons and Gloria Harris.

The following American Red Cross national headquarters Health and Safety paid and volunteer staff provided guidance and review: Frank Carroll, Manager, Israel Zuniga, Associate, and Stephen Silverman, Ed.D., National Volunteer Consultant, Program Development; Karen White, Marketing Specialist, External Relations; and Kathy Oberlin, Associate, Operations.

The Mosby-Year Book Production team included: Virgil Mette, Executive Vice President; David T. Culverwell, Vice President and Publisher; Richard A. Weimer, Executive Editor; Mary Beth Warthen, Developmental Editor; Carol S. Wiseman, Project Manager; David S. Brown, Production Editor; Kay Kramer, Director of Design; Jerry A. Wood, Director of Manufacturing, Patricia Stinecipher, Special Product Manager; and Theresa Fuchs, Manufacturing Supervisor.

Special thanks go to Tom Lochhaas, Ed.D., Developmental Editor; Joseph Matthews, Elizabeth Roll, and Daniel Cima, Photographers; Jane Moore, Desktop Publishing Specialist, and to Michael Espino, Director of Health and Safety Services, American Red Cross, Santa Barbara County Chapter, for his work on the Water Safety Instructor Aide course.

We would also like to thank the American Red Cross at Fort Belvoir, Virginia, and the management and staff of the Benyaurd Pool (Community Recreation Division) at Fort Belvoir and the Fairfax County Park Authority—Providence Recreation Center for providing locations and talent for the photographs in this manual.

The following American Red Cross chapters assisted with pilot testing sections of the instructor's manual:

Mid-America Chapter, Chicago, Illinois

American Red Cross of Massachusetts Bay, Boston, Massachusetts

Syracuse & Onondaga County Chapter, Syracuse, New York

Lancaster County Chapter, Lancaster, Pennsylvania

Summit County Chapter, Akron, Ohio

Greater Cleveland Chapter, Cleveland, Ohio

Palm Beach County Chapter, West Palm Beach, Florida

Lehigh Valley Chapter, Bethlehem, Pennsylvania

Dutchess County Chapter, Poughkeepsie, New York

Southeastern Michigan Chapter, Detroit, Michigan

Greater Houston Area Chapter, Houston, Texas

Dallas Area Chapter, Dallas, Texas

Knoxville Area Chapter, Knoxville, Tennessee

Bluegrass Area Chapter, Lexington, Kentucky

Santa Barbara County Chapter, Santa Barbara, California

Tucson Chapter, Tucson, Arizona

Central Arizona Chapter, Phoenix, Arizona

Oregon Trail Chapter, Portland, Oregon

Central Massachusetts Chapter, Worcester, Massachusetts

Pensacola Chapter, Pensacola, Florida

American Red Cross in Greater New York, New York, New York

Central Florida Chapter, Orlando, Florida

Indianapolis Area Chapter, Indianapolis, Indiana

Oklahoma County Chapter, Oklahoma City, Oklahoma

Seattle-King County Chapter, Seattle, Washington

Guidance and review were also provided by members of the American Red Cross Swimming Advisory Committee:

Stephen Langendorfer, Ph.D., Committee Chair, and Associate Professor of Motor Development/Developmental Aquatics, School of Physical Education, Recreation, and Dance Kent State University, Kent, Ohio

Elaine Bird, M.Ed., Committee Vice Chair and Associate Director and Aquatic Director, Division of Leisure Sports, Louisiana State University, Baton Rouge, Louisiana and Field Service Chairman, American Red Cross, Region 3, Territory 11, Baton Rouge, Louisiana

Chrys Baird, Health Specialist, American Red Cross, Montgomery County Chapter, Silver Spring, Maryland

Bruce Carney, M.A. Ed., Deputy Director of Safety & Health, American Red Cross in Greater New York, New York, New York

Paul Crutchfield, Assistant Director of Parks and Recreation, Spokane Parks and Recreation Department, Spokane, Washington, and Member, Board of Directors, American Red Cross, Inland Empire Chapter, Spokane, Washington

Gerald DeMers, Ph.D., Assistant Professor and Director, Aquatic Program, Physical Education and Recreation Administration Department, California Polytechnic State University, San Luis Obispo, California, and Health & Safety Volunteer Specialist, American Red Cross, San Luis Obispo Chapter, San Luis Obispo, California

Terri Elder, M.Ed., Aquatic Coordinator, The Heskett Center, Wichita State University, Wichita, Kansas, and Volunteer Safety Specialist in Water Safety, American Red Cross, Region 3, Territory 2, Wichita, Kansas

Susan Grosse, M.S., Physical Education Instructor, Milwaukee High School of the Arts, Milwaukee, Wisconsin, and Volunteer Instructor Trainer, American Red Cross, Greater Milwaukee Chapter, Milwaukee, Wisconsin

Mark Hokkanen, M.S.T., Director, Aquatic and Wellness Center, Oklahoma City Community College, Oklahoma City, Oklahoma, and Volunteer Instructor Trainer, American Red Cross, Oklahoma County Chapter, Oklahoma City, Oklahoma

Neill Miller, M.S., Associate Professor of Physical Education, Department of Sport and Recreational Sciences, Barry University, Miami Shores, Florida, and Member, Health and Safety Committee, American Red Cross, Greater Miami Chapter, Miami, Florida

Ed Morford, M.Ed., Director of Aquatics, State University of New York, Delhi, New York, and Volunteer Instructor Trainer, American Red Cross, Delaware County Chapter, Delhi, New York

Fontaine Piper, Ph.D., Director and Associate Professor, Biomechanics/Motor Learning Laboratory, Division of Health and Exercise Science, Northeast Missouri State University, Kirksville, Missouri, and Adjunct Associate Professor of Anatomy, Department of Anatomy, Kirksville College of Osteopathic Medicine, Kirksville, Missouri, and Volunteer Instructor Trainer, American Red Cross, Adair County Chapter, Kirksville, Missouri

Craig Ritz, M.Ed., Aquatics Coordinator, Office of Recreational Services, Rutgers University, New Brunswick, New Jersey, and Past Chair, American Alliance for Health, Physical Education, Recreation &, Dance—Aquatics Council, Reston, Virginia, and Volunteer Aquatics Coordinator, Health and Safety Committee, American Red Cross, Central New Jersey Chapter, New Brunswick, New Jersey

External review was provided by the following organizations and individuals:

R. Ann Hood Weiser, M.S., M.F.A., Coordinator of Aquatics Instruction, University of North Carolina, Greensboro, North Carolina

Dennis A. Munroe, M.S., Director of Aquatics, University of Oregon, Eugene, Oregon

Tom Griffiths, Ed.D., Director of Aquatics, The Pennsylvania State University, University Park, Pennsylvania

Virginia Reister, M.Ed., Aquatics and Rehabilitation Management Consultant, Johnson City, Tennessee

Liane M. Summerfield, Ph.D., Professor of Physical Fitness Management and Department Chair, Marymount University, Arlington, Virginia

Diane Davis, Ph.D., Director of Student Teaching, Bowie State University, Bowie, Maryland

Jim R. Wenhold, M.A., Aquatic Director, University of Maryland, College Park, Maryland

TABLE OF CONTENTS

administration

A

1 | introduction

This manual is a resource for those authorized by the American Red Cross to teach the following American Red Cross Swimming and Water Safety courses:

- Infant and Preschool Aquatics Program (IPAP)
- Water Exploration (Level I in the American Red Cross Learn to Swim program)
- Primary Skills (Level II)
- Stroke Readiness (Level III)
- Stroke Development (Level IV)
- Stroke Refinement (Level V)
- Skill Proficiency (Level VI)
- Advanced Skills (Level VII)
- Basic Water Safety
- Emergency Water Safety
- Water Safety Instructor Aide

All Water Safety Instructors are authorized to teach these courses. Selected Water Safety Instructors may teach the Safety Training for Swim Coaches course.

This manual provides information and teaching suggestions to help you plan and conduct these courses safely and effectively, maintaining Red Cross standards. Before you teach any of these courses, you should be familiar with *American Red Cross Swimming and Diving* (Stock No. 652000), this instructor's manual, and the relevant materials listed on pages 6–8 and in Appendix A.

This manual also contains suggestions for teaching people who may have special needs—infants and preschoolers, people with disabilities, adult beginners, and older adults. Also included are resources to help you to add fitness components and games and water activities to your courses. Instructors eligible to teach the Safety Training for Swim Coaches course must also use *American Red Cross Safety Training for Swim Coaches* (Stock No. 329449) and *American Red Cross Safety Training for Swim Coaches Instructor's Manual* (Stock No. 329450). The Basic Water Safety and the Emergency Water Safety courses are also treated in the *American Red Cross Basic Water Safety and Emergency Water Safety Instructor's Manual* (Stock No. 329314).

PURPOSE OF THE PROGRAM

The primary purpose of the American Red Cross Swimming and Water Safety program is to help people learn to be safe when they are in, on, or around water. The program covers skills and knowledge in a logical progression for aquatic skill development. As participants develop these skills, they will become safer and better swimmers.

COURSE OBJECTIVES

The objectives of each course are provided along with the outline for that course. Appendix B, Performance Standards, describes how well participants should perform strokes in the American Red Cross Learn to Swim program.

PURPOSE AND FORMAT OF THE INSTRUCTOR'S MANUAL

This instructor's manual has eight parts.

Part A, Administration, introduces the Swimming and Water Safety program, tells how to set up and teach courses, describes course organization, gives administrative information about program operation, discusses risk management, and describes course completion procedures.

Part B, Learning Theory, discusses the teaching and learning process in detail, including the principles of motor learning. It contains suggestions you can use in teaching your courses.

Part C, Elements of Course Design, explains how to prepare block plans and lesson plans for a full course. Part C also includes information on drills, formations, and the assembly line method of teaching.

Part D, The Infant and Preschool Aquatics Program (IPAP), covers what you need to teach infants, toddlers, and preschool students. It discusses issues that affect young learners and how to orient parents to the program. Part D gives outlines for the three levels of this program and progressions you can use to teach the skills.

Part E, The Learn to Swim Program, contains outlines for the seven courses in this program. It includes a discussion of support techniques and teaching progressions for basic skills, strokes, diving, and starts and turns.

Part F, Customizing the Program, helps you adapt your teaching approach when there are people with disabilities or adult beginners in your class. It also shows how to include fitness components and games and water activities in your program and how to help participants meet their individual goals and objectives.

Part G, Basic Water Safety and Emergency Water Safety, presents course outlines and lesson plans for the Basic Water Safety course and the Emergency Water Safety course.

Part H, Training Water Safety Instructor Aides, contains a course outline for the Water Safety Instructor Aide course.

Appendixes contain useful supplementary material and are referred to in appropriate places in the text.

INSTRUCTOR'S RESPONSIBILITIES

Your responsibilities as an American Red Cross Water Safety Instructor are to—
- Represent the American Red Cross in a positive manner.
- Be familiar with course materials and know how to use them effectively.
- Plan, coordinate, and manage courses in conjunction with the local Red Cross unit.
- Create a nonthreatening environment encouraging participants to meet course objectives.
- Remain alert to your own cultural and ethnic stereotypes and be creative and flexible in presenting material in a culturally sensitive and effective manner.
- Be prepared to answer participants' questions, or know where to find the answers.

- Adapt your teaching approaches to the experience, ability, and culture of participants so that they can meet course objectives.
- Provide for the health and safety of participants, including making sure that all teaching and practice areas are free of hazards and that materials and equipment are safe.
- Organize the class environment to enhance individual and group performance and to minimize distractions.
- Cover all material required in a course.
- Be able to demonstrate the skills required for completion of the Water Safety Instructor course.
- Use corrective feedback to evaluate participants' progress and correct problems.
- Supervise and give guidance to any Water Safety Instructor Aides assisting with a course.
- Administer and score the final examination when applicable.
- Ensure that participants meet course completion requirements.
- Submit completed course records and reports to Red Cross within the time required by the local Red Cross unit.
- Issue course-completion certificates.
- Be familiar with the Red Cross publications and brochures available at the local Red Cross unit.
- Identify potential instructor or instructor aide candidates and refer them to the appropriate Red Cross course.
- Promote other Red Cross courses and volunteer opportunities to course participants. Other Red Cross courses are listed on the inside back cover of *Swimming and Diving*.
- Meet the obligations in the *Instructor Agreement* (Form 6574) and, if applicable, the *Authorized Provider Agreement* (Form 6575).

> *Note:* Appendix C, Administrative Terms and Procedures, defines many of the terms and procedures you need to know as a Red Cross instructor. Appendix D discusses cultural diversity.

2 organizing and conducting courses

This chapter explains how to organize and conduct courses in the American Red Cross Swimming and Water Safety program. Chapter 3 discusses program planning for Water Safety Instructors who are program administrators.

PLANNING

You should start planning several months before the first lesson. Meet with your local Red Cross unit to discuss your proposed program. The unit may want to know the dates, times, and locations of the course(s). The unit will also assist you with—

■ Your authorization to teach.
■ The *Instructor Agreement* (Form 6574) and, if applicable, the *Authorized Provider Agreement* (Form 6575).
■ Local policies and procedures in addition to national guidelines.

Contact your local Red Cross unit for any other information you need before your first lesson and any time thereafter you have questions.

COURSE PARTICIPANTS

Instruction in the Red Cross Learn to Swim program involves no age requirements except in IPAP, where an infant must be at least 6 months old. There are no other restrictions on participation. In general, try to compose your class with participants of similar abilities and ages so you can more easily plan appropriate activities. Chapters 22 and 23 can help you plan for adult beginners and mainstream people with disabilities into your courses.

INSTRUCTOR-PARTICIPANT RATIO

The American Red Cross recommends that there be at least one instructor for every 10 participants in a course. With more than 10 participants, you should have a co-instructor or aide. Close supervi-

sion is needed to make practice effective and the class safe. You can help your participants reach their goals more easily if you keep the class size small. At least six participants per class are required for a course. For a class of fewer than six, prior written approval is needed from the local Red Cross unit. Recommended class sizes in the infant and preschool program vary with the age and ability of the children in the course. For more information, see page 54.

If you have participants with disabilities, you might want to have a smaller class or obtain additional help. Chapter 22 explains how to customize your course to meet the needs of these participants.

WATER SAFETY INSTRUCTOR AIDES

Guidelines for training Water Safety Instructor Aides are in Chapter 28. Instructor aides can help make large classes more successful since participants get more individual attention. The more trained instructor aides you use, the more individual attention can be given and the faster your participants can progress. Instructor aides are not a substitute for a second instructor.

To find candidates for Water Safety Instructor Aides, consider good swimmers aged 10 and older who might not have the age prerequisite, interest, or skills to become Water Safety Instructors but who want to help with water safety courses. Older adults are potential aide candidates and should not be overlooked.

FACILITIES AND STAFFING

To ensure your course is safe and successful, be sure your swimming facility has the right dimensions for your course. The course requirements in Chapter 16 may be modified if the water is too deep for participants to stand. The requirements must be modified if the water is not deep enough for safe diving. If you use open water, it should be free of surf and large enough to practice skills. It should have a clearly marked safe swimming area that is large enough and deep enough for your program. Courses for infants, toddlers, and preschoolers should not be conducted in open water, which is more likely than chlorinated pools to carry harmful organisms. If you are unsure whether your swimming area is appropriate, contact your local Red Cross unit for advice before offering courses.

At least one lifeguard should be present for all swimming lessons. The lifeguard's *only* duty should be to lifeguard the swimming area during lessons. (For more information on lifeguards, see page 11.) In addition, the facility should have an emergency action plan. This is a written plan detailing roles, responsibilities, and procedures in the event of an emergency. For more information see *Swimming and Diving,* page 27, and *American Red Cross Lifeguarding Instructor's Manual* (Stock No. 329453), pages 167–169. Be sure you know your responsibilities in such a plan, as well as the expectations for any co-instructors and instructor aides assisting you in a course. Your responsibilities are detailed in Chapter 4.

COURSE MATERIALS AND EQUIPMENT

American Red Cross Swimming and Diving

The basic resource for participants and instructors is *American Red Cross Swimming and Diving* (Stock No. 652000). The book describes and illustrates all the skills for the Swimming and Water Safety courses.

The book can help both you and the participants learn and understand the material. It includes the following features:

- **Key Terms**
  At the beginning of each chapter are listed key terms the participant needs to know to understand the chapter. Some key terms are listed in more than one chapter when they are essential to the material in each. In the chapter, key

terms are printed in bold italic type the first time they are discussed.

- **Learning Objectives**
  After the key terms is a list of objectives that participants should be able to meet after reading the chapter and participating in appropriate class activities.

- **Sidebars**
  Small articles inside the chapters give additional information to enhance the main text. They appear in a contrasting background. Included is a variety of material ranging from historical information to further applications of information in the chapter. This feature makes the book more interesting.

- **Figures**
  Extensive photographs and illustrations reinforce chapter concepts and information and vividly show how to do the aquatic skills.

- **Appendixes**
  The book contains six appendixes:
  - Appendix A lists organizations that promote aquatics.
  - Appendix B discusses exercises for stretching and aquatic exercise.
  - Appendix C contains blank tables for calculating target heart rate ranges.
  - Appendix D discusses equipment used in aquatic activities.
  - Appendix E describes the Emergency Medical Services (EMS) system and provides a form for making emergency telephone calls.
  - Appendix F tells how to respond to breathing and choking emergencies.

- **Glossary**
  The glossary defines the key terms and other specialized terms used in the text. Also included is a guide to pronunciation.

- **Sources**
  The sources section is a list of books and articles used in development of the book. These may provide additional information for those interested.

Audiovisuals

Several videos and films can help you as teaching aids for the Swimming and Water Safety courses. Your local Red Cross unit should be able to provide these for you:

- American Red Cross *Swimming and Diving Skills* (Stock No. 652005)
- American Red Cross *Infant and Preschool Aquatic Program* (Stock No. 329322)
- American Red Cross *Home Pool Safety: It Only Takes a Minute* (Stock No. 329474)
- American Red Cross *Water: The Deceptive Power* (Stock No. 329475)
- American Red Cross *Longfellow's Whale Tales* (Stock No. 329338)
- American Red Cross *Selected Aquatics* (Stock No. 321895); which contains the following five water safety videos:
  - *Snorkeling Skills and Rescue Techniques*
  - *Survival Swimming*
  - *Nonswimming Rescues* (also available as a separate video—7 minutes) (Stock No. 321650)
  - *Preventive Lifeguarding*
  - *Boating Safety and Rescues*
- American Red Cross *Emergency Aquatic Skills* (Stock No. 329331)
- *American Red Cross Responding to Emergencies* (Stock No. 650018)
- *American Red Cross Adult CPR* (Stock No. 329130)
- *American Red Cross Community CPR* (Stock No. 329371)
- *American Red Cross CPR: Infant and Child* (Stock No. 329378)
- American Red Cross *Spinal Injury Management* (Stock No. 329328)

Instructor References

Depending on the course(s) you teach, you may also find it useful to consult the following publications:

- *American Red Cross Instructor Candidates Training Participant's Manual* (Stock No. 329741), especially the section on learning theory, teaching styles, and class organization.

- *American Red Cross Lifeguarding Textbook* (Stock No. 329452) and *American Red Cross Lifeguarding Instructor's Manual* (Stock No. 329453), especially the sections on emergency action plans, lifeguard skills and responsibilities, and facility management.
- *American Red Cross Safety Training for Swim Coaches* (Stock No. 329449)
- *American Red Cross Safety Training for Swim Coaches Instructor's Manual* (Stock No. 329450)
- *American Red Cross Basic Water Safety and Emergency Water Safety Instructor's Manual* (Stock No. 329314)
- *American Red Cross Infant and Preschool Aquatic Program Parent's Guide* (Stock No. 329320)
- *American Red Cross Basic Water Safety Textbook* (Stock No. 329312)
- *American Red Cross Emergency Water Safety Textbook* (Stock No. 329313)
- *American Red Cross Rescue Breathing and Choking Supplement* (Stock No. 329286)
- *American Red Cross Adult CPR* (Stock No. 329128)
- *American Red Cross CPR Instructor's Manual* (Stock No. 329367)
- *American Red Cross Community CPR Workbook* (Stock No. 329364)
- *American Red Cross Standard First Aid Workbook* (Stock No. 329380)
- *American Red Cross Standard First Aid Instructor's Manual* (Stock No. 329381)
- *American Red Cross Swim and Stay Fit Program: Information for Chapters and the Monitor* (ARC 2149)

Supplementary Materials

Participants may find the following items helpful. Contact your local Red Cross unit for details.

- *Waddles Presents AQUACKtic Safety* (Stock No. 652002). This children's activity book is a colorful fun book for participants to learn, with Waddles the Duck, what swimming lessons are all about. You may want to use it and make it available at your facility.

- *Longfellow's Whale Tales* (Stock No. 329338). This packet of instructional material for children in grades K-6 presents safety lessons. This can be appropriate take-home material or it can be used with the related video in your classes on rainy days.
- *Swimming and Diving Wall Charts* (Stock No. 652007). This set of 13 wall charts on water-resistant paper includes photos and instructions on strokes, starts, turns, and dives. An additional poster in the set lists the skills and course completion requirements for the American Red Cross Learn to Swim program. They should be a valuable tool at poolside for you, as well as for participants and parents.
- *American Red Cross Swim and Stay Fit Individual Record* (Form 5347)
- *American Red Cross Swim and Stay Fit Wall Charts* (Form 5348)
- American Red Cross Aquatics brochure

Equipment

Suggested and required equipment is listed in the course outlines and in Appendix A. Make sure all equipment is ready and in working order before your course begins. If your facility does not have the needed equipment, check with the local Red Cross unit to see if they have it available and follow their procedures for reserving it. Some local units have a rental fee. If you have signed an *Authorized Provider Agreement* (Form 6575), it may cover the use of equipment. A Water Safety Instructor's Sports Bag (Stock No. 652009) is available for purchase or order through your local Red Cross unit. It measures 15 by 12 by 8 inches, has two video side compartments, an adjustable shoulder strap and two handles, a large ventilated side pocket, and ample space for course materials, the Instructor's Portfolio, bathing suits, and personal belongings. You may find the Instructor Portfolio (Stock No. 652008) useful for lesson planning.

3 | program planning

his chapter discusses program planning for Water Safety Instructors who are program administrators. Usually Water Safety Instructors teach courses in programs set up and administered by someone else. Sometimes, however, you may be responsible for setting up a program. The following sections can assist you in this.

ROLE OF THE RED CROSS UNIT

Your local Red Cross unit may have a Health and Safety Director who supervises swimming and water safety, first aid, and CPR courses. If not, the unit manager can refer you to the volunteer or staff person who handles the Swimming and Water Safety program.

Your unit's health and safety committee, if it has one, is an important resource for you. Many units also have water safety committees. Both committees may include representatives of community groups concerned with safety, such as schools, recreation departments, youth groups, and service organizations. Most Red Cross units have active Water Safety Instructors on the committee and, if possible, representatives from the unit's other safety committees. This committee helps develop the health and safety goals for the unit.

WORKING WITH THE COMMUNITY

Community service activities include promoting water safety by offering demonstrations, talks, videos, and displays and by distributing educational materials through public information outlets. Since community support is essential to a successful program, investigate ways to advertise your program in the community. Your local Red Cross unit can often be helpful with this.

REGISTRATION

To start a new program, you must develop procedures and policies for registration. To determine how many and what type of swim classes to offer, consider the size of the facility, the deck and water areas, availability of periods in the day for younger and older populations, the number of instructors available, budget, and number of programming hours available. Courses are commonly made up of 10 lessons, 30 to 45 minutes each. Once you decide on your program, prepare and distribute a chart of swim classes, times, and locations.

STAFFING

Staffing the program is your next concern. You should decide early in the planning process who will hire, supervise, and evaluate staff. Many programs have an on-site program coordinator as well as instructors, instructor aides, and lifeguards. All personnel should be oriented to the specific facility and its emergency action plan.

BUDGETING

In your budget planning, consider the agreements you reach with your local Red Cross unit about authorized provider fees. Fees and charges should be based on local standards, in cooperation with your local Red Cross unit. Be sure to plan for scholarship funding so that no one is kept from participating because of financial problems. Your organization may consider fund-raising events to increase resources.

RECORDS AND REPORTS

Records and reports are critical to authorized providers and the local Red Cross unit. When you meet with the local unit, develop a list of required records and reports. Red Cross records and reports are standardized throughout the country, and your attention to detail in completing them speeds the certificate process. Courses taught by Water Safety Instructors that include certificates for successful completion include the seven levels of the American Red Cross Learn to Swim program, the Emergency Water Safety course, and the Water Safety Instructor Aide course. Some Water Safety Instructors may also teach and issue certificates in Safety Training for Swim Coaches. Certificates of participation are given in the Infant and Preschool Aquatics Program (IPAP) and the Basic Water Safety course.

Your local Red Cross unit can advise you of the local policies and procedures for submitting these documents. Work closely with your local unit to meet the deadlines. With prior written permission from your local Red Cross unit, schools, camps, and similar institutions may submit the *Course Record* (Form 6418) with the top portion completed and a list attached (such as a grade book, handwritten roster, or computer printout) of participant names and grades.

4 | risk management

Risk management is identifying, analyzing, and evaluating risks that may affect an organization or individual and then devising ways to minimize or eliminate those risks. As an American Red Cross Water Safety Instructor, you must make your teaching environment as safe as possible. In many cases, you will have to make others aware of the importance of risk management for the organization and/or the facility.

NEED FOR RISK MANAGEMENT

The primary goal of risk management is to ensure the *safety of participants.* Participants expect and deserve a safe and healthy learning environment. If it is not safe, your participants may become distracted, be afraid to participate, or even be at risk of injury. In addition, if you yourself become distracted because of hazardous conditions, your program and participants will suffer. Some state recreational bathing and health codes require meeting certain standards before the course begins. These may include requirements for lifeguards, safety equipment, and proper water chemistry. You should know the requirements for your state and local jurisdictions. Regardless of whether there are regulations, you have ultimate responsibility for the safety of the participants in your classes.

FACTORS AFFECTING RISK MANAGEMENT

Effective risk management starts with *your* awareness that risks may be present. Safety awareness is necessary for recognizing risks so that the condition can be corrected or controlled. Many other factors also affect the safety of your program, as discussed in the following sections.

Supervision

During your lessons, you are observing participants, making suggestions, and evaluating individual performance. You cannot keep a watchful eye on everyone all the time. Since any swimming class not properly supervised faces potential hazards, all participants *must* be accounted for throughout each lesson. *Adequate supervision must be maintained at all times.* A qualified lifeguard should be on duty at all times during all lessons. This will—
- Improve the instruction by letting you concentrate on teaching.
- Increase the safety of participants.
- Provide an additional trained person to respond in an emergency.

Instructor Preparation

You can improve your program by being thoroughly prepared. Careful preparation includes considering possible risks and managing safety concerns before the program starts. Often you can foresee risks and eliminate or control them long before participants step into the water.

Assistant Instructors and Instructor Aides

Co-instructors, assistant instructors, and instructor aides can help decrease risks by giving more supervision and reducing the instructor-participant ratio. Participation and learning are also increased with greater attention to individual participants. However, an assistant or instructor aide is not a substitute for having a lifeguard on duty.

The key element when using additional staff is to define their roles and responsibilities clearly. This helps eliminate confusion and lapses in supervision. Remember, you have the ultimate responsibility for your participants' safety. Be sure your instructor aides have been trained according to the guidelines in Chapter 28.

To determine your staffing needs, consider the different ages of participants, the level of the program, and the individual abilities of participants in that program. A larger number of participants in your program may require additional staffing or increased lifeguard supervision.

Participants

The participants themselves greatly affect how you manage risks in the class. Be sure your participants know and follow the facility's and program's rules and regulations. Explain and enforce all rules and regulations consistently. At all times, safety is your primary concern.

Safety Equipment and Instructional Aids

Your instructor training has taught you how to use safety equipment and instructional aids. You should request and receive orientation on the location and use of the equipment in any facility where you teach. Always check instructional aids before you use them to ensure they are safe.

Teaching Environment

The teaching environment may involve risks you need to eliminate or minimize. Hazards in permanent or semi-permanent structures cannot easily be altered, such as the natural hazards of a pool or lake, deck areas, and permanent equipment such as diving boards. Be alert for potential hazards. Document and report your concerns to the facility manager and/or program administrator, and retain a copy for your records. Adjust your program to reduce such risks to your participants if you cannot completely eliminate them. Some conditions may require temporary adjustments or suspending a class, such as during poor water conditions and weather situations like electrical storms. Note these conditions on the *Course Record* (Form 6418).

Facility Policies and Procedures

Besides being prepared to teach, you should be prepared to react appropriately in a serious emergency. Know the facility's emergency action plan to ensure your safety and that of your participants. Know the location of emergency equipment, telephones, first aid supplies, and additional personnel. Be sure you know where emergency phone numbers are posted, including police, ambulance, fire, poison control, security, and facility management. You do not have time to find this information when an accident occurs. (Appendix E in *Swimming and Diving* tells how to make emergency telephone calls.)

All facility policies and procedures, including how to activate the emergency action plan, should be in writing and available to you. You should have your own copy, and it is your responsibility to know how the plan pertains to you and your classes. Be sure your duties and responsibilities are clearly outlined and documented to avoid misunderstandings.

Costs Related to Effective Risk Management

Risk management is sometimes narrowly considered only in terms of the immediate financial costs, but good risk management is cost effective. It does cost money to supply lifeguards in addition to instructors, to provide enough proper equipment for participants, and to maintain the facility correctly and safely. However, not managing risks effectively may be far more costly in the long run. Budgetary concerns do not justify poor risk management. Inadequate risk management can lead to injury and lawsuits, both of which can be extremely expensive.

Just by staying alert for potential risks, you are taking a big step toward effective risk management. Before you teach your courses, personally inspect the teaching area and every piece of equipment you will use. Maintaining recommended instructor-participant ratios also decreases risks.

THE AMERICAN RED CROSS AS A RISK MANAGEMENT RESOURCE

The American Red Cross can be a prime resource for effective risk management. To start, this manual gives you information and procedures to help in preparing, conducting, and reporting programs. *American Red Cross Lifeguarding Textbook* (Stock No. 329452) contains additional helpful information.

Your local Red Cross unit may also have risk management information and resources provided by national headquarters. They may have safety equipment and instructional aids as well. Before you start your program, find out what support your local unit can provide.

Summary

Risk management involves being well prepared and having an attitude of watchfulness. The more you do to make the learning environment safe, the more you and your participants will benefit.

5 | course completion

CRITERIA FOR GRADING PARTICIPANTS

The *Course Record* (Form 6418) and the *Course Record Addendum* (Form 6418A) require that you enter a grade of pass, fail, or incomplete for each participant. The correct grade is assigned by these criteria:

- "Pass" (P) is entered for a participant who has passed all the required course skills, the final skills test, and the final written test, if applicable.
- "Fail" (F) is entered for a participant who has not passed all the required course skills and final skills test or written test at the completion of the course.
- "Incomplete" (I) is entered for a participant who could not complete the course because of circumstances that prevented attendance. A grade of incomplete should be given only when arrangements have been made for the participant to complete the training. These arrangements should be noted on the *Course Record* (Form 6418) in the section for instructor's comments.

There are no grading criteria for the Infant and Preschool Aquatics Program or the Basic Water Safety course except full participation. The goal of these programs is to provide information and help the participants learn techniques to be comfortable in and around the water, to develop a readiness for learning to swim, and to learn safety fundamentals. Therefore, the completion of these courses reflects "participation" in a program rather than a "pass/fail" criterion. For these courses, a passing (P) grade is recorded on the *Course Record* (Form 6418) to indicate attendance and participation.

REPORTING PROCEDURES

At the conclusion of the course, you must complete, sign, and promptly turn in the American Red Cross *Course Record* (Form 6418) and *Course Record Addendum* (Form 6418A) to your local Red Cross unit to receive course completion certificates. You should keep a copy for your records and give a copy to the institution or organization where the course was conducted. Your local Red Cross unit may require you to complete other forms such as an equipment log sheet. Report problems with equipment to your local unit if you used its equipment.

AWARDING CERTIFICATES

Discuss with your local Red Cross unit the procedures for obtaining American Red Cross course-completion certificates for participants in your courses. Be sure to follow approved procedures. Sign the certificates before giving them to the participants. If you will receive the certificates after the course is over, make arrangements to get them to the participants.

Course Evaluation

Receiving feedback from participants is important in any evaluation. Participants or parents should have an opportunity to tell you what they thought about the course. Have them complete an evaluation in every course you teach. This information gives you feedback about the course and its instruction, and it helps you and the Red Cross maintain the highest quality in its courses.

Appendix E contains sample course evaluation forms for participants and parents. You may photocopy these forms for each participant or parent. It need not be signed, so comments can be anonymous. This evaluation, or a similar one used by your local Red Cross unit, should be used at the end of each course. Your local Red Cross unit may want to read these evaluations.

Instructor's Evaluation

To continue to improve its courses, the American Red Cross needs your help. After you teach a course the first time, use the feedback from participants and/or parents to help you complete the Instructor Course Evaluation form (Appendix F). Return the completed evaluation to—

American Red Cross National Headquarters
Health and Safety Course Evaluations
17th and D Streets, N.W.
Washington, DC 20006–5399

We also invite you to share your thoughts and suggestions about the courses at any time by sending in additional evaluation forms or by writing to the address above.

- learning and development
- motor learning principles
- teaching principles

learning theory

B

6 learning and development

As in any American Red Cross health and safety course, participants learn a variety of skills in Swimming and Water Safety courses. You may give information on how to develop a stroke or on the principles that make it effective. You discuss safety issues and what participants can do to prevent aquatic emergencies. Participants may discover other applications for aquatic skills such as competitive swimming or leisure activities such as SCUBA diving or boating. The majority of participants' time is spent learning motor skills.

You learned several strategies for helping others learn in the American Red Cross Instructor Candidate Training course. This chapter and the two that follow build on that course by discussing principles of learning and development. These are based on the way persons of different ages, skills, and abilities change the way they perform motor tasks. These learning and developmental principles are based on observations that people have certain things in common as they acquire and refine motor skills. You will be a more effective instructor if your teaching practices reflect these general principles for the way people learn.

Part B has three chapters. This chapter discusses the developmental learning process. It serves as background for the more specific material in the next two chapters. Chapter 7 discusses how the learning process affects the learner, focusing on individual factors that help or inhibit learning. Chapter 8 discusses how you, as an instructor, can help the learner through the learning process. It explains the importance of using progressions for teaching motor skills, referred to here as teaching progressions, and it contains concrete measures for improving your teaching style.

FACTORS THAT INFLUENCE LEARNING

Learning involves changes in behavior that result from practice or experience. As an instructor you can make this process work best by focusing on four influences on learning: setting goals, encouraging practice, giving feedback, and providing motivation.

Setting Goals

To change or improve their performance, participants must first understand the goal. For young students you set the goals. As students mature, they can participate in setting goals for themselves. See pages 164–166 for additional information on adults' involvement in goal setting. The first step in the learning process is to present the goal clearly. Methods to accomplish this include—

- Verbal explanations (discussions, descriptions).
- Visual descriptions (posters, slides, illustrations, videos, films).
- Instructor demonstrations.
- Peer demonstrations.

Each of these methods is effective with certain learners, situations, and skills. With young participants, a peer demonstration can be very effective in helping to set goals. The demonstration not only shows the correct way to perform a skill but may lead young participants to think, "If she can do it, so can I." With adults, on the other hand, you might only have to state, after demonstrating a skill, "By the end of this lesson you should be able to do this skill fairly well. We're going to practice it so you can achieve that goal."

When setting goals, consider participant factors such as these:
- Age (children or adults)
- Disabilities and other conditions
- The level of cognitive and motor skill development
- Learning stage
- Language differences
- Level of motivation

Encouraging Practice

Practice is essential for both learning and improving motor skills. Using a variety of practice situations leads to better learning. Variety and frequent changes in tempo help keep participants interested. For example, practicing kicking in several situations (e.g., at poolside, with instructor support, and with a kickboard) will lead to more effective learning of kicking skills than simply practicing the flutter kick at the side of the pool. In addition, increased practice time improves skill proficiency.

Giving Feedback

Information participants receive about how they just performed a skill is called feedback. You can use feedback to help participants learn to repeat desired responses, such as performing a skill correctly. Without feedback, participants might not improve much in swimming or other motor skills. The more precise the feedback, the more useful it is. Participants need positive feedback when they are doing something right and corrective feedback when they are not. Feedback as it relates to the learner is discussed in more detail in Chapter 7. Techniques for providing feedback are given in Chapter 8.

Providing Motivation

People come to aquatics classes for many reasons. Participants can range from the fearful child to the self-directed adult, from the determined person with a disability to the eager competitor, from the person who enjoys socializing to a student who is required to take a course. As an instructor you must understand and recognize the variety of motives of your participants and be able to encourage all of them if they begin to lose interest.

Motivation brings the discussion on learning full circle. Motivations can be translated into goals. Goals give purpose and direction to practice time. Effective practice involves getting feedback, and feedback that one has reached a goal is a great way to boost motivation and

enthusiasm for aquatics. In Chapters 7 and 8 you will learn how to use these learning principles as you plan your courses and develop teaching skills.

STAGES OF LEARNING

A popular theory about how motor skills are learned is that of Paul Fitts and Michael Posner. They explain that an individual progresses through three identifiable stages of learning, known as the cognitive, the associative, and the autonomic.

The first stage, the cognitive, is marked by awkward, slow movements that the learner is consciously trying to control. The person has to think before doing the movement. Performance in this stage is generally poor, and the person makes many errors in these slow movements.

For example, remember the first time you tried to drive a car. Recall the thoughts that raced through your head. Where is the brake? How far before the corner do I put on my turn signal? Because you had to think through every move, your reactions were slow and awkward. In general, your performance in this stage was poor.

As you gained experience and as your instructor explained things in different ways, your performance improved. You made fewer errors, and your responses were faster. Now you had a general understanding of each movement.

According to Fitts and Posner, you had progressed to the associative stage. In this stage, one spends less time thinking about every detail and begins to associate the movement one is learning with another movement already known. For example, when you learned to drive, you did not have to think about all the separate tasks that were part of a certain skill (such as using the turn signal, applying the brake, and looking both ways when you stop to turn at an intersection).

Finally your driving performance reached an acceptable level. Your movements were accurate and rapid; you seemed to know instinctively what to do in almost every situation. When you did make an error, you realized it immediately and found ways to correct it.

This is the final stage in motor skill acquisition, the autonomous stage. At this stage learning is mostly complete, although the individual can continue to refine the skill through practice. This stage is called autonomous because the learner no longer needs to depend on the instructor for all feedback about performance.

Your students go through these same stages as they learn motor skills. Different people in the same class may be in different stages. A person can be in the cognitive stage of learning one skill and in the autonomous stage of learning another.

THE DEVELOPMENTAL PERSPECTIVE

In addition to the specific changes that happen when a person learns a skill, everyone goes through more gradual changes throughout their lifespan. Change is not limited to infancy and childhood. Nor does change depend on specific experiences. This way of understanding people is called a developmental perspective, which looks at how changes in behavior occur in a regular and orderly manner throughout life. These changes can be understood in terms of natural patterns, or developmental principles, as defined and explained in the following sections.

Qualitative Nature of Change

Developmental change is qualitative in its very nature. Changes do not simply increase quantity, such as weight or height. Rather, developmental changes involve the appearance of something new and different from previous behavior. For example, a young child or an adult beginner first trying to kick in the water performs a distinct flexion and extension leg action that looks like "running" or "bicycling." With time and experience, the kicking changes to a more fully extended position and actually becomes a true flutter kick. This change is not simply an increase in speed, range of motion, or strength. It is a change into a new and different coordinated muscle action.

Increasing Complexity

Developmental changes also involve increasing complexity. Basic forms of a behavior lead to more advanced forms. Changes do not occur randomly but happen in a definite sequence. For example, in prone swimming, inexperienced people tend to keep their arms under water even during recovery, while more experienced swimmers get their arms out and over the water during recovery. More rudimentary behaviors (such as underwater recovery) are often prerequisite to later, more advanced skills (such as above-water recovery). You can apply this principle in teaching skill sequences.

Increasing Integration and Coordination

Another crucial principle of developmental change is that behaviors become more closely connected with other behaviors. Skilled swimmers doing the front crawl move through the water with apparent ease because rotary breathing is tightly integrated and coordinated with the arm pull and proper body roll. In contrast, beginners often pull their arms rapidly for a time, then stop their arms while they catch a large breath, and finally resume the arm pulling. A key difference here is the degree of integration and coordination between arm stroking and breathing. This principle highlights the importance of helping swimmers integrate and coordinate different parts of the aquatic skills you teach them.

Increasing Differentiation and Specialization

As developmental changes occur over time, behaviors and skills become more differentiated and specialized. Young swimmers often use one general method for moving in the water. As noted above, the first attempts at kicking often look like "running" in the water. Over time, the person differentiates between the "running" action used on land and the "flutter" action that is more successful in the water. You should note these attempts to use general responses and patiently help the person specialize that response for more efficient swimming.

Stability Over Time

It may seem strange, but developmental change is very consistent at any point in time. For instance, a child may seem to vary greatly in the performance of a skill (such as holding the breath for 2 seconds one time and 8 seconds at another or covering 10 yards one time and only 10 feet the next). In fact, the way in which the child performs the skill (breath control, stroke pattern) is remarkably consistent over short periods of time. The fundamental parts of a person's stroke (e.g., an above-water arm recovery or the rate of kicking and arm pulling) change only gradually, but qualitatively, over time.

Age Relationships

Time is a convenient "marker" most people use to understand developmental changes. Chronological age is frequently used as a developmental marker. For example, we mark our progress through life through the annual celebration of our birthdays. We also identify behaviors by identifying them with ages, such as the "terrible twos" of toddlers and "difficult teens" and "sweet sixteen" stages for adolescents.

Unfortunately, since age is generally linked to development, many people think that an increase in age automatically causes certain developments. This leads to many mistaken assumptions and unfortunate practices, such as assuming all people of a certain age are alike. For example, parents may ask, "Why can all my daughter's friends swim and she can't?"

The assumption that there is a cause-and-effect relationship between age and development often leads to the practice of grouping children of similar ages together in the hope of producing similar behaviors and learning. School grades, athletic teams, and even swim classes are often grouped almost solely by chronological age. In reality, people of similar ages vary greatly in their body sizes, skills, personalities, and experiences and are only similar in some very general ways.

With this developmental perspective, you can see that a person's behavior and qualities involve a complex interaction of age, specific and general experiences, and the person's genetic endowment. Consider all these characteristics carefully when you try to determine a person's developmental stage.

SUMMARY

No matter how random it may appear, human learning follows some very clear principles. Goal setting, focused practice, corrective feedback, and effective motivation help students to learn.

Acquiring motor skills involves three distinct phases from cognitive learning to autonomous performance. Finally, learning follows a developmental pattern; simple skills must be learned before more complicated tasks are attempted. Your teaching will be more effective if you remember and use these principles. The next two chapters can help you further understand the process of learning and give you skills you can use to improve your teaching methods.

7 | motor learning principles

A motor skill involves using part or all of the body. Motor learning is the process of learning a motor skill so that it is permanent. Motor learning in a class depends on three elements:

- The skills to be acquired. These are outlined later in this manual, aquatic skills in Parts D and E and safety skills in Part G.
- Your contribution as instructor presenting the skills and guiding the learner's progress. These are discussed in Chapter 8.
- The active participation of the learner in acquiring and/or perfecting the skills, as discussed in this chapter.

Motor skills involve both physiological and psychological factors. The physiological factors include changes in heart rate, the utilization of oxygen, and the conversion of fat, carbohydrates, and protein into mechanical energy. Chapter 10 in *Swimming and Diving* discusses many of these factors. These physiological factors do not significantly affect the learning of participants in your class. Therefore, this chapter focuses on psychological factors, the role of the learner in the learning process.

In Instructor Candidate Training, you learned an acronym, **MARS**, to help you remember four elements of learning: **M**otivation, **A**ssociation, **R**epetition, and use of the **S**enses. This chapter is structured around these themes. The first section discusses the interactive nature of change and the learner's internal control of the learning process, especially through motivation. The second section discusses the role of memory in motor learning, to give background for the next three sections. The third section explains the process by which learning skills involves transfer from skills already known, using association. The fourth section discusses the importance of repetition in practice. Adults' use of cognitive strategies is discussed in that section. The final section discusses the role of the senses in learning,

including how intrinsic feedback, or "listening to the body," is important for developing motor skills.

The learner's role in the learning process is affected by the "outside" influences of the class setting and the instructor's teaching style. To help you understand the different roles of learner and instructor in a clear and orderly way, these contributions are discussed in separate chapters. Thus, your full understanding of the learning principles in this chapter depends also on reading Chapter 8.

INTERACTIVE NATURE OF CHANGE

For a long time, developmental change was thought to result from maturation, a gradual process of change considered to be controlled mainly by genetics. In this view, one only needed to let the nervous system "do its thing" and the person would change (e.g., get bigger, smarter, more skillful). We now understand that not even pure "maturation" occurs in isolation. Optimal developmental change requires the active participation of the person along with a generally supportive environment. The interaction between a person and the environment stimulates a person to grow throughout life. For example, most people do not learn to swim simply by looking at pictures, videos, or films. They must get in the water and try it. On the other hand, not everyone who gets in the water learns to swim or swim efficiently. This is part of the mystery of the interaction between person and environment that leads to developmental change.

Internal Control of Change

One of the most important principles here is that the learner fundamentally controls the change process. As an instructor, you can support changes, but you cannot *cause* them to occur. Not even the best teaching progressions, drills, and games can ensure that learning and development will occur without the learner's active involvement. For this to happen, as discussed in Chapter 6, the learner must have a clear goal for a task, assimilate feedback given about performance, and practice actively. This assumes, of course, that the person *wants* to learn the skill in the first place.

The Role of Motivation

Motivation is the internal drive that keeps people moving toward a goal. Motivation can lead an individual to start, maintain, or modify a behavior. Three factors influence motivation: anxiety, reinforcement, and goal setting. Each of these is discussed below.

Anxiety is the stress people feel in the performance settings. This can be either trait anxiety or state anxiety. Trait anxiety is a person's normal tendency to feel stress in some situations or even in anticipation of a situation. Consider the participants who show little apprehension about standing on a 3-meter diving board and jumping or diving off. They ascend the ladder with self-confidence and minimal hesitation. They do feel a little more nervous, however, because they want to perform the skill well. This normal attitude is classified as trait anxiety.

State anxiety is the stress that may be caused solely by the task being performed. Picture now the same confident, calm participants as they approach the ladder to the 3-meter diving board to perform a reverse dive. Their lack of confidence is generally temporary and is state anxiety. As the participants gain confidence, they have no more anxiety than before they were asked to perform a reverse dive.

Reinforcement, the second influence on motivation, is anything that increases the likelihood that a person will perform a given task as desired. Positive reinforcers are responses to the desired behavior that are pleasing to the person. Negative reinforcers are responses such as punishment or harsh words that cause the person to perform the desired behavior so they can avoid the negative response. Most psychologists believe that positive reinforcers are more effective than negative reinforcers in shaping learning. A good form of positive reinforcement is the personal praise you give when someone performs a skill properly. The more a participant feels that his or her efforts are noticed and appreciated, the more likely it is that he or she will repeat and thus learn the desired behavior.

Motivation is also increased when participants set goals and then meet them. Goals help focus participants' efforts and shape their motivation. Participants need both short-term and long-term goals. A short-term goal may be something that the person can achieve by the end of a given lesson or by the end of the week. A long-term goal might take several weeks, or longer, and is met as the person successfully meets a series of short-term goals. The skill progressions in Chapters 18 to 21 can be guidelines for setting short-term goals. Some participants may need even shorter-term goals so they do not feel frustrated by what seems like a lack of progress. Success and motivation strongly influence each other. As success increases, motivation grows, and when motivation grows, success increases.

It is very important for the goals to be realistic. If the goals are too low, the person does not accomplish much. If they are unrealistically high, the person is likely to fail and the motivation diminishes. Motivation remains strong if goals are realistic, based upon prior experience, measurable, and above all, meaningful.

STAGES OF MEMORY

To repeat a particular motor skill, a person must remember how to perform it. Information must therefore first be *in* the person's memory. While this seems like a rather obvious principle, you must realize that even things the person repeats several times are not *necessarily* placed in the person's memory to be later remembered and used.

The person's ability to recall information is a key function of memory and shows whether that person has permanently stored the information. In one theory, there are three stages to memory: short-term sensory memory, short-term memory, and long-term memory. These stages differ in how much information they can handle and how long they retain this information.

Short-term sensory memory (STSM) is the most limited stage of memory in both how much and how long information is retained. In general, information is held in STSM for 15 seconds or less. If a person doesn't repeat the task in that time, the memory of how to perform the task is lost and the learning process must start over again.

For example, you can introduce the concept of lift by having your students slice their arms through the water. When they feel the pressure on their hands and arms, STSM is being activated. They must perform the slicing motion correctly before too much time passes or they will not learn the skill.

If the person uses or repeats the information held in STSM, it is stored in short-term memory (STM). STM can hold a small amount of information for only a few minutes. Information that is transferred from STSM to STM is re-coded, so that individual bits of information are grouped together through a process called "chunking".

It is generally believed that the capacity to retain information in STM is limited to nine independent items. Chunking increases the amount of information that STM can hold, since a given chunk represents 1 item of information rather than the 8 to 10 individual bits that are grouped together. Thus, by making connections between items of information, learners decrease the number of independent items, making room for more information. The more information that can be chunked without losing its original meaning, the greater the capacity of STM and the greater the chance that learning will occur.

To continue the example from above, once students have learned to experience lift in a horizontal sweep of the arm, you can direct them to try slicing their arms in different directions, such as diagonal and vertical. By this time, they have probably learned that holding the hand and

wrist in a certain position creates the most lift. They have "chunked" this part of their learning experience so that they can focus now on the differences of slicing through the water in different directions.

New information the learner thinks is important or associates with previously learned information is stored in long-term memory (LTM). LTM has unlimited capacity and unlimited duration. Information placed in LTM is never lost from storage, but people can lose the ability to retrieve the information because they have forgotten where they put it.

As the final part of the example, once students have experienced lift and learned how it applies to sweeps in various directions, they can associate this with the components of an arm stroke. They realize, for instance, that in the front crawl, lift applies to the catch, the outsweep, and the insweep and that the hand and arm must be positioned differently in each phase of the stroke. What began as a simple experiment in experiencing lift has become a complex set of motor skills put into long-term memory for use throughout life.

When people are confronted with a large quantity of information, they tend to remember the first and last items presented and forget the information in the middle. This is called the *primacy-recency effect*. One possible explanation is that people tend to be more alert when an explanation begins. As the explanation continues, attentiveness decreases. When the presentation draws to a close, attention increases again, perhaps as the learner waits for the chance to perform the skill. Therefore, you should not present too much information at one time because much of that information will not retained.

TRANSFER OF LEARNING

Information may be placed in LTM if it is associated with something already known. Transfer of learning is the process in which a previously learned skill affects the learning of a new skill. Transfer of learning can be positive, negative, or zero. Zero transfer occurs when an instructor tries to relate two skills that have no connection with each other. For instance, the flutter kick and the breaststroke kick are both kicks, but they are not connected in any way. In fact, the flutter kick requires floppy ankles while the breaststroke kick works best when the ankles keep the feet in a very definite position. Because there is no transfer here, learning the second skill is not made any easier by knowing the first skill.

Negative transfer happens when a previously learned skill hinders the learning of a new skill. This occurs when the old skill is so ingrained that the motor patterns automatically come to the fore. For example, a swimmer who has used a straight-arm recovery in the front crawl may have difficulty learning to recover with a bent elbow. The tendency is for the old task to override the new skill, thereby hindering the learning process.

Positive transfer is the best form of transfer because it eases the learning of a new task. Positive transfer depends on several factors:

- The learner must have enough experience with the first skill.
- The new task must be highly similar to the first skill.
- The learner must be able to identify those similarities, as well as what is different about the new skill.
- The learner must be given a variety of examples of the new skill.

The ability to transfer learning also depends on the person's stage of learning for that skill. During the cognitive stage, people have only a limited capacity to retain information. However, if they are beyond the cognitive stage, learning occurs mostly by association. The more connections they can make between the new skill and known skills, the easier it will be to learn the desired new skill.

One problem with the transfer of learning in aquatics happens because locomotion in the water is very different from movement on land. Few skills done on land can be transferred directly to skills in the water. It may take you some effort to identify land skills that can be adapted to skills in

the water. For example, the sculling motion of the hands in treading water can be likened to the movements of the hands smoothing a pile of sand.

THE ROLE OF REPETITION

In the earlier discussion of short-term sensory memory, it was noted, that a skill has to be repeated for learning to occur. For learning in general, the learner who repeats small bits of information several times has a better chance of retaining them and the learner's progress is more rapid.

Another factor that is very important to learning motor skills is the amount of time the person spends practicing the task. People who spend more time actively practicing a skill learn more quickly than those who spend less time practicing. The *way* people practice also affects how quickly they learn. Those who practice a *specific* task perform better than those in a general activity. For example, the person who spends 30 minutes working on the specific task of rhythmic breathing in the front crawl performs better than someone who spends 30 minutes practicing the front crawl by just swimming up and down the pool without any specific guidance. Thus, focused practice time, which is also called time spent on task, is a very important factor in motor learning.

Cognitive Strategies

Some learners are more successful if they use cognitive strategies. These are psychological skills or processes that help increase attention, thinking, learning, and remembering. Following are some of these strategies:

- **Self-verbalization**. Learners talk through the skill in their own words. They may verbalize to themselves or back to you so you can check their understanding.
- **Labeling**. Learners identify skills with key words or images. For example, they might use the face of a clock to identify the position of the correct hand entry for the back crawl.
- **Directed attention**. Learners focus on a critical step of the skill. For example, they

might not think about recovering their legs during the scissors kick and concentrate just on the power phase.

- **Imagery**. Learners visualize the skill; they "see themselves doing the skill."
- **Rhythm**. Learners identify a certain rhythm or cadence for performing a skill, such as using a sing-song version of "breathe and blow and breathe and blow."

APPLYING THE SENSES

In general, the more senses one engages in learning and practicing a skill, the more quickly and precisely one learns it. Thus, a class that sees a video or a demonstration and is then led through a dry land drill learns the skill more easily than a class that is only given an oral description.

The Role of Intrinsic Feedback

Chapter 6 explains feedback as the information a person receives about how he or she performed a task. The two kinds of feedback are augmented and intrinsic. Augmented feedback, the information about the performance from a coach or teacher, is discussed at some length in Chapter 8. Intrinsic feedback is information about the task performance that the learner receives from his or her own senses.

Many experts believe that true learning does not occur until a person can feel what he or she is doing. Corrections from the instructor have little effect if the learner does not yet have a personal sense of the performance. If your participants believe they are moving their arms and legs in a certain way, even if they are not, they will not understand your correction until they have a clear sense of the actual movement. However, when they can "feel" their own performance, they have that internal control of the learning process that is so important.

SUMMARY

Memory, motivation, repetition, and association all affect the speed and ease with which participants acquire and develop motor skills. The more you understand and use these principles, the more effective you will be at teaching participants how to swim.

8 | teaching principles

Chapter 7 notes that motor learning in a Swimming and Water Safety class depends on three elements: the skill itself, the learner's active participation, and the instructor's skill and guidance. This chapter discusses the third element, your contribution as an instructor to the learning of your participants. As in Chapter 7, the presentation is loosely structured around the MARS acronym for learning: motivation, association, repetition, and use of the senses.

MOTIVATING PARTICIPANTS

Chapter 7 explains that the learner's motivation is crucial in the learning process. You can support and enhance the motivation of your participants in several ways. One way is to plan your lessons such that each of the participants will succeed in some way each time. Even if that success is relatively minor, each participant needs to feel that he or she has accomplished something. It is also important that you, the instructor, recognize the success as worthwhile.

Success depends on having realistic goals. If the goals you help the learner set are unrealistically high, the learner is likely to fail and the motivation to continue diminishes. If the goals are too low, the learner is held back. If your expectations are low, the participant's performance will be low, but if you present realistic expectations, learners are more likely to improve their performance in ways that are satisfying to them and to you.

Giving feedback is an important task for you as an instructor. Positive feedback helps motivate participants. It tells them that you are paying attention to what they are doing and that you care enough to let them know. Remarks such as "good job," or "that looks right," or "I can tell you are really trying" are very important to the participants' motivation and success, especially when the task is difficult.

Positive attitude and success go hand in hand for you, the instructor, just as motivation and success go together for the learner. A successful instructor generally has a positive, upbeat attitude during class. If you plan, are prepared, and expect success from your participants, they will see you in a positive light.

Thorndike's Laws of Learning

A learning theorist, Edward Thorndike, said that learning depends on three principles, which he named the laws of effect, readiness, and frequency. The law of effect states that a learner tends to repeat those things that are pleasing and not to repeat those things that are displeasing. The law of readiness simply means that individuals perform a task when they are ready, both physically and psychologically, to perform. The law of frequency states that learning requires repetition for the skill to be mastered.

When instructors evaluate an individual's performance, they often overlook two of Thorndike's laws, the law of effect and the law of readiness. The law of effect is overlooked, for example, when a beginner is forced into activities and skills because *someone else* believes the activity is fun. If a beginner has an inherent fear of the water, no skill is fun. Learners must first enjoy what they are doing and feel relaxed before true learning can take place. If individuals are to learn to swim, they must enjoy all aspects of the learning process.

Thorndike's law of readiness is also often overlooked. Someone is not ready to perform a precise task if he or she has not yet learned the underlying gross motor movements. For example, participants are not likely to attempt turning over in the water if they have not first learned to float and how to recover from a floating position. This underscores the importance, with any aquatic skill, of teaching (or correcting) broad elements such as body position in a stroke before trying to teach fine points like the correct hand position for the catch.

By being aware of these three laws, you may be able to see when an individual's motivation is sagging. Then you can adjust the learning situation so it meets the needs of that person.

Dealing With Anxiety

Fear or anxiety can also lessen participants' motivation. The instructor should watch for actions that suggest that participants are anxious. The following are the most common avoidance behaviors revealing anxiety:

- Making excuses
- Huddling (rounding the shoulders too much and making the chest concave, especially when in a prone position)
- Wiping the face often to remove hair and/or water from the eyes
- Holding the body rigid, particularly the shoulders and legs
- Clenching fists
- Pursing or biting the lips
- Shivering (Someone who is frightened will shiver no matter how warm the water.)
- Clinging to supports when practicing skills, especially floating
- Gripping the instructor, especially during floating and submersion skills practice
- Moving unnecessarily (such as kicking when they should be floating motionless)
- Performing strokes that are too short, too shallow, too rigid, and/or too fast

If apprehensive participants are to learn successfully, the following three conditions are essential:

1. The participants must have a strong desire to learn. Without motivation it is too easy to give up when the task seems threatening. Remind them of the goals they have set for themselves and praise them for the skills they have already acquired.
2. Tasks must be broken down into smaller skills with maximum opportunities for success. The component parts of skills are more manageable and reduce the anxiety of performance demands. You must be patient and encourage participants at every step. Practicing skills they already know can help participants gain confidence to try the next step in a skill progression. This also helps reinforce the transfer of learning, as discussed in Chapter 7.
3. The participants should be allowed to control their fear. They should never be forced to try something they perceive as very threatening, nor should they be criticized for avoiding a fearful situation. For successful learning the participants must develop self-confidence and trust in you, the instructor.

You can help participants feel in control and gain self-confidence by taking special care to prepare them for each new experience. Verbalize the new task. Discuss the task and the outcomes. Direct the participants to imagine themselves successfully completing the task. When the participants feel ready to attempt the new task, encourage and reward each attempt as a success.

PRESENTING INFORMATION

Association is an important part of learning motor skills. Help participants make connections between what they know and what they are learning by presenting new information in a careful, logical way. Anything you want to teach must be received and understood by the participants to be of any value. The next section offers ways to present motor skill information effectively, both verbally and by demonstration.

Communication

Everybody perceives information differently. What and how we perceive something depends largely on our age, experience, and maturity. It is important to communicate at the appropriate level for your participants. Knowing your subject matter well is not enough to be an effective instructor.

There are several ways to check if you are communicating at the right level. The simplest way is just to ask the participants if they understood what you just said. You can tell how much they understand by asking them to explain it back to you. If your participants seem uninterested or distracted, you may be talking over their heads. Finally, if their movements are nothing like what you explained, you should suspect that you failed to communicate the information at the right level.

It is easy to give too much information. The description of even a simple motor skill involves an enormous amount of information. If you describe (and ask participants to perform) a simple skill broken down in all its parts, you are giving them a large amount of information to absorb all at once. Since they are more likely to remember the first and last things you say, your communication will be more effective if you give the information in smaller amounts. This is especially true with younger or beginning students.

When you are verbally describing a motor skill, you are in a sense painting a picture in the minds of your participants. The challenge is to paint a clear picture using as few words as possible. Choose your words carefully. Develop a vocabulary that describes what you want to see in a skill. If you want a flutter kick with the muscles in the lower leg loose and relaxed, you might tell the participants to use "floppy ankles." Use and reuse those words or phrases so they become part of the participants' vocabulary as well.

Pick words and phrases that are precise and concise. Vague terms such as "in front," "wide," and "long" used in directions like "put your hands *in front* of your body when pulling in the crawl," "pull *wide* in the breast stroke," "pull and glide *long* in the elementary backstroke" lead to questions like: where "in front," how "wide," and how "long." Directional and spatial descriptions should tell *exactly* where movements should be. For example:

- "Your hands should enter directly forward of your shoulders and with the elbow bent slightly."

- "Pull to 10 and 2 o'clock before you sweep during the breaststroke pull."
- "Glide for the count of two or until you are almost stopped when you swim elementary backstroke."

The use of simile, metaphor, and analogy (ways of making comparisons) can effectively and quickly convey much information. The simile, "kick like a dolphin," paints a picture because many people are familiar with a dolphin and how it propels itself through the water. A direction such as, "stretch like you're hanging from a tree," helps them associate something they already know with something they are learning. An example of a metaphor is "boil the water" with your feet when you flutter kick. Because people know what boiling water looks like, this phrase takes a concept that otherwise is difficult to explain and describes it in just three words.

A new instructor should not expect to come up with a perfect descriptive phrase, simile, or analogy spontaneously. It takes both experience and preparation. Effective communication may sound spontaneous and unrehearsed, but it seldom is. Good teachers consciously develop a vocabulary that suits their needs. These words and phrases become teaching cues you can use over and over. Start thinking about brief, highly descriptive ways to explain what you want to communicate.

Demonstration

When done properly, demonstrations are a powerful and effective way to present information about motor skills. To demonstrate well, you must be knowledgeable about the subject and proficient at the skills as well. Presenting information through demonstration has many parallels to presenting information verbally. Sometimes you may prefer to have an aide demonstrate a skill while you comment on the demonstration. Another valuable tool for demonstration and review is the American Red Cross *Swimming and Diving Skills* video. Make it available at poolside whenever possible. You may want to use it to demonstrate complex skills such as springboard diving or the butterfly. The American Red Cross *Swimming and Diving Wall Charts* also can help you describe aquatic skills.

A demonstration must be at the appropriate level for the participants. If the participants are just starting to learn the front crawl, for example, conduct the demonstration very slowly and with exaggerated movements, such as lifting the arms way out of the water. Demonstrate the elementary backstroke with a noticeable hesitation between the recovery phase and the propulsion phase. This way of demonstrating slows down the skill and gives the participants a chance to see all components of a movement.

Keep information to a minimum at any one time. For example, to show rotary breathing for the front crawl, you may demonstrate it by standing in waist-deep water and leaning over with just your head in the water. You don't have to perform the entire stroke. Another way to simplify a demonstration is to do it on dry land before you demonstrate it in the water. Even advanced participants can have trouble paying attention to all the aspects of a stroke (body position, kick, pull, timing), so just concentrate on one aspect at a time.

Although chunking information is a natural process, some participants may need to be taught how to do it. You can help them learn by pointing out relationships between items whenever you present them. This allows participants to get a better grasp of the total process.

To make the most of a demonstration, ask participants to pay attention to exactly what you want them to see by first describing what they are about to see. If you want them to see a starting position for a good breaststroke kick, tell them precisely what to look for: knees approximately shoulder-width apart, feet wider than the knees, and the feet pulled up and turned out.

You must also make sure participants are in a position to see the skill clearly. In general, participants can see demonstrations better when they are completely out of the water standing on the edge of the deck. Don't let anyone stand behind anyone else. You may decide to show a

side view and a head-on view. You have spent a fair amount of time explaining the skill and getting them out of the water to see you do it, so now give them several opportunities to observe it. Ask them to "take a picture" of the skill in their mind so they see themselves doing it.

Once they have seen the skill, get them to perform it as soon as possible. Ask them to try to see the picture they made of you when you were presenting the skill and duplicate that movement. Give them corrective feedback, if necessary.

Present a skill in as many ways as you can, sometimes by combining methods. For instance, give a verbal description and a demonstration of a skill at the same time, whenever possible. If you are describing a hand stroking motion, do the motion while you describe it. Talk with your body as well as your mouth. You can also have a participant or an aide demonstrate while you talk. Learning motor skills is simpler when participants receive information they can see as well as hear. This is a powerful form of communication because it imparts more information in the same amount of time and uses multiple senses in the learning process.

When your participants have a complete and correct understanding of the skill you are teaching, they are more likely to learn the skill quickly. If you describe and demonstrate the skills well, you speed their process of "getting the idea." Both you and the participants will feel rewarded by these efforts.

Using Teaching Progressions

The teaching progressions in Parts D and E have been designed according to the principles of learning discussed so far. When you lead participants through these progressions, you are using a teaching strategy that is:

- **Developmental**. Motor skills are best learned when the skill is broken into steps that are taught logically, each leading directly to the next. This applies the principle of association in learning theory. In addition, since each new detail or refinement of a skill is added incrementally to what the participants already know, they can integrate the new skill with what they have already learned. The result is a qualitative change in their abilities.

■ **Familiar**. The teaching progressions rely on the principle that people learn a variety of skills more easily when the skills are taught in a standardized way. The familiarity that comes from this approach helps participants anticipate the next step of a progression even as they improve the skills they know.

■ **Measurable**. Since the teaching progressions are divided into small measurable steps, you and the participants have a useful standard for setting goals. Thus, you can use the teaching progressions to assess participants' readiness to attempt a new skill (or the next step of a complex skill) and to evaluate their performance of a skill after they have practiced it. This approach also helps you deal with any anxiety participants may have about attempting a skill.

Generic Outline for Teaching Aquatic Skills

As you present skills, you might find it helpful to follow most or all of the steps in the box to the right. (A more detailed version of this list appears on page 123.)

GUIDING PRACTICE

The chapters in this unit emphasize that motor skills are best learned through repetition. For practice to help, however, the learner must be performing the appropriate skill at the appropriate level with corrective feedback. To repeat a skill wrong not only impedes learning but also creates a pattern of behavior the learner must overcome before learning the correct action.

The most important contribution you make to the participants' practice is the feedback you give. Augmented feedback, discussed in Chapter 7, is the feedback you give to the learner. There are many ways to give feedback. For example, you can give feedback while the participants are moving by mirroring their arm action in the sidestroke as they do it. You can also give verbal

---

Teaching Aquatic Skills

1. Demonstrate and explain the mechanics of the skill, including its components. The demonstration should be slow and be repeated several times.
2. Conduct a movement-exploration drill or whole approach drill.
3. Demonstrate the skill on dry land, if possible.
4. Have the participants practice a dry land drill, if feasible. Depending on the skill, participants may be standing, seated at pool-side, or lying down.
5. Demonstrate the skill in the water. For more complex skills, demonstrate the skill in separate components.
6. Have the participants practice the skill in the water. Participants may be supported by aides, partners, or flotation devices as necessary.
7. Demonstrate the skill and explain its mechanics again.

---

feedback during the action. Normally, when you give feedback as the person practices, you can see if the feedback has the desired effect simply by seeing if the participant improves in the skill. Sometimes this method is not effective because it is too much for the participant to attend to the skill and listen to feedback at the same time.

The *American Red Cross Instructor Candidate Training Participant's Manual* identifies three types of feedback: negative, positive, and corrective. Negative feedback, even if used with good intentions, is usually not productive. It can hurt the learner's motivation and inhibit learning. Positive feedback, on the other hand, shows that you appreciate the effort, see an improvement, or see a positive result of the participants' behavior. Corrective feedback is not necessarily positive or negative. Corrective feedback identifies the behavior as not matching the goal and provides specific corrective information to help the participants attain the goal.

Following are examples of negative, positive, and corrective feedback in a teaching situation. In this example, you are trying to correct the body position of a participant doing the elementary backstroke with hips too low in the water.

Negative feedback: "No, you're not doing it right." This response may imply that the participant is not trying or is incapable of doing the skill. It may hurt motivation or frustrate a participant who is striving to improve.

Positive feedback: "I can tell you are trying, and you are doing better. You'll get it soon, I'm sure." This response is not helpful. It neither identifies what is wrong nor gives any prescriptive measures. You are making the participant figure out on his or her own what is wrong and what to do to correct it.

Corrective (positive) feedback: "This is (1) a good effort, but (2) your hips are still too low because your head is out of the water. (3) Try to keep your head back and your ears in the water and you'll improve." The three separate elements within this response are: (1) a positive manner, (2) error identification, and (3) prescriptive measure. It is positive because it praises a good effort and encourages the person to continue. It also states what the flaw is and prescribes a way to correct the flaw.

As an instructor you will probably spend most of your attention and energy responding to and correcting skill imperfections. You should also identify and respond when participants are performing a skill correctly, for two reasons. First, success is a powerful way to set the psychological stage for learning. When participants are doing something correctly, they must be made aware of it.

Second, participants might not know that they are performing the skill correctly. If you do not reinforce the correct movement with feedback and then have the participant repeat it, the participant may lose the correct skill. If you identify correct performance and have participants repeat it, they will learn it.

The following are examples of negative, positive, and reinforced (positive) feedback in a situation where the participant is performing the skill correctly.

Negative feedback: "You finally got it right." This response implies that the participant was not trying earlier or is somehow a slow learner. This type of statement, even if made in jest, is inappropriate for learning and can be damaging to a person's self-esteem.

Positive feedback: "Good, that's it!" This response recognizes the success, but it does not carry any information other than something was done right.

Reinforced (positive) feedback: "Great job, your hips are right at the surface and your head is in the water. Keep your head back and your ears in the water and you will have your hips at the surface where you want them." This response is positive and rewards the success by giving praise, but it also reinforces what the participant is supposed to do (keep the hips up) and reminds the participant how to accomplish it (head back, ears in the water). As in the first example, the most beneficial form of feedback is the longest and takes the most effort.

Another factor to consider when giving feedback is the timing. How long after the participant completes a task can you give corrective information? The timing of augmented feedback depends on many factors. First, consider what the information is intended to do. If the information is solely to motivate participants to keep trying, the feedback should be given as soon as possible. If the information is of a corrective nature and the learner is in the autonomous stage of learning the skill, the information can be delayed somewhat. For young learners, give the information soon enough that they can still associate it with what they just did. Augmented feedback is only useful if the learner can associate the information with the proper task. Information that becomes disassociated is of little value and only prolongs the learning time.

Feedback is typically given just after the learner completes the skill. This lets participants give their full attention to what you say. When you are more experienced, you will better understand what kind of feedback works best, and when.

FOCUSING ON SENSORY AWARENESS

Chapter 7 explains how augmented feedback can support learning but how practicing a skill with intrinsic feedback is essential for learning. Thus, the feedback you give should help participants pay attention to their intrinsic feedback. One of the best things you can do for your participants is to teach them how to listen to their bodies. You can do this in two ways: by adjusting the environment and by focusing participants' senses on what they are learning.

Adjusting the Environment

To help participants focus on their sensory and kinesthetic awareness of their performance, you can adjust the environment to help reduce distractions and establish a situation conducive to the participants' progress. The size of the class and the length of lessons are elements of good teaching, not just matters of course administration. Other factors also affect the "environment" of your classes.

The way you schedule lessons has an impact on learning. For example, twelve 30-minute classes over 3 weeks are more effective than two 3-hour classes. A well-distributed practice schedule is better for learning skills than a practice schedule grouped in large blocks. A shorter period between classes is better than long periods, for example, 24 hours instead of 7 days. Sometimes schedules are affected by outside factors such as facility availability and conflicting activities. Whenever possible, try to have classes 30 to 45 minutes long with very few days between the classes.

For some groups, time of day is critical. Classes for infants, toddlers, and preschoolers often are not effective after lunch because that is when many young children take naps. Morning is better for this group. For adults, just after work is a good time for a class because many adults use this time to relax as well as to learn.

A wide range of abilities in a class can affect the success of the participants. In most classes for motor skills, relatively homogeneous classes are easier to teach and participants are more successful. In general, classes that range widely in skills and abilities tend either to leave someone behind or to hold someone back. Try to organize classes with comparable skill levels.

Focusing Participants' Attention

Helping the participants pay attention to their bodies begins with the way you demonstrate skills. For example, if you tell participants to put their palms down on a flat surface (such as a table) and press gently, they will notice the pressure in the joints, tendons, and muscles of the body. You can then lead them to feel another kind of pressure on these body parts by having them make slicing motions through the water. Such exercises help you introduce the concept of lift, the main propulsive force in swimming, while the participants learn to pay attention to their bodies.

With such an approach, you help participants learn through intrinsic feedback. Swimmers can feel what a floppy ankle in a good flutter kick is like if you get them to pay attention to it. They can feel the water swish past the thigh on the completion of an arm stroke in the crawl if you ask them to do so. Use your imagination, creativity, and experience to develop ways to get participants to listen to their bodies.

After a skill demonstration, you can keep directing the participants' attention to their bodies by using descriptive words during drills. By telling participants to "press," "stretch," "relax," or "feel," you are urging them to listen to their bodies and the way a skill feels or should feel. Whenever possible, try to use such descriptions to help participants understand the movement. It is easier to remember a feeling than a verbal description.

You can help translate the hydrodynamic principles that underlie aquatic skills from dry abstractions to concrete experience if you include them when you focus participants' attention. For instance, when participants are comfortable with the supine float, introduce the concept of the center of buoyancy. As you show them how they can adjust their body position, tell them to try to "feel" their center of buoyancy. Newton's law of acceleration similarly can be "felt" if participants do the elementary backstroke with one arm at a time. These and other ways to illustrate hydrodynamic principles are in *Swimming and Diving*.

Try to keep participants' attention on intrinsic feedback even when you teach the most basic skills. If participants rely too much on augmented feedback in these early stages, they might not be able to focus on all the information their bodies give them during more complex skills. As their aquatic skills develop and their attentiveness to intrinsic feedback improves, they have learned how to learn to swim.

SUMMARY

Your success as an instructor depends on many factors. Some of these are in your control; others rest with the learner. In every learning situation, progress involves the successful interaction of the two most important people, the instructor and the learner. Without a harmonious relationship little can be accomplished. Participants generally come to you with a desire to learn. It is up to you to understand their hopes and fears, to relieve the fears, and to foster and nurture the hopes. Consider each participant an individual. The cloning of swimming styles is a thing of the past. Each participant comes to the learning process as an individual and must leave as an individual, but one who is improved and confident and who realizes that aquatics is fun. If you remember and apply the learning principles discussed in this chapter and Chapters 6 and 7, your participants will realize the goals and objective of the American Red Cross Swimming and Water Safety program.

- course planning
- class organization

elements of course design

9 | course planning

One of your responsibilities as an American Red Cross Water Safety Instructor is to make class time as effective and rewarding as possible for the participants. This takes careful planning and prep-aration, especially when you consider the kinds of activities that take place in a given course:

- Lectures, discussions, and videos on a variety of topics
- Demonstrations of aquatic and safety skills
- Practice time for participants
- Assignments to be given for the next lesson

In your planning, you must also take into account several other factors:

- Requirements for the course
- Differences in participant skill levels
- Concerns about communication based on language or cultural differences
- Effective strategies for meeting course objectives
- The participants' own goals for the course.

For all these reasons, no two classes are ever the same.

This chapter provides you with a framework for course planning. First there is a discussion of block plans, which you use to map out a full course. Then there is a strategy for developing individual lesson plans and translating your block plan into a day-by-day approach for teaching. You can use the templates for the block plans and lesson plans and the skills checklist (Appendix H) on a daily basis to help chart the progress of your classes. The Instructor Portfolio provides a convenient way to prepare lesson plans on waterproof acetates.

FACTORS THAT INFLUENCE PLANNING

Whether you are preparing a block plan or converting that block plan into your daily lesson plan, you should consider the following—

- **Class size**. This affects how long it takes to organize a drill, practice the skill, and give feedback to the group and to individuals. A small class (ideally 6–10 participants) needs less time per activity and thus has time for more activities per lesson. Small classes also have more time for optional skills and other activities. Depending on the participants' background and interests, you can include fitness components or games and water activities in your planning. (For more information, see Chapters 24 and 25.)

  For classes with more than 10 participants, you will be more successful with additional instructors or Water Safety Instructor Aides. Large classes require more planning to ensure the maximum involvement of all participants. Wave and stagger formations and station teaching can help you use class time wisely to provide more group practice. (For information on class organization, see Chapter 10.)

- **Participant abilities**. Developing your plans is easiest when all the participants are at the same level in prerequisite skills. If they have a wide range of skills at the beginning of the course, you should try to develop a flexible plan that does not ignore stronger swimmers or frustrate anyone struggling to keep up with the class. Take similar care when you are mainstreaming people with disabilities in your course.

- **Review skills**. The Infant and Preschool Aquatics Program (IPAP) and the American Red Cross Learn to Swim program progress from level to level. Each level builds on skills and knowledge from previous levels. Reviewing these earlier skills helps build on this progression and reinforces learning. Reviewing skills also helps you introduce new skills by relating them to familiar ones. Teaching from the known to the related unknown is a logical teaching method and helps your participants experience success.

- **New skills**. Be sure to include all required course material somewhere in your plans.

Skills for the various programs and courses are listed in the related chapters:

- Infant and Preschool Aquatics Program in Chapter 13
- Learn to Swim program in Chapter 16
- Basic Water Safety course in Chapter 26
- Emergency Water Safety course in Chapter 27
- Water Safety Instructor Aide course in Chapter 28

- **Proficiency requirements**. Greater proficiency usually results from more practice time and practice with immediate feedback. After you have introduced a skill, participants should review and practice it in subsequent lessons until they have reached the required proficiency.
- **Completion requirements**. Be sure you include the skills for successfully completing a course level. Photocopy the skills checklist in Appendix H for each course you teach prior to the first lesson. List the participants in the column at the left and copy the completion requirements from the appropriate course outline. Keep this checklist poolside as a handy reference and to chart each participant's progress.

DEVELOPING A BLOCK PLAN

The first step in effectively organizing the course is to develop a block plan. A block plan is a template that gives you an overview of the course. Each square in the template is for one lesson. By planning the main parts of your course from beginning to end, you set up logical learning sequences to ensure no skills or information is overlooked.

One of the easiest ways to develop a block plan is the calendar approach to organization. An example of a completed block plan in this format is on page 41. Appendix H gives a template you can use for your own block plans. Each block is one day in the course. The block plan should include some or all of the following:

- Safety information
- Equipment
- Review skills
- New skills

The first time you organize the block plan for a course, you may have difficulty determining which skills to review, what order to follow in introducing new skills, and how much time is needed to introduce a skill. Always allow time for the participants to practice and for you to give feedback. Experience is a good teacher. The longer you teach, the better you will be at organizing your block plans. One approach is to distribute skills across the lessons, allow several lessons for difficult skills, and integrate safety skills throughout the plan.

You may find that after the first couple of lessons you have to rearrange the block plan. This happens often, and you should not view it as a failure or lack of organization.

DEVELOPING A LESSON PLAN

When you have finished organizing the block plan, you can use it to plan daily lessons. An effective lesson plan usually includes the following:

- **Safety topics**. It is especially helpful to teach safety issues related to the skill being introduced or practiced. Check the course outlines for cross-references to safety information in *Swimming and Diving*. Use key words to remind you of the information you want to include in each day's lesson.
- **Equipment**. List all equipment needed. Be sure it is available and in good repair.
- **Opening**. All lessons should have an opening activity. This may be a land drill for a swimming skill, stretching, a water adjustment drill such as bobbing or rhythmic breathing, or a drill to review a skill. These activities should last 5–10 minutes depending on the length of the lesson and the age of the participants. (Suggestions for customizing your lessons are included in Chapters 22–25. For instance, older

BLOCK PLAN

Instructor **Miss LaPink**	Course Level **II—Primary Skills**
# of Students **8** # of Days **10**	Length of Lesson **45 minutes**
Dates **6–10 thru 6–28** Aides **Zeke**	

Safety Topic: Reaching Assists	Date 6/10
Equipment: Kickboards	

Review Skills:	New Skills:
Individual water entry	Flutter kick
Supported float	Prone float
Kick	Prone glide
Alternating arms	

Safety Topic: Assist Nonswimmer	Date 6/12
Equipment: Kickboards	

Review Skills:	New Skills:
Alternate arms	Rhythmic breathing
Flutter kick	Submerge
Prone float	Unsupported glide
Prone glide	
Back float	
Back glide	

Safety Topic: Life Jacket Safety	Date 6/14
Equipment: Life Jacket, Kickboard	

Review Skills:	New Skills:
Submerge	Recover object
Rhythmic breathing	Finning
Glides, front & back	Combined stroke front
Flutter	
Alternate arms	

Safety Topic: Extension Assist	Date 6/16
Equipment: Pole, Kickboard	

Review Skills:	New Skills:
Rhythmic breathing	Back crawl/ arms
Retrieval	
Combined stroke front	

Safety Topic: Float w/Life Jacket	Date 6/18
Equipment: Life Jacket, Kickboard	

Review Skills:	New Skills:
Back crawl/arms	Orientation to deep water
Front crawl	Exit side of pool
Back crawl/arms	
Rhythmic breathing	

Safety Topic: 911	Date 6/20
Equipment: Kickboards	

Review Skills:	New Skills:
Deep water	Level off
Front crawl	Combined back
Back crawl/arms	
Rhythmic breathing	
Exit side of pool	

Safety Topic: Rescue Breathing Intro.	Date 6/22
Equipment: VCR after class	

Review Skills:	New Skills:
Deep water	Step off and level
Rhythmic breathing	Turn front to back
Front crawl	
Back crawl	

Safety Topic: Rescue Breathing	Date 6/24
Equipment: Kickboard	

Review Skills:	New Skills:
Deep water	Turn back to front
Turn front to back	
Rhythmic breathing	
Front crawl	
Back crawl	

Safety Topic: Improvised Extension Rescues	Date 6/26
Equipment: Raft, tube	

Review Skills:	New Skills:
Deep water	Use checklist
Turn back to front	
Any safety skills	
Rhythmic breathing	
Front crawl	
Back crawl	

Safety Topic: Review Order of Assists	Date 6/28
Equipment: VCR makeup	

Review Skills:	New Skills:
Deep water	Complete checklist
Rhythmic breathing	
Front crawl	
Back crawl	

Safety Topic:	Date
Equipment:	

Review Skills:	New Skills:

Safety Topic:	Date
Equipment:	

Review Skills:	New Skills:

adults may need a longer period to become accustomed to the water temperature. Appendix B of *Swimming and Diving* includes other activities to consider.) Be sure the opening activities are appropriate for the course and the participants.

■ **Skill review**. You can review skills in several ways. You may demonstrate the skill or show a video, verbally present information about the skill, conduct a drill (land, bracket, or swimming), or give participants time to practice. Choose your methods depending on the complexity of the skill and the past accomplishments of the class. Be sure to plan enough time for feedback to the group and to individuals.

■ **New skill demonstration**. Decide how, when, and where to present and demonstrate new skills. In general, introduce each new skill with a verbal explanation and a demonstration. Be sure to perform the demonstration slowly and accurately and ensure all participants can see it. Allow for time to repeat the demonstration if necessary or to let participants see it from other angles so they can understand it better. Often it is better to have an aide or an accomplished swimmer demonstrate while you point out what to watch for. Your class may benefit from reading appropriate parts of *Swimming and Diving* or seeing the video *Swimming and Diving Skills* when they are learning strokes and diving. Participants in the Basic Water Safety and Emergency Water Safety courses are expected to read assigned material.

■ **New skill practice**. You can organize this in many ways. Participants can learn some skills by trying the whole skill immediately. Other, more complex skills should be broken down into small parts that are practiced one at a time. The part-whole approach can be very effective for teaching strokes. The progressive part approach also breaks a skill into parts but helps participants learn the skill by adding new parts to what is already known. Review the teaching methods in the *Instructor Candidate Training Participant's Manual.* You will also want to

review Chapter 8. Chapter 10 contains information on organizing the class for practice sessions.

Plan enough time to arrange the class into a practice pattern and to give positive corrective feedback to all participants. When using a drill, explain clearly what you want the class to do. Plan more drills than you think you will use so you have many options. Your participants' age and attention span, as well as the difficulty of the skill, determine how long to spend on each skill or part of a skill in each lesson. Include some fun drills or games and use a wide variety of activities to keep participants motivated.

First, have participants practice each skill or part of a skill on land if they can assume the correct body position. Then have them practice the skill in a static drill in the water, followed by a variety of fluid drills. Chapters 18–21 suggest a sequence for each skill.

■ **Closing**. The closing is the "winding down" phase of the lesson. It should include an oral review of what the participants learned in the lesson and a look ahead to the next lesson. In some courses it may include an assignment. This part of the lesson is a great opportunity for individual practice. Let participants practice something they enjoy doing, so they leave the lesson remembering the pleasure of the last activity. It is also fun to end with a game or an enjoyable stunt everyone can do or to include optional activities for that course. (Chapter 25 has suggestions for such activities.) When participants are reluctant to get out of the water at the end of a lesson, they will remember the experience as a fun activity and come to the next lesson motivated.

Writing the Lesson Plan

Now you are ready to write the lesson plan. An example of a completed lesson plan is on page 43. It uses the third block from the block plan on page 41. This sample is for a children's class. Appendix G gives a template you can use for making

LESSON PLAN

Miss LaPink	II	3	6/14	Sun.	2–2:45
Instructor	Level	Lesson #	Date	Day	Time

Safety Topics:	Equipment:
Choosing, fitting and when to wear life jacket	Life jackets, pennies, kickboards, weighted rings, plastic cups, 1 per participant

Assignment:

Time	Activity/Topic	Key words/ Phrases	Practice Method	Pattern of Organization
2–2:05	**Opening:** Attendance Follow the leader	Big bite of air Blow	Lead class into water-walk, hop, etc., duck under, march, sing, splash, etc.	Follow around teaching area, be creative w/ movement exploration
2:05– 2:10	Life jacket safety	Sizing safety	Try on and check	Sit on deck in semi-circle— face away from pool
2:10– 2:15	Rhythmic breathing	Eyes open Blow Bend Knees	Try-ring a rosy Bobbing Stand in place Travel and bob See-saw with partner Tea party Count fingers	Circle Double line
2:15– 2:20	Recover object	"Pick flowers" Open eyes	One at a time, submerge and recover (challenge w/ pennies after rings)	Near wall—may hold—away from wall—stagger on double line with partner
2:20– 2:30	Review front glide Add arms/ As ready Review back glide	Stretch Big breath Head down Stomach up Head back	With kickboard and without glide to wall if necessary, play rocket ship Walk with arms With and without support for distance	Wave, stagger One on one who need help Try for distance Wall push off Wave Stagger
2:30– 2:35	Finning Combined stroke	Push water to feet	Stand, walk, support	Line, wave, stagger
2:35– 2:40	Combined stroke front	Reach, pull	Stand at wall and pattern	Line, watch demo
2:40– 2:45	**Closing:** Skill game	Walk or kick, fast or slow	Balance plastic cup of water on kickboard and walk or kick across area	Straight lines, or circle, follow student leader— relay?

your own lesson plans. The Instructor Portfolio, available from your local Red Cross unit, has the template permanently printed on it. Waterproof overlays are included so you can write your lesson plans on them.

For each part of the lesson, you have to decide—

- How much time each activity requires.
- The key words or phrases you want to use.
- The practice method you want the participants to use.
- The pattern of organization you will use for the participants' practice.

These elements are described below.

The following is a guide for assigning times for the different parts of a lesson. Classes in the American Red Cross Learn to Swim program typically last 30 to 45 minutes. Infant and preschool programs are usually shorter. The Basic Water Safety and Emergency Water Safety courses are discussed in Chapters 26 and 27.

Opening	5–10 minutes
Practice (including practicing, review skills, demonstrations, and practicing new skills)	20–30 minutes
Closing	5–10 minutes

Follow these steps to complete the lesson plan:
1. Using your block plan, list the skills on the lesson plan in the section marked activity/topic. The activity/topic can include any or all of the following:
   - Lecture topic (may include safety information)
   - Review of part of a skill
   - Review of a whole skill
   - Demonstration of new skill(s) or parts
   - Practice of skill(s)
   - Transition from one skill or area to another
   - Game or other water activity
   - Assignment for next lesson
2. Arrange the activities so that a review skill appears before a related new skill and the demonstration occurs before the practice.

3. For each skill, identify key words appropriate for the age of participants. Try to think of different ways to say the same thing and write one- or two-word descriptions in the key word section.
4. Decide what practice method is best for teaching this activity. You may want to use a land drill, bracketing on the wall, walking drill for arm strokes, or a moving drill. List any equipment you will need. Briefly describe your practice method in the section provided.
5. The section for pattern of organization can remind you of additional information at a glance. Draw a small picture of the way you want the practice to flow.

Keep in mind that most of the lesson time is needed for practice (repetition). Each skill introduced should include practice time. You may have to change activities often. Younger participants may stay on task as little as 2 minutes and you will need to provide more ways to practice the same skill. Plan to make the lesson fun for everyone.

Lessons in the the American Red Cross Learn to Swim program are skill-intensive, so about 80 percent of the time should be planned for practice. The Basic Water Safety course and the Emergency Water Safety course include more discussion and lecture material. However, in these courses you must allow enough time for the students to master the skills. Infant and toddler courses are often less formal and are adapted for the readiness needs of each parent-child pair. Teaching the infant and preschool program is discussed in Part D.

When planning for the practice of new skills, list each drill for the practice as a separate activity in the lesson plan. For example, when you introduce a kick, you may use a mass drill bracketing on the wall and then continue with a wave drill with kickboards. Estimate the time required for each drill. Try to develop creative ways to keep the practice time fun by including games and other activities.

The lesson plan should also include time for transitions from one activity to the next. Consider how long it takes to reorganize your class to begin the next part of the lesson. Limit the number of times participants have to get in and out of the water. If they become chilled, they are not likely to make much progress.

Using Time Effectively

You can make the best use of the practice time by using the following suggested sequence for each skill:
1. Conduct a group drill.
2. Provide corrective feedback based on the needs of the group as a whole.
3. Repeat the group drill, perhaps in another version.
4. Provide corrective feedback to any individuals still having trouble with the skill.
5. Have the group repeat the same or a similar drill (or a game with the skill incorporated into it) while you help anyone still having trouble with the skill.

Guide the practice, stressing major corrections first. At first it is most important to recognize and correct body position errors. Make only one correction at a time. Review Chapter 8 for more techniques on feedback.

Adjusting the Lesson Plan

If you see that your lesson plan is not working, adjust it as needed. A drill may be too complicated or advanced for the skill level of the group. The group may need more practice with previous steps in the teaching progression, or it may take more time to address the needs of participants with a wide range of skills.

You may find that a drill inhibits the learning of the skill. Sometimes a student who could perform the whole skill has difficulty with a part or progressive-part approach. Let that person do a variation of the drill in order to stay with the group rather than risking frustration or failure.

One of the best ways to prepare for adjustments to your lesson plan is to write down a variety of methods for practicing the same skill or skill sequence. You may want to include a static drill, a moving drill, and a game. If one drill or method of practice is not working, switch to another. Chapter 10 describes some methods you may wish to incorporate.

Evaluating the Success of the Lesson Plan

Evaluation of the lesson plan is an important step for both the participants' success and your own improvement as instructor. To evaluate your plan, ask yourself these questions immediately after the lesson:
1. Did I follow my plan?
2. Did the participants have enough time to practice?
3. Did I choose the right activities, or were the drills too difficult, too time consuming, or too easy?
4. Did I use my teaching area effectively?
5. Were the drills I used right for the age and skill of the participants?
6. Did I use a variety of methods and equipment to enhance learning?
7. Did I include a variety of skills in the plan so everyone had some success?
8. Did the participants improve?

Use your answers to these questions to improve the next lesson plan. Analyze all parts of the lesson plan and decide what changes would have made it more successful.

You may find it easier to write the next lesson plan immediately after a lesson, while it is still fresh in your mind. You need to know your group and how much practice they need, which skills need only minor review, and which skills need the most time in the next lesson. All of the factors discussed above, including the size, age, and experience of the group, influence the success of your plans. If you see you are falling behind, rework your block plan and try to get additional help with your course.

Summary

The role of planning in teaching others to swim cannot be overemphasized. A successful lesson doesn't just happen. This chapter has detailed the components necessary to guide your planning. You start with a block plan, then convert each day of the block plan into a functional lesson plan. Keep handy your skills checklist to help evaluate participants' progress. Evaluate your plans soon after each lesson so you can make necessary adjustments. With enough preparation you will be able to adjust to the needs and circumstances of the participants and to make their class time rewarding and fun.

10 class organization

You need to consider many things to make your lesson plans work. Organizing the class effectively, choosing the best drills, and knowing what approach to use in a given situation all take practice. Learning from trial and error, in addition to good planning, can make you a more effective instructor. Use this chapter closely with Chapters 6–9 to plan an effective strategy for all the courses you teach.

PRINCIPLES OF CLASS ORGANIZATION

To organize the class for effective teaching and learning experiences, always arrange the class so that—

- Everyone's safety is ensured.
- Everyone can hear and see instructions.
- Everyone can hear and see demonstrations.
- Everyone has an opportunity for enough effective practice.
- Everyone has an opportunity to be checked for skill improvement.

The most important factor is the safety of the participants. Make every effort to prevent injuries. Be sure a lifeguard is on duty during instructional periods. Be familiar with the facility's emergency action plan. Explain and enforce safety rules. Never leave the teaching area until all participants are accounted for and have left the area.

PATTERNS OF CLASS ORGANIZATION

Patterns of class organization are formations you use to make sure all participants practice skills. Inactive participants may become bored, chilled, or restless and may disrupt the class.

Demonstrations

When you demonstrate a skill, whether on land or in the water, be sure all participants are close enough and positioned so everyone can see. For a demonstration of a moving skill in water, participants may stand in a single line along the edge of the teaching area (FIG. 10–1, *A*). For a demon-

stration of a stationary skill in water, participants may stand or sit in an "L" formation around the corner of the teaching area (FIG. 10–1, *B*) or in parallel or multiple lines (FIG. 10–2, *A* and *B*). You can reinforce the demonstration by showing the American Red Cross *Swimming and Diving Skills* video or by having it demonstrated by a skilled swimmer.

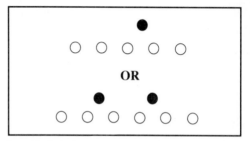

FIG. 10–1, *A* Samples of single line formation. Solid dots show location of instructors.

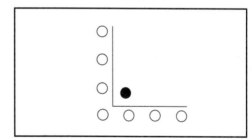

FIG. 10–1, *B* "L" formation

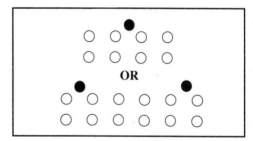

FIG. 10–2, *A* Samples of parallel lines

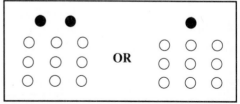

FIG. 10–2, *B* Samples of multiple lines

Static Drills

Use static drills when participants practice in one place. Static drills are appropriate for skills such as kicking on the wall, treading water, and isolating part of a skill to practice it without movement. Participants can be in any safe arrangement along the sides of the pool, standing in lines, or randomly scattered. The shape, size, and depth of your teaching area is a major factor. Be sure to position yourself where you can see all participants at all times. Most of your time will be in the water so that you can readily provide hands-on feedback as well as encouragement and corrections.

Fluid Drills

Use fluid drills to help participants improve their skills and physical endurance and to evaluate their performance. Vary the type and formation of drills to keep the practice interesting and help participants meet the course requirements. Consider the following factors when choosing drills:

- The participants' skill proficiency
- The participants' physical condition
- The intensity level of each drill
- The frequency and length of rest periods

Individual Instruction

Observe your participants one at a time in skills that involve extra safety considerations. Carefully monitor skills like entering deep water for the first time, floating on the back, diving skills, and any other skill that makes participants fearful. Giving feedback to one participant at a time is not very efficient with larger classes, since other participants have to wait, so you may want to provide another activity for the rest of the class. Use a previously learned drill or activity, if possible one that is related to the skill you are observing individually or that leads up to it. If you have enough instructors and aides, individualized instruction is a very useful teaching method.

Wave

You may divide a large group into smaller units for maximum supervised practice. Participants count off by number, and each group then performs as a unit. This method lets you watch smaller groups and give better feedback. It also makes better use of a small practice area (FIG. 10–3).

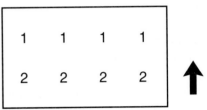

FIG. 10–3 Wave pattern. Arrow indicates direction of travel.

Stagger

In the stagger formation (FIG. 10–4) the class remains in a single line. You signal the first in line to start swimming. The next in line starts when the person ahead reaches a certain spot. This lets you follow the progress of each participant for a few body lengths. It also lets you speak to each participant as he or she finishes the swim and still have time to focus on the next participant. This method gives a large amount of practice time on a skill, as well as individual feedback. It also gives participants a short rest period while they wait their turn. Finally, it lets participants who are not ready to perform the particular skill or drill do a modified version and receive feedback on their progress. Water Safety Instructor Aides can also give feedback at the other end of the line.

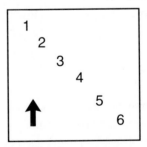

FIG. 10–4 Stagger pattern. Arrow indicates direction of travel.

Circle Swimming

For longer-distance swims to build endurance, you may have participants use the pool lanes. Have them keep to the right and remain in one lane as they turn and continue swimming (FIG. 10–5). Another option is a circuit swim in which the participants first swim in one lane and then move over a lane to swim in the other direction (always keeping to the right side of the lane). You can continue this pattern so participants use all the available lanes. With this method you can interrupt the participants at any time to make corrections and give feedback. Participants can also perform different phases of the same drill depending on their progress.

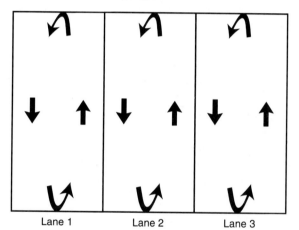

| Lane 1 | Lane 2 | Lane 3 |

FIG. 10–5 Circle Swimming

Paired Coaching

With adults and students at higher levels, it can be very effective to have them observe and help each other. Each participant learns better as he or she also practices observing.

Summary of Other Options

The more flexibility and variety that you build into your lesson plan drills, the more successful and effective the lessons are apt to be. You can choose perimeter, circle, stagger, diagonal, or other formation drills. Be creative in using whatever variety of patterns the swimming area permits.

Assembly Lines and Stations

Assembly line and station teaching are proven methods of class organization that use multiple instructors efficiently and help participants most fully. In the Instructor Candidate Training course and video, you saw examples of these methods. There are many variations on assembly line and station teaching, depending on the numbers of participants, instructors, and aides. In your planning, consider the participants' age and experience and the goals of the lesson.

Station Teaching

In the most common use of stations, participants begin in a single group to receive all the information for the day's lesson. Then they are directed to stations at various parts of the facility, each equipped with appropriate equipment and written instructions for practice. The participants perform the skills at that station until signaled to rotate to the next practice area. You can move from station to station to give as much feedback as possible. Having an assistant or trained aide at each station makes this method more effective. Rotating through stations is an efficient way to review previous skills and to prepare for a new skill. This promotes a high level of participant involvement. Ensure safety with station teaching by having enough lifeguards on duty.

Station teaching works best when participants take some responsibility for their own progress. Safety skills are often taught effectively in this format. After all participants have completed each station, you may review the material with the whole group and lead group drills to reinforce or check skills.

Assembly Line Within One Level

The assembly line method of teaching works best when you have enough instructors and trained aides and you have participants at about the same skill level. Each instructor or aide conducts a particular drill or teaches a specific skill. One way to use this method is to teach the same skill at all the stations, but with different styles, techniques, and drills. Another variation is to assign each instructor a different skill. As participants rotate from station to station, they receive a full and varied lesson in groups small enough for individualized attention. If you use this method, be sure that the activities at the different stations are compatible and that instructors teach the skills they are most proficient at teaching.

Assembly Line With More Than One Level

Another option for the assembly line method is to program the facility with several classes of participants at different but consecutive levels of the Learn to Swim program. This works best if the participants are of similar ages. Assign each instructor to a particular station. Participants remain with the same instructor until they perform the required skills well enough to advance. Some participants may move from one level to the next after only one lesson; others may need to remain in the same level for a full series of lessons. This method allows maximum flexibility for participants to proceed at their own speed, the chance to experience a variety of instructors, and the opportunity to meet new people as they move through the program.

This method also allows flexibility in class organization. Aides and other instructors can assist instructors whose groups are large or who need more help. The positions of instructors and aides may change as group structure changes. Instructors and aides can be reassigned if a large group is divided or if two small groups are combined.

SUMMARY

To organize your lessons in meaningful ways, you must consider many variables. Once you have written block plans and lesson plans for a particular group, you must decide the specific class organization that will best help them succeed. There are many techniques you can use and there may be others you develop. Remember to include time to flow from one arrangement to another and consider issues such as class size and experience as you decide what patterns of organization to include. Planning sequences, activities, and arrangements take extra time but your investment here can help the participants meet their individual goals. You will also see overall results as the participants progress towards completion requirements for each level. As you become more experienced, you will build a repertoire of activities that work well for you and the participants.

- overview of IPAP
- parent orientation
- IPAP course outlines
- holding positions for infants and young children
- aquatic skills for infants and young children

the infant and preschool aquatics program

D

11 | overview of IPAP

The American Red Cross Infant and Preschool Aquatics Program (IPAP) helps young children (aged 6 months through 5 years) become comfortable in and around the water so they are ready to learn to swim. This program is *not* designed to teach children to become good swimmers or even to survive in the water on their own. The program gives parents information and techniques to help orient their children to the water and to supervise water activities in a safe manner.

> **Instructor's note:**
> Guardians, child care providers, grandparents, other adults, and even older siblings may also participate in IPAP courses. For the sake of simplicity, however, the term *parent* is used throughout.

This chapter provides basic information about IPAP. General administrative notes are covered first, followed by a discussion of issues you may face in teaching infants and young children. Finally, there are some notes about common health and safety concerns. Chapter 12 discusses the parent orientation for IPAP. Chapters 13–15 present the course outlines, holding positions, and skill progressions you should use in teaching IPAP courses.

ADMINISTRATIVE NOTES

The following points apply to the Infant and Preschool Aquatics Program:

Prerequisites

There are no skill prerequisites for IPAP. An infant must be at least 6 months old to be enrolled in IPAP. IPAP introduces infants and young children to aquatics in three age groups:
1. Infant Level: 6–18 months
   (Parent/adult accompaniment in the water is required.)
2. Toddler Level: 18–36 months
   (Parent/adult accompaniment in the water is required.)
3. Preschool Level: 3–5 years
   These children might complete Level I, Water Exploration, in the American Red Cross Learn to Swim program.
   (Parent/adult accompaniment in the water is optional.)

Children in IPAP may meet the objectives of one or more levels of the American Red Cross Learn to Swim program. They should move to the Learn to Swim program as soon as they are able.

Course Length

There is no minimum or maximum course length. As a general rule, the program works well if you schedule 7–10 lessons of no more than 30 minutes, at least twice a week. Lessons for preschoolers may extend to 45 minutes each.

Scheduling

Scheduling depends on facility availability, community needs, staffing, and facility characteristics (water chemistry, air and water temperature, and depth). If possible, offer programs in the daytime and evenings, on weekdays and weekends. It is useful to schedule lessons at intervals that allow you to communicate with parents between lessons, as needed.

The ideal teaching situation is to offer separate courses for each of the three age levels. However, a practical alternative is to combine infants and toddlers (aged 6 months to 3 years), since both levels require parent accompaniment in the water.

Class Size

Enough staff must be present for the safe operation of the program. Consider increasing the staff ratio if any participants have disabilities or any special needs. The recommended ratios are as follows.

- Infants and/or toddlers:
  6 to 8 parent-child pairs per instructor.
- Preschoolers (without parent):
  - If the water is more than chest-deep, 4 or 5 children per instructor, without an aide.
  - If the water is more than chest-deep, 6 to 8 children per instructor, with an aide.
  - If the water is chest-deep or less, 4 to 6 children per instructor, without an aide.
  - If the water is chest-deep or less, 8 to 10 children per instructor, with an aide.

Facility

It is recommended that IPAP courses be taught only in well-maintained swimming pools. Open bodies of water such as lakes, streams, and ponds are more likely to carry harmful organisms.

Conditions at the facility can make your program more successful. When possible, a facility for IPAP classes should have—

- Dry, comfortable changing tables.
- Sanitary crawling areas.
- Adequate garbage disposal, especially for soiled diapers.
- Adequate air circulation and warm air temperatures.
- Secured pool entrances when class is not in session.
- A storage space for instructional aids and toys. This helps to keep these objects out of sight and reach when not in use.

Temperature

Infants and young children are more susceptible to hypothermia than older children, even at relatively warm temperatures. Take the following measures to keep infants and young children from getting chilled:

- Be sure the water temperature is at least 82 degrees F (28 degrees C). A temperature of 86 degrees F (30 degrees C) is preferable.
- Keep the air temperature at least 3 degrees F (2 degrees C) above water temperature.
- If you cannot control water and air temperature, keep the lessons short.

Depth

Young children learn best when actively exploring the aquatic environment under their own power. When the water is too deep for children to stand safely and comfortably, seek ways to reduce the depth.

- Use a facility with a gradually sloping shallow area and/or graduated steps so that a child of average size can stand alone in waist- or chest-deep water.
- Construct or purchase teaching platforms on which children can stand safely.
- When the depth cannot be controlled or with infants, a parent or instructor may support the child, or a flotation device may be used.

Noise and Distractions

You must control sights and sounds in the environment since infants and young children are easily distracted. Consider the following points:

- Limit loud, distorted sounds as much as possible.
- Limit the number of other children who may be moving about and shouting or crying.
- Encourage people to talk in normal voices and not shout over the noise.
- Store unused toys and equipment out of sight.
- Take any child who is over-stimulated to a quieter area of the pool to calm down and adjust to the environment.

Certificates

IPAP certificates (Cert. 3400) are awarded on the basis of participation alone. Certificates given in IPAP reflect the age of the child (see page 53). (For more information on awarding certificates, completing records, and conducting course evaluations, see Chapter 5.)

TEACHING INFANTS AND YOUNG CHILDREN

To teach aquatic skills to infants and young children, you need an extra dose of patience and additional teaching skills. The following sections give essential information for orienting infants and young children to the water and for preparing them for entry into the American Red Cross Learn to Swim program.

Despite the similarities between young children, each one is unique. Each child has individual qualities that make him or her different. Children learn new motor skills at different ages. They learn at different rates, and they have different preferences for activities and learning styles. They are often affected by their parent's comfort in and around the water. For example, the parent may be fearful of the water or have different cultural or social attitudes toward swimming.

Children also differ in their learning styles. Some children want to be shown how to do something, while others want to hear how to do it. The younger the child, the less likely it is that verbal explanations alone are enough. If you spend too much time talking about how to do something, children who learn better by seeing or feeling how it is done will not learn as quickly. Be aware of such differences when you plan your presentations of skills for the class.

The Infant and Toddler Levels require a parent to participate in the water with the child. Therefore you are more of a facilitator of parent-child interaction than an instructor for the child.

Children progress at their own rates through the skills in this program. You guide, instruct, and provide positive corrective feedback to help the parents as their children explore the aquatic world. Holding positions are described in Chapter 14; aquatic skills for infants and young children are in Chapter 15.

Learning and Development in Children

Infants and young children undergo rapid and remarkable changes between birth and the fifth year. During this time, a child's ability to think, feel, move, and play all change dramatically. Because a child is so different from an adult, you must understand these complex learning and developmental changes.

The learning process is one way parents and instructors see how young children grow. Learning involves changes in behavior that result from practice or experience. The parent or instructor can control the factors that influence a young child's learning in the home or teaching environment. As an instructor, you direct the learning process by setting goals, encouraging practice, and providing feedback and motivation. However, you must focus on the child's learning rather than on your teaching. Instruction is only one of many influences on learning in young children.

Practice is essential for learning motor skills. Infants and young children usually benefit most from distributed practice, with frequent rest periods throughout the practice. A distributed practice schedule has three benefits:

- It minimizes fatigue.
- It gives time for the child to assimilate learning.
- It helps the child stay motivated and interested in the activity.

Applying these principles in your IPAP courses means that your classes should meet more often for shorter periods of time. For example, five 20-minute lessons per week help young children learn better than two 50-minute lessons. Other factors that influence learning are explained in Chapters 6–8.

The Fearful Child

One challenge you may face with young children is dealing with their fears about water. Infants and young children are often reluctant to approach the pool, work with an instructor or any adult other than the parent, go into the water itself, or submerge. To understand the fearful child, you must understand children's learning and development processes.

Some fears are related to the child's developmental level. At about 8 months, an infant starts to express stranger or separation anxiety. As infants recognize the difference between a parent and others, they may react by crying, screaming, or becoming withdrawn. Some infants react with anger often marked by stiffening their bodies. One way to reduce fear is to be consistent in your lessons. If you start, end, and organize each lesson the same way, the child becomes familiar with the routine and may participate more easily.

After 2 years of age, the child's emerging memory and active imagination may trigger fears of the unknown. The child's fantasies can be distressing to both adults and the child. The imagination can conjure monsters, scary animals, and other fearful images. Sometimes the fears make the child less willing to try a new skill.

Other fears come from experience. For instance, an unpleasant experience with water may provoke fear when an adult encourages the child to try a new aquatic skill or even to enter the water. Coach the parent to be patient and not force the child to progress before he or she is ready. Remind parents that their children's moods often reflect the parent's feelings, so that if parents maintain a positive attitude toward swimming, their children will be less likely to be afraid.

Theories of social learning and development suggest ways you can reduce or eliminate fearful behavior in young children. First, you can reduce the impact of learned fears by anticipating possible problems. Be aware of those developmental stages when children are most likely to have fears. If you anticipate infant separation anxiety, you can avoid activities that separate infants from parents. You can reduce other problems related to fears by presenting progressions carefully, giving enough time in the lesson to play, and paying attention to the individual needs of the children in your courses.

To reduce the impact of learned fears, plan carefully and give a lot of positive reinforcement. Children enjoy the water more when they can take their own time, experience success, practice repeatedly, and receive praise for their efforts. For

example, before young children go under water for the first time, they need to understand what is going to happen, to be ready and agree to go under water, and be told how well they did.

COMMON HEALTH AND SAFETY CONCERNS

Aquatics programs for young children involve some controversy about the health and safety of participants. Some concerns, summarized below, have not been completely resolved. The Council for National Cooperation in Aquatics (CNCA) has guidelines for aquatics programs for children under the age of three. (See Appendix I.)

Risk of Drowning

Statistics show that children under the age of six are at greater risk of death by drowning than any other age group except young adults. Most drownings of young children occur in unsupervised water situations involving bath tubs, backyard pools, and hot tubs. Nevertheless, as an instructor you must give careful attention to the safety of participants during lessons. Remind parents that even if their children have learned to move in the water, they still lack the judgment to recognize dangerous situations and the ability to swim to safety if necessary.

Disease and Infection

Pediatricians and other doctors recommend that a child with a fever, rash, or any symptom of an infection not participate in an aquatics program. Infections usually spread among children by direct contact and not through the water, particularly when correct pool water chemistry is maintained.

Aquatics programs for infants and young children should have a clear, well-defined policy restricting participation by children or parents with any contagious illness. It is also essential to maintain proper water chemistry to prevent the spread of infections.

Ear Infections

Ear infections are a very common reason that children are restricted from participating in aquatics programs. Exposure to water has been blamed for causing ear infections. Pediatricians have kept children with tympanotomy tubes in the ear canal from participating in programs. Since medical professionals disagree about swimming, ear infections, and tympanotomy tubes, advise parents to follow their pediatrician's instructions.

Other Water-Related Conditions

Two other conditions related to infants in aquatics programs have been publicized in the popular and medical press. The first, giardia, is a parasitic infection usually transmitted through the water supply. It is most common in high altitudes and rural areas where the water has been contaminated. Giardia is controlled by chlorination and proper pool chemistry.

The second condition, hyponatremia (better known as "water intoxication"), is an imbalance of electrolytes, especially sodium, in the bloodstream. Although hyponatremia is extremely rare, you should not let young children submerge more than three times in a lesson. (For more information, see the CNCA statement in Appendix I).

SUMMARY

The Infant and Preschool Aquatics Program is a wonderful and rewarding way to use your skills and abilities. However, you must take extra precautions and have some additional teaching skills. Extra precautions include being watchful for overstimulation or excessive fatigue in the child and controlling facility variables, such as water temperature.

Children learn and develop at different rates, but you can use the principles of development and learning to make your IPAP courses fun and successful. With your help, parents can forestall or ease problems if their children are afraid of the water. Lots of patience and awareness of children's learning style can help you and the children get the most out of IPAP.

12 parent orientation

An orientation session helps prepare parents and their children for the program, particularly by building their trust and confidence. They also become familiar with the facility, so they know what to expect, and they meet the other participants. This chapter discusses how to hold an orientation session, lists materials to use, and gives an outline for the session.

SCHEDULING

Give the orientation either as the first lesson of the course or before the first lesson. You may use a single orientation session for parents, whether their children are infants, toddlers, or preschoolers. Encourage all the adults who might be active participants in the IPAP course to come to the orientation. Consider scheduling the orientation to coincide with the last lesson of a previous IPAP course so you can demonstrate the program to new participants. During the orientation, participants are not required to enter the water. (Appendix J contains a sample letter to parents.)

MATERIALS

You may wish to use some or all of the following in the orientation.
- *American Red Cross Infant and Preschool Aquatic Program Parent's Guide.* The Parent's Guide introduces the program, so you should highlight it in your presentation. It includes the following information:
  - Description of the program (goal and purpose)
  - Answers to questions frequently asked by parents
  - Role of the Red Cross Water Safety Instructor
  - Role of the parent
  - Lists of skills participants can be expected to learn
  - Recommended readings

- The segment, "A Good Beginning," in the American Red Cross *Infant and Preschool Aquatic Program* video. This segment for parents reinforces the information in the guide. It is a motivational and educational tool for the program.
- *Waddles Presents AQUACKtic Safety.* This combination storybook and activity book for children describes what happens in a swimming class and teaches important safety rules.
- Appropriate facility handouts, including information such as the following:
  - Policies and procedures for the class and the facility
  - Qualifications of Water Safety Instructors and other staff
  - Other programs and services at the facility
- Certificates and ancillary materials. Show parents a sample of the course participation certificate and any promotional items such as tee-shirts and emblems that may be available. The certificates recognize the participants' accomplishments. The promotional items give the program visibility in the community.

Distribute written materials to parents at registration if possible and ask them to read them before the orientation.

SUGGESTED OUTLINE

Following is an outline you may use for the orientation:

1. Welcome and introductions. Introduce yourself and the staff, stating the qualifications of those directly involved in the program. Those you might introduce include—
   - All instructors assisting with the class.
   - In-water and on-deck aides.
   - Locker or changing room attendants.
   - Lifeguards.
   - Cashiers.
   - Facility and/or program manager.

- Sponsor representative.
- Representative from the local Red Cross unit.

2. Review the program's goal and purpose.

   A. The purpose is to develop in young children:
      - Comfort level in and around the water
      - Readiness for learning to swim

   B. The goal of this nationally standardized aquatics program for infants, toddlers, and preschoolers is to promote the following:
      - Water safety knowledge and practices
      - Aquatic adjustment and swimming readiness skills
      - Fun and enjoyment in the water
      - Participant socialization
      - Parental involvement
      - Preparation for a lifetime of aquatic activity

3. Show the segment, "A Good Beginning," in the American Red Cross *Infant and Preschool Aquatic Program* video, 9 minutes.

4. Highlight the *American Red Cross Infant and Preschool Aquatic Program Parent's Guide,* particularly—
   Chapter 3: "Your Instructor" (instructor responsibilities)
   Chapter 4: "How You Can Help" (parental responsibilities)

5. Review facility policies and procedures.

   A. Schedule
      - Session starting and ending dates
      - Number and length of lessons
      - Days of the week and time lessons are held
      - Alternate class times in case of conflicts with naps or other activities
      - Arrival and departure times for each class (these should give an unhurried atmosphere)
      - Absence policy, make-up days (if available)
      - Refund policy

- Promotion of other services offered by the facility
- Promotion of other American Red Cross Health and Safety classes available

   B. Class rules (especially for a class of young children and their parents)
      - Parent and child enter the water only on the instructor's cue.
      - Child enters the water only on the parent's cue.
      - Parent and child stay with the class and follow the instructor's guidance.
      - The instructor is in charge at all times.

   C. Appropriate swimming apparel and gear
      - Swimsuits for parents should withstand tugging and stretching by little hands and feet.
      - Swimsuits for children should be snug around the legs, or children should wear training pants underneath suits.
      - Parents should follow facility rules for children who are not toilet trained.
      - Goggles, ear plugs, and noseclips are not recommended as they generally do not fit young children properly.
      - Parents should not wear jewelry and watches since the children may be easily scratched.
      - Parents should bring enough towels for themselves and their children.

   D. Health and medical information
      - Ask parents to tell you about any known medical problems that might affect participation.
      - Stipulate the daily class health requirement—no one with a cough, cold, fever, infection, open sore, rash, or who looks or acts sick may participate.
      - Collect medical forms, if required.

   E. Facility rules
      - Parental supervision of children
      - Safe behavior in the changing rooms
      - Use of equipment/toys
      - Food, drink, and gum

- Showering
- Arrival times
- Pool rules (walking on deck, no-diving areas, etc.)
- Emergency action plan

6. General Discussion.

Let the parents ask questions or raise concerns. You might also cover the following points:

- Be sure the purpose of the course is clear, so parents do not have false impressions or unrealistic expectations.
- Discuss the responsibilities of parents and staff so these are clear before the lessons start. Be clear what you want parents to do—or not do—in case of emergency.
- Explain why and how cuing is used. Before practicing each skill, the parent cues the child. A cue is a short sentence preparing the child for the action. Effective cues are simple and rhythmical. Each time they are repeated exactly the same way. Examples include:

Ready? Set…Go!
Take a deep breath…hold it…
Ready? 1,2,3…Jump!
Let's blow bubbles!
Kick, kick.
Reach, pull.

You may use different cues for each skill or you may prefer always to use the same cue to prepare the child for the coming action.

Explain that if a parent has a fear of water, he or she may want to take Level I of the American Red Cross Learn to Swim program or have another adult participate in IPAP with the child.

7. Facility tour. Give a complete tour of the facility to introduce parents and children to the changing rooms, pool (including the specific teaching area), and equipment and toys. Be sure to mention any facility restrictions on spectators.

SUMMARY

An effective orientation lays the foundation for a successful course. Helping parents understand what to expect from an aquatics program for infants and young children increases the program's value for them and their children. A good orientation helps make children and parents eager to participate in the first lesson. Parents can also set more realistic goals and know what to expect for themselves and their children. You can enforce rules and regulations more easily when participants know the reason for them.

13 | IPAP course outlines

The foundation of the Infant and Preschool Aquatics Program is the basic learning progression for the Infant Level. A toddler starts with the infant progressions until he or she is relatively adept at those skills. The Toddler Level then builds on them to increase the child's endurance and teach new aquatic skills appropriate for his or her age and readiness. Because of their greater physical and mental development, children of preschool age sometimes complete the Preschool Level quickly and enter the level of the American Red Cross Learn to Swim program appropriate for them.

> **Instructor's note:**
> Many of the names used for skills in this program give you a familiar point of reference, not necessarily an intended result.

Equipment

For all levels of IPAP, the only required equipment is Coast Guard-approved life jackets of appropriate sizes for parents and children.

SKILLS TO BE TAUGHT TO PARENTS

- Holding positions and when to use them
- The importance of cues and how to use them
- Roles for helping the child learn and practice skills appropriate for his or her age
- Life jackets: how to use them and how to fit them onto their child
- Basic safety skills: reaching, extension, throwing, and wading assists

SKILLS TO BE TAUGHT TO INFANTS

A. Water adjustment
  1. Getting wet
  2. Water entry
    - Lifting in
B. Exploring the pool
C. Front kick

D. Prone glide
  1. Readiness
  2. Passing
  3. Drafting
E. Underwater exploration
  1. Readiness
  2. Bubble blowing
  3. Scooping
F. Back float
  1. Adjusting to water in back position
  2. Readiness
G. Arm movement, prone position
  1. Arm stroke alone
  2. Combined skills
H. Rolling over
  1. Rolling back to front
  2. Rolling front to back
I. Introduction to life jackets
  - Experiencing buoyancy
J. Water exit
  1. With ladder
  2. At side of pool

SKILLS TO BE TAUGHT TO TODDLERS

Young children who can walk unassisted can progress through some skills more quickly than infants. In classes for toddlers, you first cover the skills for infants and then work with the toddlers (and their parents) to improve the skills they have learned and introduce more advanced skills. For the most part, toddlers are taught the skills in the following list. Those with an asterisk go beyond Infant Level skills.

A. Water adjustment
  1. Getting wet
  2. Water entry
    a. Parent carrying toddler
    b. Using ladder*
    c. Rolling from side of pool*

d. Seated at side of pool
e. Jumping in*

B. Exploring the pool

C. Front kick

D. Prone glide
1. Readiness
2. Passing
3. Drafting
4. Drafting with breathing*
5. Glide*

E. Underwater exploration
1. Readiness
2. Bubble blowing
   ▪ Bobbing*
3. Scooping
4. Opening eyes*

F. Back float
1. Adjusting to water in back position
2. Readiness

G. Back glide*

H. Arm movement on back*
1. Finning*
2. Finning combined with kicking*

I. Arm movement, prone position
1. Arm stroke alone
2. Combined skills

J. Rolling over
1. Rolling back to front
2. Rolling front to back

K. Using life jackets
1. Putting on correctly
2. Rolling over (both directions)*
3. Jumping in and swimming to wall*
4. Floating, H.E.L.P. position, and huddle position*

L. Changing positions*
1. Vertical to prone*
2. Vertical to back float position*

M. Kick up to surface*

N. Water exit
1. Pulling self out at side of pool*
2. Using ladder or stairs*

SKILLS TO BE TAUGHT TO PRESCHOOL CHILDREN

Many preschool children are independent enough to participate in swimming classes without a parent. These children should be placed in the appropriate level of the American Red Cross Learn to Swim program with children of similar abilities.

For some preschoolers, especially those who have not had water experiences or who show fear, having parents with them may be helpful, at least for the first several lessons. Start with the infant and toddler skills and let the children progress at their own speed. Once they have mastered all the infant and toddler skills, they may join the Learn to Swim program at the level that corresponds to their ability. Another option is to continue with a small preschool class but progress through the Learn to Swim levels as participants are ready.

14 holding positions for infants and young children

Parents can use several holding positions to give support and reassurance to their children while they explore the water and learn and practice new skills. Parents can vary the positions as they get used to their own needs and the child's needs. Factors such as the weight of the child, personal preference, and the need for variety determine what positions to use. The position names describe what they look like or how the child's body is supported by the adult.

> **Safety note:**
> Before participants enter the water, be sure to point out the limits of the teaching area. These limits will depend on the age, height, and comfort level of the children; height and confidence level of the parents; and the characteristics of the pool that influence water depth.

DANCE POSITION

Parents use this position with infants for water adjustment, bubble blowing, entry, and exit. They can use it in various depths of water, depending on the skill the infant is learning. Parents may stoop so water level is appropriate for child. Depending on a child's fear of water, parent may begin with only part of the child's body immersed and gradually increase depth till water comes to child's chest.

Facing the parent, the child straddles the parent's hip, and the parent's arm supports the child's back by reaching around the child to hold the upper thigh. The parent's other hand holds the child's hand (Fig. 14–1).

Fig. 14–1

HUG POSITION

Parents use this position with infants for water adjustment and for learning the front kick. A parent can try this position and the dance position to see which the child prefers. The water comes up to the child's upper chest and the parent's shoulders. The parent may also stoop so the water comes up to the child's shoulder.

The child's head rests on the parent's shoulder and the child's arms rest loosely over the parent's shoulders. The child's legs are extended, with the parent supporting the child's thighs and knees from behind (Fig. 14–2).

Fig. 14–2

FACE-TO-FACE POSITIONS

Parents use the face-to-face holding positions to introduce the child to prone skills.

Face-to-Face: Chin Support Position

Parents use this position with infants for the front kick and bubble blowing. The water comes up to the child's chin and the parent's shoulders.

The parent's fingers and palms hold the child under the upper chest and shoulders. The child's chin rests on the heels of the parent's palms so the child's face does not accidentally submerge (FIG. 14–3).

FIG. 14–4

FIG. 14–3

Face-to-Face: Shoulder Support Position

Parents use this position with toddlers for water adjustment, front kick, prone glide, prone float, and bubble blowing. The water comes up to the child's chest and the parent's shoulders.

The parent's hands support the child at hip and abdomen from below in a horizontal position. The child's shoulders rest on the parent's forearms (FIG. 14–4).

Face-to-Face: Armpit Support Position

Parents use this position with infants for water adjustment, prone kick, prone glide, bubble blowing, underwater exploration, rolling over, and drafting. Like the previous positions described, this position is one of several a parent can choose for orienting a child to learning or skill practice. The water comes up to the child's chin and the parent's shoulders.

With arms extended, the parent holds the child under the armpits. For a lighter, confident child, the parent's hands grasp the top of the child's shoulders and back with thumbs down. For a heavier or fearful child, the parent can grasp underneath the arms and upper chest with thumbs up (FIG. 14–5).

FIG. 14–5

ARM STROKE POSITION

Parents use this position with infants for learning arm movements. The parent can brace his or her own back against the side of the pool, sit on the steps, or kneel on one knee in shallow water. The water comes up to the child's upper chest or armpit and the parent's shoulders.

The child sits on the parent's knee, facing away from the parent. One of the parent's arms keeps the child upright by circling the child's chest, and the other hand holds the child's forearm to pattern a paddling motion (FIG. 14–6, *A*).

FIG. 14–6, *A*

With more secure children, the parent can balance the child on the knee and guide both arms in an alternating underwater paddling motion (FIG. 14–6, *B)*.

FIG. 14–6, *B*

SIDE-TO-SIDE POSITION

Parents use this position for water adjustment, bubble blowing, front kick, beginning stroking, passing, and practicing combined skills. The water comes up to the child's chin or neck and the parent's hips or waist. This position gives maximum mobility in a support position.

Parent and child face the same direction. The parent holds the child at one side, the hands holding the child at the armpits to keep the child's head up. The arm or elbow of the arm going across the child's back can rest against the child's buttocks and legs to keep them under water (FIG. 14–7, *A*).

FIG. 14–7, *A*

For more support, this same arm can encircle the child and be placed palm up on the child's chest. The other arm supports the child's nearer armpit from the back. As the child becomes more confident and skilled, the parent may hold the child with both hands on the waist (FIG. 14–7, *B)*.

FIG. 14–7, *B*

CHEEK-TO-CHEEK POSITIONS

Parents use the cheek-to-cheek holding positions to introduce children to skills on the back. Most children feel less confident on their backs, so you should introduce the position gradually and be sure the parent gives firm support. Tell the parent not to continue any holding position if the child becomes distressed. Sometimes letting the child's ears stay above the surface helps him or her adjust to the position.

Cheek-to-Cheek: Back-to-Chest Support Position

Parents use this position with infants for back float and back glide readiness. The water comes up to the child's armpits and the parent's shoulders.

The parent leans back against the pool wall and supports the child on the parent's upper chest. The back of the child's head rests on the parent's shoulder, the child's cheek or side of the head touching the parent's cheek. The parent may place one hand under the child's waist to bring the child to a more horizontal position. The child's legs

point away from the parent (FIG. 14–8). If the child floats naturally to a horizontal position, the parent may hold the child with both hands on top of the child's chest.

FIG. 14–8

Cheek-to-Cheek: Sandwich Position

Parents use this position for back float and back glide readiness and for rolling over. The water comes up to the child's ears and the parent's neck.

The back of the child's head rests on the parent's shoulder, the child's cheek or side of the head touching the parent's cheek. The parent holds the child horizontal by "sandwiching" the child between the parent's hands. One hand is placed on the child's lower back and the other on the child's chest (FIG. 14–9).

FIG. 14–9

Cheek-to-Cheek: Back Support Position

Parents use this position with infants for back float and back glide readiness and for the back kick. The water comes up to the child's ears and the parent's neck.

The back of the child's head rests on the parent's shoulder, the child's cheek or side of the head touching the parent's cheek. The parent holds the child with both hands on the back to bring the body horizontal (FIG. 14–10, *A*).

FIG. 14–10, *A*

The parent's exact hand position on the child's back depends on the child's readiness and the skill to be practiced. Hands on the child's lower back lend the most support; hands on the upper back give less support but more freedom of movement. If the child is secure, the parent can reach down to the child's thighs and manipulate the kick (FIG. 14–10, *B*).

FIG. 14–10, *B*

NECK AND BACK SUPPORT POSITION

Parents use this position when maximum freedom of movement is desired on the back. The water comes up to the child's ears and the parent's hips or waist.

The parent supports the back of the child's neck with one hand and prepares to help lift the child with the other hand. The child moves into horizontal position on the back while the parent holds the child with one hand supporting the back of the child's neck. The other hand assists and stabilizes the child at the middle of the child's back (FIG. 14–11).

FIG. 14–11

CHIN AND BACK SUPPORT POSITION

Parents use this position with toddlers for back float, back glide, back kick, and combined skills. The water comes up to the child's ears and the parent's armpits.

The parent supports the child in a back float position, with one hand supporting the middle of the back and the other hand placed around the chin on the lower jaw. The parent uses this chin support to prevent the child from submerging (FIG. 14–12).

FIG. 14–12

Safety note:
Warn parents not to push on the fleshy part of the child's throat.

15 aquatic skills for infants and young children

Instructor's note:
Parents should not let infants go under water until they have adjusted to "scooping" (see page 74). Do not let infants submerge more than three times per lesson in the adjustment and initial learning phases of skills introduced at this level. Infants have passed the "initial learning phase" when they are comfortable after submerging the face. Any sputtering, coughing, or crying indicates the infant is still in the initial learning phase.

Advise parents that not all children are ready to submerge at any given time. This is a developmental issue, and parents should not worry that their child is "behind" others in the class. Warn parents *never to force a child* to do a skill; this only delays his or her readiness to try additional skills.

Safety note:
Before participants enter the water, be sure to point out the limits of the teaching area. These limits will depend on the age, height, and comfort level of the children; height and confidence level of the parents; and the characteristics of the pool that influence water depth.

SKILLS TO BE TAUGHT TO INFANTS

Water Adjustment

Getting Wet
1. Parents and infants sit on the deck and get water on each other's bodies by playing with tub toys, washcloths, etc.
2. Parents support infants and let them kick water while sitting on the edge of pool.

Instructor's note:
Some children need to go through this process at the start of several lessons until they are used to getting wet. Advise parents to take their time and not force a child to progress faster than is comfortable.

Water Entry

Instructor's note:
Practice the following entry skills without submersion in the initial learning phase. Parents should not let their children go under water until they have learned scooping (page 74).

You may have parents and infants enter the water in the following ways:
- Parents, using dance position, walk down steps or ramp.
- Instructor supports infant on pool edge while parent uses ladder and then lifts infant into water.
- At side of pool, instructor or parent supports infant while parent rolls over onto stomach on deck and slides into water. Parent then lifts infant into water.
- Once parent and infant are in water, parents turn infants to face wall and place infants' hands so they hold onto side of pool.

Lifting In

> ***Instructor's note:***
> You can use this skill with infants who can stand unassisted.

1. Parents stand in water and help infants stand on deck at edge of pool by holding them under the armpits.
2. Parents cue infants, then lift infants into water (FIG. 15–1, *A*).

FIG. 15–1, *A*

3. Parents turn infants to wall and secure infants' hands onto side of pool (FIG. 15–1, *B*).

FIG. 15–1, *B*

> ***Safety note:***
> Infants should enter the water only on the parent's cue. The parent must keep a careful grip on the infant to prevent him or her from slipping, falling backward, or submerging the head.

Exploring the Pool

1. Parents hold infants in dance or any face-to-face position.
2. Parents move around in teaching area with infants. A child who is wet is more comfortable if kept at the same depth in the water. Encourage parents to talk calmly or even sing to their children as they move around the teaching area.

Front Kick

1. Parents hold infants in hug or face-to-face: shoulder support position.
2. Parents move backward and give a verbal cue.
3. Tell parents to watch for the infant's natural leg movement and, if needed, to help move their infant's legs in up-and-down action (FIG. 15–2).

FIG. 15–2

Prone Glide

Readiness

1. Parents hold infants in hug or any face-to-face position.
2. Parents walk backward, talking calmly or humming to infant (FIG. 15–3).

FIG. 15–3

> **Instructor's note:**
> Once infants have learned bubble blowing, that may be added to this skill as a variation.

Passing

1. Hold an infant in side-to-side position with head out of water. Move forward to gain momentum (FIG. 15–4, A).

FIG. 15–4, A

2. Cue infant, then gently glide and release infant to his or her parent's arms (FIG. 15–4, B).

FIG. 15–4, B

3. Do not lose contact with infant on the first passes. Be sure the parent has made contact before you let go.
4. Parent gains control of infant in chest support position, pulls infant to chest, and gives hug and praise (FIG. 15–4, C).

FIG. 15–4, C

The pass should be smooth and gentle with the infant staying at the same level in the water. When the child becomes adjusted to scooping, passes (with the infant's face in the water) can progress to 2–3 feet between the instructor and parent. The parent may practice by gliding the infant to the wall and securing his or her hands onto the side of the pool. When the child gains confidence, the parent may pass the infant to the instructor. Parents should avoid quick or jerky movements, avoid lifting the infant totally out of the water, and avoid "shoving" the infant toward the wall or another adult.

> **Instructor's note:**
> Once the infant is comfortable putting his or her face in the water, continue this progression with drafting (page 76).

Underwater Exploration

Readiness

> **Instructor's note:**
> The procedure for getting the infant wet is expanded to include the head and face. Have the parents do this either at the beginning of the lesson when this skill is introduced or just before you present it.

1. Parents hold infants in dance position.
2. Parents follow the same procedure as before for getting infant wet. Then, as the infant's confidence builds, parent can let water fall a few inches onto back of head. Finally, parent lets water wash down infant's face.
3. Instruct parents to continue this exercise until infant can accept water flowing gently across face.

Bubble Blowing
1. Parents hold infants in dance or any face-to-face position.
2. Parents demonstrate this skill to infants by using humming sounds and blowing bubbles gently on infant's cheek or hand. Infants eventually imitate parents blowing bubbles (FIG. 15–5).

FIG. 15–5

3. Parents practice this skill while stationary and while moving backward.

> **Safety note:**
> Parents should keep infants from drinking water and take care to avoid accidental submersion.

Scooping
You may introduce this skill once the infant enjoys water on his or her face and can imitate the parent by putting mouth or face in water. If an infant objects or cries, go back to the readiness level and repeat the sequence.
1. Parents hold infants in face-to-face: armpit support position.
2. Parents cue infants, then take one or two steps backward, while tipping infant's head down, but not submerging, in a scooping motion. Repeat several times.

3. When infant is ready for immersion, parents cue infants (FIG. 15–6, A), then tip infant's head so forehead or bridge of nose enters water first. (This prevents forcing water up the nose.) In one continuous motion, parent lowers infant just under the surface (FIG. 15–6, B) and scoops him or her up to chest. Then the parent gives hug and praise (FIG. 15–6, C).

FIG. 15–6, C

FIG. 15–6, A

FIG. 15–6, B

Instructor's note:
Do this skill only once in any lesson until the infant is comfortable and is not crying, coughing, or choking.

Safety note:
Remind parents to keep both their feet on the pool bottom; caution them against forcing the infant or keeping the infant under water longer than a very brief "dip" (maximum 3 seconds). Have the parents help watch for infants expelling air bubbles under water, because they are likely to try to inhale, taking in water. A child who cries, chokes, or shows discomfort is not ready for this skill.

Drafting

Introduce this skill only after the infant is comfortable being passed with his or her face in the water.

1. Parents hold infants in face-to-face: armpit support position (FIG. 15–7, A).

FIG. 15–7, A

2. Parents walk backward with infants, then, when they gain momentum, parents cue infants and briefly release support so that infants move forward, free-floating between parent's outstretched arms (FIG. 15–7, B).

FIG. 15–7, B

3. Parents resume support by grasping infants' shoulders or armpits and then give hug and praise (FIG. 15–7, C).

FIG. 15–7, C

The infants should be unsupported with their faces in the water no more than 3 seconds. Have the parents spread out to avoid collisions with other parents. Ask parents to help watch for infants expelling air bubbles under water because they are likely to try to inhale, taking in water. Do not use drafting with an infant who cries, chokes, or shows discomfort. Remember, infants should not be allowed to submerge more than three times per class in the initial learning phase.

Back Float

Adjusting to Water in Back Float Position
1. Parents hold infants in cheek-to-cheek: sandwich or cheek-to-cheek: back-to-chest support position.
2. Parents talk or hum to infants. Parents may stay motionless or move slowly backward (FIG. 15–8).

FIG. 15–8

Readiness
1. Parents hold infants in cheek-to-cheek: back support position.
2. Parents move backward as they talk to infants and look into their eyes (FIG. 15–9).

FIG. 15–9

Arm Movement, Prone Position

Arm Stroke Alone
1. Parents hold infants in arm stroke or side-to-side position.
2. Parents guide infants' arms, using cue such as "reach," "paddle," or "dig" (FIG. 15–10).

FIG. 15–10

> **Safety note:**
> You and the parents should watch that the infant's face does not go into the water. In the side-to-side position, check that the infant's buttocks stay under the surface so the head stays up.

Combined Skills
1. Parents hold infants in side-to-side position.
2. Parents cue infants to combine arm movement, bubble blowing, and kicking (FIG. 15–11).

FIG. 15–11

Rolling Over

Rolling Back to Front
1. Parents stand a few feet from wall, facing away from wall, and hold infants in cheek-to-cheek: sandwich position (Fig. 15–12, A).

FIG. 15–12, A

2. Parents cue infants, then rotate hands while rolling infant onto stomach with head up (FIG. 15–12, B).

FIG. 15–12, B

3. Parents move their hands to hold infant in face-to-face: armpit support position.
4. Parents move backward to gently glide infant to wall, then secure infant's hands onto side of pool (FIG. 15–12, C).

FIG. 15–12, C

Rolling Front to Back

1. Parents hold infants in face-to-face: armpit support position (FIG. 15–13, *A).* One hand grasps infant's upper arm, thumb down, fingers on top. Fingers of other hand hold infant under armpit and chest, and the thumb (pointing up) holds the upper arm.

FIG. 15–13, *A*

2. Parents move backward, cue infants, then roll infants onto back (FIG. 15–13, *B).*

FIG. 15–13, *B*

3. Parents move their hands to hold infants in the neck and back support position and cue infants to look back into parents' eyes (FIG. 15–13, *C).*

FIG. 15–13, *C*

Introduction to Life Jackets

1. Parents and infants put on Coast Guard-approved life jackets of appropriate sizes.
2. Parents hold infants, wearing life jackets, in any face-to-face position, so infants can experience buoyancy (FIG. 15–14).

FIG. 15–14

Water Exit

With Ladder
1. Parents lift infants from pool and sit them on deck next to ladder.
2. Instructor holds infant while parent uses ladder to exit pool.

At Side of Pool
Depending on the infant's age and ability, the parent may assist the infant to exit the pool in the following ways:
- Parent helps infant climb out of pool, using knee or hand as step.
- Parent encourages infant to climb out unassisted. Parent does not boost the infant but lets the infant do the work (FIG. 15–15).

FIG. 15–15

SKILLS TO BE TAUGHT TO TODDLERS

Toddlers should be introduced to all the skills taught to infants. Toddlers improve on these skills and learn more advanced skills. Following are adaptations of the skills at the Infant Level and the skills that are new for the Toddler Level. (For an outline of the skills to be taught to toddlers, see pages 63–64.)

Water Entry

Using Ladder
Stronger toddlers can use the ladder with supervision. Have the parent walk down the ladder backward ahead of the child.

Rolling From Side of Pool
- Parents roll over onto stomach and slide into water feet first. Then parents cue toddlers to roll over onto stomach the same way and enter water feet first, holding onto side of pool (FIG. 15–16).

FIG. 15–16

Seated at Side of Pool

1. Toddlers sit on edge of pool, with parents standing in water facing toddlers and grasping wrists or forearms.
2. Parents cue toddlers to push off pool edge to parents (FIG. 15–17). Parents and toddlers return to side of pool, where parents place toddlers' hands on side of pool.

FIG. 15–17

Jumping In

1. Toddlers stand at edge of pool, with parent standing in water *to side of toddler,* holding the top of one of toddler's wrists or forearms.
2. Parents cue toddlers, then toddler steps or jumps into water (FIG. 15–18). Parent rotates toddler, using one or both hands. Parents and toddlers return to side of pool, where parents place toddlers' hands on side of pool.

FIG. 15–18

Front Kick

With assistance, toddlers may do some or all of the following exercises to improve their skills:

■ With parent's assistance (in hug or face-to-face shoulder support position), toddler is encouraged to kick.

■ Parent holds toddler's hands on kickboard or barbell float. Then parent gradually lessens support and contact. Parent faces child across support (FIG. 15–19).

FIG. 15–19

Prone Glide

Passing

As a variation, pass toddler to wall through hula-hoop.

Drafting With Breathing

If the toddler has completed the initial learning phase and is comfortable with submersion, have parents draft toddlers for 3 seconds. Parent uses one hand to give support under the toddler's shoulder or chest, cues the toddler, and with the other hand lifts the chin for a breath (FIG. 15–20).

FIG. 15–20

Glide

■ Parents cue toddlers, then glide toddlers to wall (FIG. 15–21). Parents then secure child's hands to wall.

FIG. 15–21

■ As a variation, toddlers stand facing pool wall, push off from bottom, and glide to wall with parent's assistance.

Underwater Exploration

Bobbing

- Parents hold toddler's hands onto edge of pool as toddler submerges (bobs) and blows bubbles (FIG. 15–22). Toddler bobs rhythmically, once every 2 or 3 seconds. Parent discourages toddler from wiping water from eyes. Remember, until toddlers have adjusted to the water, they should not be submerged more than three times in a lesson.

FIG. 15–22

Opening Eyes

1. Toddler holds up fingers under water while you or parent counts fingers.
2. Parent and toddler reverse roles so toddler goes under water to count parent's fingers. Toddler may hold parent's arm or side of pool (FIG. 15–23).

FIG. 15–23

Back Glide

1. If water is chest-deep or less for the toddlers, they can learn the back glide using the progression on page 119.
2. If water is more than chest deep, toddlers can hold onto side of pool and place feet against wall, then release the wall and gently glide backward with parent supporting head and back (FIG. 15–24).

FIG. 15–24

3. Toddlers repeat this skill with parents using chin and back support position.

Arm Movement on Back

Finning
1. Demonstrate back glide with finning arms. (See *Swimming and Diving,* page 95.)
2. Direct parent to hold toddler in back float position while you move toddler's arms and hands in finning motion (FIG. 15–25).

FIG. 15–25

Finning Combined With Kicking
1. Toddlers perform back glide with support from parent or instructor.
2. Cue toddlers to add finning and kicking to back glide (FIG. 15–26).

FIG. 15–26

Arm Movement, Prone Position

Arm Stroke
1. Parents hold toddlers in arm stroke position.
2. Demonstrate front crawl arm stroke with underwater recovery.
3. Toddlers imitate arm movement with assistance while sitting on parents' knees.
4. Parents hold toddlers in side-to-side position while toddlers practice arm movement independently (FIG. 15–27).

FIG. 15–27

Combined Skills
1. Parents hold toddlers in side-to-side position while toddlers combine arm movement, kicking, and blowing bubbles.
2. Parents walk forward so water helps support the toddler's body (FIG. 15–28).

FIG. 15–28

Using Life Jackets

1. Toddlers and parents practice putting on Coast Guard-approved life jackets correctly.
2. Toddlers, wearing life jackets, and parents face each other in the water. Parents support toddlers if needed (FIG. 15–29, A).

FIG. 15–29, A

3. Parents cue toddlers, then toddlers roll over onto back. Then toddlers roll over onto front and return to the wall (FIG. 15–29, B).

FIG. 15–29, B

4. With parents in the water to assist as needed, parents cue toddlers, then toddlers jump into water wearing life jackets and return to the wall using front crawl arm stroke with underwater recovery (FIG. 15–29, C).

FIG. 15–29, C

5. Toddlers practice floating in life jackets. Toddlers may wear lightweight clothes under life jackets (e.g., tee-shirt and shorts; no jeans or sweat shirts/pants) and float in water. Limit this activity to a few minutes.
6. Toddlers and parents practice "H.E.L.P." and "huddle" positions. (See *Swimming and Diving*, page 40.)

> **Safety note**:
> Check the life jackets to make sure they meet Coast Guard specifications and fit the individual toddlers properly.

Changing Positions

Vertical to Prone

1. Toddlers sit on parents' knees facing wall but just beyond reach of it (FIG. 15–30, *A).*

FIG. 15–30, *A*

2. Parents cue toddlers to move to the wall.
3. Parents guide toddlers into horizontal position and help toddlers grasp wall (FIG. 15–30, *B).*

FIG. 15–30, *B*

Vertical to Back Float Position

1. Toddler faces away from parent, holding side of pool or standing.
2. Parent supports toddler with neck and back or chin and back holding position (FIG. 15–31, *A).*

FIG. 15–31, *A*

3. Parent cues toddler to look up and back at parent's eyes.
4. Parent steps backward, allowing toddler's feet to rise toward surface (FIG. 15–31, *B).*

FIG. 15–31, *B*

> **Safety note:**
> Do not allow toddler's head to submerge.

Kick Up to Surface

1. Parents cue toddlers, then parents stay above water and lower toddlers, feet first, just below surface (FIG. 15–32, *A*).

FIG. 15–32, *A*

2. Parents release toddlers briefly to let toddlers kick to surface. Parents assist toddlers to reach surface, if needed (FIG. 15–32, *B*).

FIG. 15–32, *B*

3. Parents cue toddlers to go under water independently.

Water Exit

- With parents' supervision, toddlers pull themselves out of pool onto deck.
- Toddlers who are able may use ladder and stairs.

Safety note:
Watch for toddlers slipping on the steps or stairs or running away from their parents.

P A R T

E

- outlines for learn to swim courses
- support techniques
- teaching basic skills
- teaching strokes
- teaching diving
- teaching starts and turns

the learn to swim program

16 outlines for Learn to Swim courses

The American Red Cross Learn to Swim program teaches aquatic and safety skills in a logical progression. The program comprises seven courses:

- Level I: Water Exploration
- Level II: Primary Skills
- Level III: Stroke Readiness
- Level IV: Stroke Development
- Level V: Stroke Refinement
- Level VI: Skill Proficiency
- Level VII: Advanced Skills

The objective of the program is to teach people to swim and to be safe in, on, and around the water.

There are six categories of skills:

- Water adjustment
- Buoyancy and breath control
- Water entry and exit
- Locomotion
- Turns
- Personal safety and rescue

Not every level includes skills in all categories. Nor is it necessary to introduce the skills in the order of categories listed above. In fact, it is very important to introduce safety skills in the first lesson of a Level I course, so participants start to be aware of what they can do to be safe around the water.

The program is designed to give students a positive learning experience. Students in Level I are oriented to the aquatic environment and gain some basic skills in each category. At later levels, students build on their basic skills to learn propulsive movements on both the front and back. They learn different strokes at various levels and then refine them at later levels. Personal safety and rescue skills are included to help students meet safety goals. By the end of Level VII, students have all the prerequisite skills and have developed the necessary fitness level for entrance into the American Red Cross Lifeguarding courses.

This chapter provides the information you need to conduct courses in the Learn to Swim program. General administrative notes are covered first, followed by descriptions of the courses, a list of required and optional equipment, and tables of required and optional skills.

ADMINISTRATIVE NOTES

The following points apply to all levels of the Learn to Swim program:

Prerequisites

There are no prerequisites for Level I. For Levels II–VII, students must have a certificate for the preceding level or be able to demonstrate all the completion requirements at the previous level. You may want to pretest all students in a course, regardless of level, so you can recommend an appropriate starting point for each. There is no minimum or maximum age for any level.

Course Length

No level has a minimum or maximum length. In general, the program works well in 8–10 lessons of 30–45 minutes each.

Scheduling

It may be helpful to schedule courses at adjacent levels together (for example, a Level II course at the same time as a Level I course). In this way students who complete the requirements for the lower level course can transfer to the higher level course.

Class Size

At least six students are required in a course except with prior permission of the local Red Cross unit. For classes with 10 or more students, you should have additional instructors or aides. Regardless of class size, you can use assistants or aides for more flexibility and to give more individualized attention to students. A qualified lifeguard should be on duty during lessons. (For more information on risk management, see Chapter 4.)

Facility

The course requirements are based on the assumption that the facility has water shallow enough for students to stand and, for some levels, deep enough to learn diving skills. (The Red Cross recommends a minimum of 9 feet for diving. If state or local regulations require greater depth, you must abide by those rules.) If your facility does not meet these guidelines, the following applies:

- If the facility does not have water shallow enough for students to stand, see the tables of skills and course requirements for alternative standards.
- If the facility does not have water deep enough for diving, you SHOULD NOT teach diving skills. In such circumstances, diving skills are not required for the level. As an alternative, if possible, move the class to another facility with proper depth and teach diving skills there.

For other notes on facilities, see Chapter 4.

Course Requirements

For each of the seven levels in the Learn to Swim program, there are required skills with completion requirements given in the tables on pages 96–109. In addition, Appendix B describes the performance standards students should meet to complete each level. As your class proceeds, use the skills checklist (in Appendix H) to chart students' progress in satisfying the requirements. To be certified at a given level, students must meet the requirements for the course, except for diving skills if the water is not deep enough.

Extenuating circumstances (such as restricted motion in a joint) may keep a student from meeting the performance standards. In such cases, you may award a certificate if the student meets the objective for the level. Base your judgment in

such cases on whether the student performs the skill as close to the standard as his or her condition allows. You must be flexible in applying performance standards. The objective is to customize swimming strokes to match the swimmers. (For more information on customizing a program, see Chapters 22–24.)

Optional Skills and Activities

Besides the skills required for a course, you may teach optional skills and use other activities, such as games, to help students learn and to enrich the program. You may also use optional skills with more advanced students while others are practicing the required skills. You may use skills required for the next level as optional skills for the preceding level.

On pages 97–109 there are lists of optional skills and activities. You may use some or all of these—or add to the list—as long as your course meets the needs and interests of your students. Do not introduce skills too advanced for the level you are teaching. Urge your students to develop proficiency in the skills they know, not just to acquire new skills.

Certificates

Students who meet the requirements for a level are eligible to receive a certificate for their achievement. The following is a list of certificates that may be awarded in the Learn to Swim program:

- Level I: Water Exploration   (Cert. 653431)
- Level II: Primary Skills   (Cert. 653432)
- Level III: Stroke Readiness   (Cert. 653433)
- Level IV: Stroke Development   (Cert. 653434)
- Level V: Stroke Refinement   (Cert. 653435)
- Level VI: Skill Proficiency   (Cert. 653436)
- Level VII: Advanced Skills   (Cert. 653437)

(For more information on awarding certificates, completing records, and conducting course evaluations, see Chapter 5.)

DESCRIPTIONS OF THE COURSES

Level I: Water Exploration

The objective of Level I is to help students feel comfortable in the water and to enjoy the water safely. In Level I, you teach elementary aquatic skills, which students build on as they progress through the Learn to Swim program. At this level your students also start developing good attitudes and safe practices around the water. Some students will have some experience with the water and may begin the program at a higher level.

Students who have had pleasant water experiences complete this level quickly. However, fear of the water may be a major issue for some students regardless of age. Before students enter the water the first time, show them the area in which they will be swimming. Explain the safety rules for your facility. Explain the buddy system and pair off students. Emphasize that this system helps students help each other learn and provides added safety. If the students are old enough, explain and demonstrate how buoyancy helps keep them at the surface. Impress on all students, and especially younger ones, that they can and will learn to swim if they follow your directions (and other instructors or aides) and are willing to try out new things.

Let students ask questions, so you can begin to address and allay any fears. As the course progresses, provide a wide variety of experiences to meet the course objectives. If you approach your task with creativity and enthusiasm, learning to swim will be fun, safe and rewarding for everyone.

There are no prerequisites for this course.

Level II: Primary Skills

The objective of Level II is to give students success with fundamental skills. Students learn to float without support and to recover to a vertical position. This level marks the beginning of true locomotion skills and adds to the self-help and basic rescue skills begun in Level I.

Students entering this course must have a Level I certificate or must be able to demonstrate all the completion requirements in Level I.

Level III: Stroke Readiness

The objective of Level III is to build on the skills in Level II by providing additional guided practice. You teach students to coordinate the front crawl and back crawl. You introduce the elementary backstroke and the fundamentals of treading water. Students should also learn rules for safe diving and begin to learn to dive from the side of the pool (if the water is deep enough). As in all levels, you present additional safety skills.

Students entering this course must have a Level II certificate or must be able to demonstrate all the completion requirements in Level II.

Level IV: Stroke Development

The objective of Level IV is to develop confidence in the strokes learned thus far and to improve other aquatic skills. You help students increase their endurance by swimming familiar strokes (elementary backstroke, front crawl, and back crawl) for greater distances than at Level III. You introduce the breaststroke and sidestroke and the basics of turning at a wall.

Students entering this course must have a Level III certificate or must be able to demonstrate all the completion requirements in Level III.

Level V: Stroke Refinement

The objective of Level V is coordination and refinement of key strokes. You introduce the butterfly, open turns, the feet-first surface dive, and springboard diving (if the water is deep enough). Participants learn to perform the front crawl and back crawl for increased distances and to perform the sidestroke and breaststroke.

Students entering this course must have a Level IV certificate or must be able to demonstrate all the course requirements in Level IV.

Level VI: Skill Proficiency

The objective of Level VI is to polish strokes so students swim them with more ease, efficiency, power, and smoothness over greater distances. Students develop considerable endurance by the end of this course. You introduce additional turns as well as the pike and tuck surface dives.

Students entering this course must have a Level V certificate or must be able to demonstrate all the skills required to complete Level V.

Level VII: Advanced Skills

The objective of Level VII is to perfect strokes and to develop good fitness habits. Participants are urged to use aquatic activities throughout life to maintain their physical condition. You teach springboard diving (if the water is deep enough) and advanced rescue skills. This is also a good time to introduce other aquatic activities. As time allows, you may incorporate elements of water polo, synchronized swimming, skin diving, and competition to enrich the class and broaden participants' horizons.

Participants entering this course must have a Level VI certificate or must be able to demonstrate all the completion requirements in Level VI.

You should customize this level as much as possible to meet the objectives of the participants. For instance, you can promote the course for participants who want to enter competition or who want to achieve a higher level of fitness. You can also structure this course around a different aquatic sport each time you give it. Participants who want to enter the Water Safety Instructor course or courses in the Lifeguard Training program can use this level to practice the prerequisites for those courses. Because of the variety this course can offer, participants can repeat this level to focus on different goals each time.

REQUIRED AND OPTIONAL EQUIPMENT

Level I: Water Exploration

■ The only required equipment is Coast Guard-approved life jackets, which should be the right size for the students.

Level II: Primary Skills

■ The only required equipment is Coast Guard-approved life jackets, which should be the right size for the participants, and equipment for reaching assists.
■ You may find it useful to have kickboards or other flotation devices for students to use in drills. (See Chapter 17.)
■ To show a video segment on rescue breathing, you need a half-inch videocassette recorder (VCR) and monitor. The following videos contain segments on rescue breathing:
    ■ *American Red Cross Responding to Emergencies*
    ■ *American Red Cross Adult CPR*
    ■ *American Red Cross CPR: Infant and Child*
    ■ *American Red Cross Community CPR*

Level III: Stroke Readiness

■ The only required equipment is Coast Guard-approved life jackets, which should be the right size for the participants.
■ You may find it useful to have kickboards or other flotation devices for students to use in drills. (See Chapter 17.)
■ If you use manikins to teach rescue breathing, be sure to arrange for the proper equipment beforehand. Also see Appendix K, Manikin Use and Decontamination.

Level IV: Stroke Development

- You may find it useful to have kickboards or similar flotation devices for students to use in drills.
- If you show a video on CPR, you will need a VCR and monitor. The following videos contain segments on CPR:
  - *American Red Cross Responding to Emergencies*
  - *American Red Cross Adult CPR*
  - *American Red Cross CPR: Infant and Child*
  - *American Red Cross Community CPR*
- If you use manikins to teach rescue breathing, be sure to arrange for the proper equipment beforehand. Also see Appendix K, Manikin Use and Decontamination.

Level V: Stroke Refinement

- You may find it useful to have kickboards or other flotation devices for students to use in drills. (See Chapter 17.)

Level VI: Skill Proficiency

- You may find it useful to have kickboards or similar flotation devices for students to use in drills.
- To teach throwing rescues, you need one or several pieces of equipment used for such rescues.

Level VII: Advanced Skills

- Required equipment includes a rescue tube or other device for in-water rescue, a diving brick, a backboard, and safety devices used in the Basic Water Safety course. (For a list of equipment for the Basic Water Safety Course, see Appendix A.)

REQUIRED AND OPTIONAL SKILLS

On the pages that follow there is a table of required skills for each level. Each table lists required skills, completion requirements for each skill, and cross-references to material in *Swimming and Diving* and in Chapters 18–21, the teaching progressions. Optional skills with cross-references are also listed for each level.

LEVEL I: WATER EXPLORATION

REQUIRED SKILLS		
Skill[1]	**Completion Requirement[2]**	***References**
Water Adjustment Fully submerge face	3 seconds	
Buoyancy and Breath Control Experience buoyancy	Bounce up and down in chest-deep water maintaining upright position for 10 bounces **OR[3]** Bob to chin level, with support, 10 times	
Supported float on front	Demonstrate	*IM*, pp. 69, 115
Supported float on back	Demonstrate	*IM*, pp. 69, 115
Bubble Blowing	Demonstrate	*IM*, p. 74
Water Entry and Exit Enter and exit water independently using ladder, ramp, steps, or side of pool	Demonstrate	*IM*, p. 80
Locomotion Move through water comfortably	Walk 5 yards in chest-deep water, maintaining balance **OR[3]** Move 5 yards along side of pool maintaining contact with wall	
Supported kicking on front	Demonstrate	*IM*, pp. 72, 82, 112
Supported kicking on back	Demonstrate	*IM*, p. 113
Introduction to alternating arm action	Walk 5 yards in chest-deep water, alternating arms **OR[3]** Demonstrate alternating arm action for 10 seconds, holding overflow trough	

* *S&D = Swimming and Diving   IM = Instructor's Manual*

REQUIRED SKILLS		
Skill[1]	**Completion Requirement[2]**	***References**
Personal Safety and Rescue		
Learn basic water safety rules	Discuss importance of following rules	*S&D*, pp. 33, 39
Familiarity with getting help	Discuss role of safety personnel and EMS	*S&D*, p. 286; *IM*, p. 195
Reaching assists without equipment	Demonstrate	*S&D*, p. 291
Release cramp	Demonstrate	*S&D*, p. 37
Wear life jacket on deck and enter shallow water	Demonstrate	*S&D*, p. 29

[1]Skills may be taught in any order within a level.

[2]Times and distances listed are the minimum to meet the requirement.

[3]Whenever possible, the first requirement should be met. In those cases where participants cannot touch bottom, the alternative requirement must be met.

* *S&D = Swimming and Diving   IM = Instructor's Manual*

OPTIONAL SKILLS AND ACTIVITIES

- View videos: *Longfellow's Whale Tales* (for children up to 10 years) or *Water, the Deceptive Power* or *Home Pool Safety*
- Games that increase students' relaxation and comfort in the water (see Chapter 25)
- Skills from Level II, especially breath control and floating

Encourage students to progress to the next level as soon as they are ready.

Level II: Primary Skills

<table>
<tr><th colspan="3">REQUIRED SKILLS</th></tr>
<tr><th>Skill[1]</th><th>Completion Requirement[2]</th><th>*References</th></tr>
<tr>
<td>Water Adjustment
Hold breath and fully submerge head

Retrieve objects

Orientation to deep water</td>
<td>3 seconds

Submerge and retrieve object in chest-deep water
OR[3]
Submerge and retrieve object that is suspended at appropriate depth
Explore deep water with support</td>
<td></td>
</tr>
<tr>
<td>Buoyancy and Breath Control
Prone float or glide, unsupported, and recovery
Supine float or glide, unsupported, and recovery
Leveling off from a vertical position
Rhythmic breathing, with or without support</td>
<td>
5 seconds

5 seconds

Demonstrate
Bob 10 times, support optional</td>
<td>
S&D, p. 95;
IM, p. 118
S&D, p. 95;
IM, p. 119

S&D, p. 120;
IM, p. 83, 117–118</td>
</tr>
<tr>
<td>Water Entry and Exit
Step from the side into chest-deep water and recover to a vertical position
Get out at side of pool</td>
<td>
Demonstrate

Demonstrate</td>
<td>
IM, p. 120</td>
</tr>
<tr>
<td>Locomotion
Flutter kick on front
Flutter kick on back
Finning on back
Back crawl arm action

Combined stroke front, using kick and alternating arm action
Combined stroke back, using kick and choice of arm movement</td>
<td>
Demonstrate, support optional
Demonstrate, support optional
Demonstrate
Demonstrate

5 yards

5 yards</td>
<td>
S&D, p. 118;
S&D, p. 148;
IM, p. 119
S&D, pp. 144–147;
IM, p. 126–127
S&D, pp. 121–122
IM, 124–125
S&D, pp. 122–125;
142–148;
IM, 126–127</td>
</tr>
</table>

* S&D = Swimming and Diving   IM = Instructor's Manual

REQUIRED SKILLS		
Skill[1]	**Completion Requirement[2]**	***References**
Turns		
Turning over, front to back	Demonstrate	*S&D*, p. 98
Turning over, back to front	Demonstrate	*S&D*, p. 98
Personal Safety and Rescue		
Float in life jacket with face out of water	Put on life jacket in shallow water and float for 1 minute in face-up position **OR[3]** Put on life jacket, enter water, and float for 1 minute in face-up position	
Perform reaching and extension assist from deck	Demonstrate	*S&D*, p. 288
Assist nonswimmer to feet	Demonstrate	*S&D*, p. 291
Become familiar with rescue breathing	Watch video or demonstration	

[1]Skills may be taught in any order within a level.

[2]Times and distances listed are the minimum to meet the requirement.

[3]Whenever possible, the first requirement should be met. In those cases where participants cannot touch bottom, the alternative requirement must be met.

* *S&D = Swimming and Diving   IM = Instructor's Manual*

Optional Skills and Activities

■ Throwing assists, *S&D*, pp. 289–290
■ Games and stunts that reinforce required skills, especially breath control and submerging comfortably (see Chapter 25)
■ Skills from Level III, especially locomotion

Encourage participants to progress to the next level as soon as they are ready.

LEVEL III: STROKE READINESS

<table>
<tr><th colspan="3">REQUIRED SKILLS</th></tr>
<tr><th>Skill[1]</th><th>Completion Requirement[2]</th><th>*References</th></tr>
<tr>
<td>Water Adjustment
Retrieve object, eyes open, no support</td>
<td>Retrieve object from bottom in chest-deep water
        OR[3]
Retrieve object that is suspended at appropriate depth</td>
<td></td>
</tr>
<tr>
<td>Buoyancy and Breath Control
Bob, submerging head completely</td>
<td>15 times in chest-deep water
        OR[3]
10 times, with support</td>
<td>S&D, p. 92</td>
</tr>
<tr>
<td>Bob in water slightly over head to travel to safe area</td>
<td>Bob to standing depth
        OR[3]
Bob to side of pool</td>
<td>S&D, p. 92</td>
</tr>
<tr>
<td>Water Entry and Exit
Jump into deep water from side of pool</td>
<td>Demonstrate</td>
<td></td>
</tr>
<tr>
<td>Dive[4] from side of pool from kneeling and compact positions</td>
<td>Dive[4] from either position</td>
<td>S&D, p. 190;
IM, pp. 137–138</td>
</tr>
<tr>
<td>Locomotion
Prone glide with push-off</td>
<td>Demonstrate, 2 body lengths</td>
<td>S&D, p. 102;
IM, pp. 118–119</td>
</tr>
<tr>
<td>Supine glide with push-off</td>
<td>Demonstrate, 2 body lengths</td>
<td>S&D, p. 104;
IM, p. 119</td>
</tr>
<tr>
<td>Coordinate arm stroke for front crawl with breathing to the side</td>
<td>Swim front crawl, breathing as necessary to front or side, 10 yards</td>
<td>S&D, p. 121</td>
</tr>
<tr>
<td>Coordinate back crawl</td>
<td>Swim back crawl 10 yards</td>
<td>S&D, p. 149</td>
</tr>
<tr>
<td>Elementary backstroke[5]</td>
<td>Elementary backstroke kick 10 yards, with or without kickboard</td>
<td>S&D, pp. 122–127;
IM, p. 129</td>
</tr>
<tr>
<td>Turns
Reverse direction while swimming on front</td>
<td>Demonstrate</td>
<td>S&D, p. 99</td>
</tr>
<tr>
<td>Reverse direction while swimming on back</td>
<td>Demonstrate</td>
<td>S&D, p. 95</td>
</tr>
</table>

* S&D = Swimming and Diving   IM = Instructor's Manual

REQUIRED SKILLS		
Skill[1]	**Completion Requirement[2]**	***References**
Personal Safety and Rescue		
Learn safe diving rules	Discussion	*S&D*, pp. 57, 59–60
Tread water	Demonstrate	*S&D*, pp. 96–97
Jump into deep water with life jacket on	Demonstrate	
H.E.L.P. position	Demonstrate, 1 minute	*S&D*, p. 40; *IM*, p. 203
Huddle position	Demonstrate in groups of three, 1 minute	*S&D*, p. 40; *IM*, p. 203
Learn how to open airway for rescue breathing	Demonstrate correct technique	*S&D*, pp. 300; *IM*, p. 204

[1]Skills may be taught in any order within a level.

[2]Times and distances listed are the minimum to meet the requirement.

[3]Whenever possible, the first requirement should be met. In those cases where participants cannot touch bottom, the alternative requirement must be met.

[4]If pool depth does not meet minimum standards (American Red Cross guidelines or state or local regulations) instructors SHOULD NOT teach diving skills.

[5]Entire stroke is introduced at this level, but only the kick is required for completion.

* *S&D = Swimming and Diving   IM = Instructor's Manual*

OPTIONAL SKILLS AND ACTIVITIES

- Survival floating, *S&D*, pp. 30–31
- Treading water with a variety of kicks, *S&D*, pp. 96–97
- Sitting dive
- Human chain rescue, *S&D*, p. 291
- Putting on life jacket in deep water
- Retrieving objects in deep water, *S&D*, pp. 99–103
- Water volleyball or basketball

Encourage students to progress as far as possible with front crawl and back crawl for technique and endurance.

LEVEL IV: STROKE DEVELOPMENT

<table>
<tr><th colspan="3">REQUIRED SKILLS</th></tr>
<tr><th>Skill[1]</th><th>Completion Requirement[2]</th><th>*References</th></tr>
<tr>
<td>Buoyancy and Breath Control
Deep-water bobbing</td>
<td>Demonstrate</td>
<td>S&D, p. 92</td>
</tr>
<tr>
<td>Experiment with buoyancy and floating position</td>
<td>Demonstrate</td>
<td>S&D, pp. 93–95</td>
</tr>
<tr>
<td>Rotary breathing</td>
<td>Demonstrate in chest-deep water
OR[3]
Demonstrate in dry land drill</td>
<td>S&D, pp. 120–121;
IM, pp. 117–118</td>
</tr>
<tr>
<td>Water Entry and Exit
Dive[4] from side of pool from stride and standing positions</td>
<td>Standing front dive</td>
<td>S&D, p. 191;
IM, pp. 139–140</td>
</tr>
<tr>
<td>Locomotion
Elementary backstroke</td>
<td>10 yards</td>
<td>S&D, pp. 122–127;
IM, p. 129</td>
</tr>
<tr>
<td>Sculling on the back</td>
<td>5 yards or 15 seconds</td>
<td>S&D, p. 98;
IM, p. 119</td>
</tr>
<tr>
<td>Front crawl</td>
<td>25 yards[6], rotary breathing</td>
<td>S&D, pp. 112–121;
IM, pp. 124–125</td>
</tr>
<tr>
<td>Back crawl</td>
<td>25 yards[6]</td>
<td>S&D, pp. 142–149;
IM, pp. 126–127</td>
</tr>
<tr>
<td>Breaststroke[5]</td>
<td>Breaststroke kick 10 yards, with or without kickboard</td>
<td>S&D, pp. 128-133;
IM, pp. 130-131</td>
</tr>
<tr>
<td>Sidestroke[5]</td>
<td>Scissors kick 10 yards, with or without kickboard</td>
<td>S&D, pp. 134-141;
IM, p. 128</td>
</tr>
<tr>
<td>Turns
Introduction to turning at wall</td>
<td>Demonstrate change of direction at wall</td>
<td>S&D, p. 105;
IM, p. 120</td>
</tr>
</table>

* <i>S&D = Swimming and Diving   IM = Instructor's Manual</i>

REQUIRED SKILLS		
Skill[1]	**Completion Requirement**[2]	***References**
Personal Safety and Rescue		
Tread water with modified scissors, modified breast-stroke, and rotary kicks	2 minutes, using any kick	*S&D*, p. 96
Learn rescue breathing	Demonstrate without mouth-to-mouth contact	*S&D*, p. 300
Become familiar with CPR	Watch video or demonstration	

[1]Skills may be taught in any order within a level.

[2]Times and distances listed are the minimum to meet the requirement.

[3]Whenever possible, the first requirement should be met. In those cases where participants cannot touch bottom, the alternative requirement must be met.

[4]If pool depth does not meet minimum standards (American Red Cross guidelines or state or local regulations) instructors SHOULD NOT teach diving skills.

[5]Entire stroke is introduced at this level, but only the kick is required for completion.

[6]A turn is *not* required for meeting the criterion.

* *S&D = Swimming and Diving   IM = Instructor's Manual*

Optional Skills and Activities

- Fitness activities (see Chapter 24 and *S&D*, Appendix B)
- Inner tube water polo (see Chapter 25)
- Synchronized swimming figures and variations (see Chapter 25 and *S&D*, pp. 277–278)
- Butterfly lead-up skills, *S&D*, pp.150–159
- Stride jump entry
- Skills from Level V that promote coordination and increase endurance

LEVEL V: STROKE REFINEMENT

<table>
<tr><td colspan="3" align="center">REQUIRED SKILLS</td></tr>
<tr><td>Skill[1]</td><td>Completion Requirement[2]</td><td>*References</td></tr>
<tr><td>**Buoyancy and Breath Control**
Alternate breathing</td><td>Demonstrate</td><td>*S&D*, p. 121</td></tr>
<tr><td>**Water Entry and Exit**
Stride jump entry</td><td>Demonstrate</td><td>*S&D*, pp. 291</td></tr>
<tr><td>Beginner diving[3] progression
  from diving board</td><td>Standing dive from board</td><td>*S&D*, pp. 192–199;
IM, pp. 140–141</td></tr>
<tr><td>Long shallow dive[3]</td><td>Demonstrate</td><td>*S&D*, pp. 104–105</td></tr>
<tr><td>**Locomotion**
Breaststroke</td><td>10 yards</td><td>*S&D*, pp. 128–133;
IM, pp. 130–131</td></tr>
<tr><td>Sidestroke</td><td>10 yards</td><td>*S&D*, pp. 134–141;
IM, p. 128</td></tr>
<tr><td>Swimming under water</td><td>3 body lengths</td><td>*S&D*, p. 101;
IM, p. 121</td></tr>
<tr><td>Elementary backstroke</td><td>25 yards[5]</td><td>*S&D*, pp. 122–127;
IM, p. 129</td></tr>
<tr><td>Butterfly[4]</td><td>Dolphin kick 10 yards, kickboard
  optional</td><td>*S&D*, pp. 150–159;
IM, pp. 132–133</td></tr>
<tr><td>Front crawl</td><td>50 yards</td><td>*S&D*, pp. 112–121;
IM, pp. 124–125</td></tr>
<tr><td>Back crawl</td><td>50 yards</td><td>*S&D*, pp. 142–149;
IM, pp. 126–127</td></tr>
<tr><td>**Turns**
Open turn on front</td><td>Demonstrate</td><td>*S&D*, p. 105;
IM, p. 120</td></tr>
<tr><td>Open turn on back</td><td>Demonstrate</td><td>*S&D*, pp. 106;
IM, p. 120</td></tr>
</table>

* *S&D = Swimming and Diving   IM = Instructor's Manual*

REQUIRED SKILLS		
Skill[1]	**Completion Requirement[2]**	***References**
Personal Safety and Rescue		
Rules for safe diving from board	Discussion	*S&D*, pp. 57, 60, 62
Recognition of spinal injury	Discussion	*S&D*, pp. 302–303
Hip/shoulder support	Demonstrate	*S&D*, p. 306
Feet-first surface dive	Demonstrate	*S&D*, p. 100; *IM*, p. 121
Tread water	2 minutes total with 2 different kicks	*S&D*, p. 96; *IM*, p. 198

[1]Skills may be taught in any order within a level.

[2]Times and distances listed are the minimum to meet the requirement.

[3]If pool depth does not meet minimum standards (American Red Cross guidelines or state or local regulations) instructors SHOULD NOT teach diving skills.

[4]Entire stroke is introduced at this level, but only the kick is required for completion.

[5]A turn is not required for meeting the criterion.

* *S&D = Swimming and Diving   IM = Instructor's Manual*

Optional Skills and Activities

- Scissors kick to both sides
- Approach stroke, *S&D*, p. 293
- Use of a throw bag, *S&D*, p. 290
- Introduction of mask, fins, and snorkel, IM, pp. 209, 217–219
- Inverted scissors kick, *S&D*, p. 138
- Skills from Level VI that promote coordination and increase endurance

LEVEL VI: SKILL PROFICIENCY

<table>
<tr><th colspan="3">REQUIRED SKILLS</th></tr>
<tr><th>Skill[1]</th><th>Completion Requirement[2]</th><th>*References</th></tr>
<tr><td>**Water Entry and Exit**
Approach and hurdle on diving board[3]</td><td>Demonstrate</td><td>*S&D*, p. 192;
IM, pp. 141–143</td></tr>
<tr><td>Jump tuck from diving board[3]</td><td>Demonstrate</td><td>*S&D*, pp. 198–199;
IM, p. 144</td></tr>
<tr><td>**Locomotion**
Front crawl</td><td>100 yards, 1 turn minimum</td><td>*S&D*, pp. 112–121;
IM, pp. 124–125</td></tr>
<tr><td>Back crawl</td><td>100 yards, 1 turn minimum</td><td>*S&D*, pp. 142–149;
IM, pp. 126–127</td></tr>
<tr><td>Breaststroke</td><td>25 yards</td><td>*S&D*, pp. 128–133;
IM, pp. 130–131</td></tr>
<tr><td>Sidestroke</td><td>25 yards</td><td>*S&D*, pp. 134–141;
IM, p. 128</td></tr>
<tr><td>Butterfly</td><td>10 yards</td><td>*S&D*, pp. 150–159;
IM, pp. 132–133</td></tr>
<tr><td>Approach stroke</td><td>25 yards[4]</td><td>*S&D*, p. 293</td></tr>
<tr><td>**Turns**
Breaststroke turn</td><td>Demonstrate</td><td>*S&D*, p. 106;
IM, p. 149</td></tr>
<tr><td>Sidestroke turn</td><td>Demonstrate</td><td>*S&D*, p. 106;
IM, p. 120</td></tr>
<tr><td>Speed turn and pull-out for breaststroke</td><td>Demonstrate</td><td>*S&D*, pp. 173–175;
IM, pp. 149–150</td></tr>
<tr><td>Flip turn for front crawl</td><td>Demonstrate</td><td>*S&D*, pp. 170–171;
IM, pp. 147–148</td></tr>
</table>

* *S&D = Swimming and Diving   IM = Instructor's Manual*

REQUIRED SKILLS		
Skill[1]	**Completion Requirement[2]**	***References**
Personal Safety and Rescue		
Pike surface dive	Demonstrate	*S&D*, pp. 101; *IM*, p. 121
Tuck surface dive	Demonstrate	*S&D*, p. 100; *IM*, p. 121
Alternative kicks for treading water	Tread water for 3 minutes, 1 minute with no hands	*S&D*, p. 96
Throwing rescue	Demonstrate	*S&D*, pp. 289–290; *IM*, p. 199
Roll spinal injury victim face up	Demonstrate	*S&D*, p. 298, 307

[1]Skills may be taught in any order within a level.

[2]Times and distances listed are the minimum to meet the requirement.

[3]If pool depth does not meet minimum standards (American Red Cross guidelines or state or local regulations) instructors SHOULD NOT teach diving skills.

[4]A turn is *not* required for meeting the criterion.

**S&D = Swimming and Diving   IM = Instructor's Manual*

Optional Skills and Activities

- Survival swimming, *S&D*, pp. 30–31
- Lap swimming for fitness and endurance (including pulse check), *S&D*, pp. 236–239
- Trudgen and trudgen crawl, *S&D*, pp. 112–113
- Canoe, torpedo, and stationary sculls, *S&D*, p. 99
- Passing a ball while treading water and other water polo variations
- Safety skills from the Emergency Water Safety course (see Appendix M)
- Mini swim meets
- Swimming to music
- Skills from Level VII that meet students' needs and interests

LEVEL VII: ADVANCED SKILLS

<table>
<tr><th colspan="3">REQUIRED SKILLS</th></tr>
<tr><th>Skill[1]</th><th>Completion Requirement[2]</th><th>*References</th></tr>
<tr><td>Water Entry and Exit
Springboard dive[3] in tuck and pike positions</td><td>Front dive from diving board, 1 position</td><td>S&D, pp. 200–201;
IM, p. 144</td></tr>
<tr><td>Locomotion
Review all strokes, turns, and skills taught in previous levels</td><td>Swim continuously, any combination of strokes, 500 yards</td><td></td></tr>
<tr><td>Front crawl</td><td>200 yards</td><td>S&D, pp. 112–121;
IM, pp. 124–125</td></tr>
<tr><td>Swimming under water</td><td>15 yards</td><td>S&D, p. 101;
IM, p. 121</td></tr>
<tr><td>Back crawl</td><td>100 yards</td><td>S&D, pp. 142–149;
IM, pp. 126–127</td></tr>
<tr><td>Breaststroke</td><td>50 yards</td><td>S&D, pp. 128–133;
IM, pp. 130–131</td></tr>
<tr><td>Sidestroke</td><td>50 yards</td><td>S&D, pp. 130–141;
IM, p. 128</td></tr>
<tr><td>Butterfly</td><td>25 yards[4]</td><td>S&D, pp. 150–159;
IM, pp. 132–133</td></tr>
<tr><td>Turns
Backstroke flip turn</td><td>Demonstrate</td><td>S&D, pp. 176–177;
IM, pp. 148–149</td></tr>
<tr><td>Personal Safety and Rescue
In-water rescue using equipment</td><td>Demonstrate</td><td>S&D, p. 297;
IM, p. 200</td></tr>
<tr><td>Conditioning principles</td><td>Discussion</td><td>S&D, pp. 254–256</td></tr>
<tr><td>Check heart rate</td><td>Demonstrate</td><td>S&D, pp. 230–231</td></tr>
<tr><td>Retrieve diving brick, deep water</td><td>Demonstrate in 8-10 feet</td><td>S&D, pp. 99–101</td></tr>
<tr><td>Review Basic Water Safety skills</td><td></td><td>S&D, pp. 22–51</td></tr>
<tr><td>Tread water</td><td>5 minutes</td><td>S&D, p. 96;
IM, p. 198</td></tr>
<tr><td>Assist with backboard rescue</td><td>Demonstrate</td><td>S&D, pp. 308–309;
IM, p. 216</td></tr>
</table>

S&D = Swimming and Diving   IM = Instructor's Manual

Optional Skills and Activities

- Participate in the Red Cross Swim and Stay Fit program, IM, p. 171
- Complete the 12-minute Cooper swim test, *S&D*, p. 239
- Develop a personal swim for fitness program, *S&D*, pp. 233–240
- Aerobic water exercise, *S&D*, p. 226
- Intramural mini swim or dive meet
- Synchronized swimming routines, *S&D*, pp. 277–278
- Sculling positions and skills, *S&D*, pp. 98–99
- Water polo, *S&D*, pp. 279–280
- Selected skills from the Emergency Water Safety course (see Chapter 27)
- Water test from the Emergency Water Safety course (see Chapter 27)
- Water basketball
- Inverted breaststroke, *S&D*, p. 127
- Overarm sidestroke, *S&D*, p. 135
- Competitive backstroke start, *S&D*, pp. 168–169 (be sure water is deep enough to teach this skill)
- Grab Start, *S&D*, pp. 166–167 (be sure water is deep enough to teach this skill)

17 | support techniques

You can use a variety of support techniques to help students learn. Supports and support positions can enhance learning and make practice sessions more rewarding for students. With support, the student can assume the correct position for learning or practicing a skill. This helps students develop confidence. When they know they will not submerge accidentally, they can relax and focus on the skill being learned.

This chapter describes three types of supports: flotation devices, stationary supports, and hand supports. These may be effective for students who need individual assistance and practice, or they may be used for group practice. Persons with physical disabilities in your classes may find that flotation devices enable them to progress more quickly.

FLOTATION DEVICES

There are two categories of flotation devices for providing support:

1. Those attached to the body, such as life jackets, inflatable arm bands, and styrofoam floats.
2. Those the student holds onto, such as kickboards, pull buoys, and barbell floats.

These devices are discussed in some detail later in this chapter.

Allow nonswimmers in your classes to use attached flotation devices only in a very limited way. Nonswimmers should stay in shallow areas, and they *should not become dependent on an aid.* Teach nonswimmers and their parents about the potential hazards of such aids when used for recreational swimming or practicing skills without a qualified instructor's supervision. Children in particular may get a false sense of security. A child who is used to such a device may drown if he or she goes into the water without it. Emphasize, as well, that such aids do not take the place

of Coast Guard-approved life jackets. Nonswimmers should wear Coast Guard-approved life jackets in any situation where there is a chance they may fall into the water.

For maximum effectiveness, a flotation device attached to the body should—

- Support the body in the proper position for the skill to be learned.
- Be placed on the part of the body requiring support without interfering with movements of other body parts.
- Be secured so it does not slip or come loose.
- Be constructed so it cannot deflate accidentally.

You may use a variety of free-floating supports to support the body to help the student practice with one or both arms, with or without breathing, and/or utilizing various kicks. Students grasp these supports with one or both hands or hold them between the thighs or lower legs. Such supports include kickboards, pull buoys, and barbell floats. Maintaining correct body position using a leg support can be difficult and only advanced swimmers should use these devices.

Attached Supports

Life Jackets

Using a properly fitted Coast Guard-approved life jacket can be helpful in building a student's confidence and promoting relaxation (FIG. 17–1). Attached securely and fastened correctly, a life jacket provides support for back float and kicking positions. Holding the life jacket under the chin and chest provides enough buoyancy and proper body position to practice treading water.

Life jackets have limited usefulness as teaching aids since their bulk reduces effectiveness in performing skills. They also can promote poor body position. If the life jackets do not fit correctly they can endanger a panicky child and cause him or her to float face down.

FIG. 17–1

Inflatable Arm Bands

These aides are sometimes called "muscles", "wings", or "swimmies" (FIG. 17–2). They are used only for very small children and even that use should be severely limited. They can keep a child's head above water and permit the child to move independently. This frees the parent to assist with the manipulation of the limbs. They may be useful for water adjustment, but they tend to reinforce a false sense of security in the child who cannot reason that the artificial device is providing the flotation. These devices readily develop leaks and tend to slip off. They raise the child's center of buoyancy and actually impair progress if he or she becomes accustomed to kicking in a vertical position.

FIG. 17–2

Styrofoam Floats

These attachable devices come in a variety of shapes and provide enough buoyancy to support small children. They can help build strength and endurance since the child can practice longer in water over his or her head. They can be useful in beginning coordination practice of combined skills. To enable the child to float on the stomach, the device is placed on the back. To enable the child to float on the back the device is placed on the stomach.

The disadvantages often outweigh the advantages as parents and children alike may become overconfident of the child's ability and safety. A poorly positioned device can submerge the child's face. Parent's should be strongly warned not to depend on any artificial device for their child's safety. These devices cannot substitute for Coast Guard-approved flotation devices for emergency situations.

Free Floating Supports

Kickboard

The most common and probably the most useful teaching aide is a kickboard (FIG. 17–3). Kickboards can be used at all levels with varying degrees of assistance. Small children can be held on the kickboard by their parents as they explore the water. They may also enjoy the independence of exploring alone. Be sure to observe carefully, since the kickboard may slip out of the child's grasp or flip over.

FIG. 17–3

Students learning to kick can hold the kickboard to simulate proper flotation position so that they can concentrate on kicking. For practicing kicks on the front, the student holds the kickboard in front with the arms outstretched. The swimmer who is very buoyant can hold the end of the kickboard, while the less-buoyant swimmer may need to stretch the arms to the top of the kickboard allowing the arms to rest on it. Check to see if students are simulating a streamlined swimming position when they practice. The head may be held out of the water so that breathing does not interfere with kicking practice. To practice back position floating and kicking the student holds the kickboard across the stomach. The hands hold the far side of the kickboard and may rest on the board. More skilled swimmers can manipulate the kickboard in the water overhead. In those cases where the use of the kickboard alters body position or is too cumbersome, its use should be discontinued. Be sure the kickboard does not become a substitute for correct body position.

Pull Buoys

Commonly used in the upper levels of the Learn to Swim program and in competitive training, these foam devices are held between the student's thighs, knees, or ankles to provide buoyancy and to allow the student to concentrate on arm stroking (FIG. 17–4). The placement of the device depends on how much buoyancy the swimmer needs. Be sure the student remains in good body position. A very buoyant swimmer may be equally successful without artificial flotation. You should never permit a device to be tied to a student's legs.

Barbell Floats

These instructional aides are available in different sizes and materials, so you can use the appropriate size for each student. The support consists of a bar with a float on each end (FIG. 17–5). The student holds the barbell in front with arms stretched straight and uses it much like a kickboard. Because the bar is easier to grasp than a kickboard, these aids are most useful with small children or students who have problems with kickboards. The greatest value of the barbell float is for the child to practice relatively unencumbered arm movement. The barbell is placed under the armpits for support and the child can stroke ahead of it without fear of sinking. You or the parent can face the child and offer encouragement and stay close enough to catch the child if the barbell float slips away.

FIG. 17–4

FIG. 17–5

STATIONARY SUPPORTS

Stationary supports include the deck or the side of a pool or a dock, the bottom of a shallow water area, and the ladders or steps into the water. The body can be supported in several ways to allow practice of leg movements.

Students should learn to bracket themselves to practice leg actions in proper body position. Bracketing is a technique in which the student balances and controls his or her body position while holding onto the side of the pool or the dock. Practicing in this position helps students develop correct form. Students may find ways to bracket themselves other than those described here.

Bracketing in the Prone Position

Students grasp the gutter with one hand while pressing the other hand against the pool wall, below the water line, fingers pointing down (FIG. 17–6). The submerged hand should be deep enough to give enough leverage to stay in correct body position. Students keep their arms extended and their heads low in the water to let the hips and legs rise toward the surface. Students may keep the face out of the water for easy breathing or keep it in the water and lift it for each breath.

FIG. 17–6

Bracketing in a Side-Lying Position

Students grasp the gutter with the hand of the upper arm and place the palm of the lower hand, fingers toward the bottom, against the wall directly under the top hand at a comfortable distance beneath the surface. Students keep the body straight, stretched, and perpendicular to the wall, with the lower ear in the water (FIG. 17–7).

FIG. 17–7

In this position the lower hand gives most of the support and control for the body. If students sway forward or backward, they can slide the lower hand in the direction of the sway and exert pressure against the wall to push the body back into position. This position gives stable support to practice the scissors kick.

HAND SUPPORTS

Hand support from the instructor, an aide, or a partner can be helpful for timid beginners because it helps them feel secure. The person giving support holds the student's body in a natural floating position, not a raised position. The body must be positioned properly for the skill being practiced. The person can be supported prone (FIG. 17–8) or supine (FIG. 17–9), depending on the skill. The most common support positions are described with the progressions for learning prone and supine floats (pages 118–119).

FIG. 17–8

FIG. 17–9

18 | teaching basic skills

This chapter focuses on ways to give participants a firm foundation for their progress in swimming. Teaching progressions are provided here for your lesson plans. The mechanics of these skills are described in detail in Chapter 5 of *Swimming and Diving*.

Chapter 8 discusses how to teach aquatic skills through logical progressions. You probably change the way you teach a skill depending on your experience, the participants' skill level and age, and any special needs or conditions of participants. Included here are TIPS (Tips to Insure Participants' Success) for teaching. As your experience grows, you will develop your own TIPS. The box on page 33 lists the steps you should follow in teaching aquatic skills.

WATER ORIENTATION AND ADJUSTMENT

The first step in learning to swim is to become comfortable in the water. The student's adjustment and orientation to the water is the basis for later success. You may use any or all of the following activities in Levels I and II to help students build confidence. Some students might need to do all of these, but others may need additional transitional steps. You do not have to follow the order of bulleted items.

- Students cup hands and bring water first to chin, then to nose, and then to eyes.
- Students place cupped hands in water beneath surface and then lower face into cupped hands.
- Students bend forward at the waist and submerge the face, first with support from aide or partner and then without support.
- Students submerge the face several times, taking a breath after each submersion.
- Partners hold hands and take turns submerging their faces.
- Students walk through waist- or chest-depth water holding onto the wall.
- Students walk through the water with support from instructor, aide, or partner.

- Students walk by themselves away from the wall.
- Students hold onto the gutter and move along the pool edge through deeper water by sliding their hands.

> **Safety note:**
> Be sure you can adequately supervise students before allowing them to try this.

- Partners hold hands and take turns submerging their whole bodies.
- Students submerge by themselves. Encourage them to open their eyes when they are submerged and to avoid wiping their eyes when they come back up.
- Plan games for younger students in which they see objects under water and retrieve them. (For more information on games and water activities, see Chapter 25.)

BREATH CONTROL AND RHYTHMIC BREATHING

Participants need to learn correct breathing early because breath control is basic to later aquatic skills. Teach breath control in easy steps with lots of practice in each lesson. Explain that breathing in and out properly is needed in all swimming strokes. Point out that swimmers should inhale through the mouth and exhale through the mouth and nose. Use the following steps in numerical order to teach or review breath control.

1. With face out of water, participants feel what it is like to expel air through the mouth and the nose. They hold the nose closed and exhale through the mouth. Then they keep the mouth closed and exhale through the nose.
2. Participants scoop water in cupped hands and blow water from hands by exhaling through the mouth. They repeat this but exhale through the nose only, and then from both mouth and

117 ◀

nose together. When exhaling through the nose only, they should exhale slowly so a steady stream of air exits the nose.

3. Participants stand, holding onto the gutter or other support, then bend forward at the waist, lower the face into the water, and repeat Step 2.
4. Participants hold onto the gutter or other support, inhale, submerge vertically, and exhale.
5. Participants move away from the wall and repeat Step 3.
6. Partners hold hands and take turns performing Step 5 away from the wall.
7. Front crawl rotary breathing drill. Participants stand, holding onto the side or other support with the left hand. They bend forward from the waist, lower the face into the water and exhale, turn face to the right to raise the mouth out of the water, and inhale. If they breathe to the right, they may lower the right arm to the side. They should keep their eyes open and the cheek and ear in the water when turning the face to the side. They should move the head on a single axis (an imaginary line that runs through the neck to the top of the head). Have them do this step several times and then repeat the drill, turning the head to the other side. (Remind them to switch hands when they practice to the other side.) You can also have them practice breathing drills without wall support. They can gain additional practice in the shower by turning the face away from the stream of water and inhaling and then turning the face back into the water and exhaling.

FLOATING AND GLIDING

As they first learn to move the body through the water, students often do not maintain good body alignment, so you may need to help them at first and then gradually decrease your support. Remember that body composition affects how each person floats. Those less buoyant can glide more easily than they can float. Some students may never be able to float motionless, but this should

not affect their swimming progress. Help build students' confidence and gain their trust. At this stage your goal is to help them feel comfortable by themselves in the water.

Prone (Front) Float

1. Work with each student in turn. In waist- or chest-deep water, student bends forward at the waist, extends both arms forward on the surface, and lowers the face into the water between the arms. (This skill is the same with students pushing off gently from the wall.) The student lets the upper body be supported by the water. Stand in front of the student and gently grasp the wrists.
2. Student pushes up gently off the bottom. Remember that the feet will return to the bottom if the water is not deep enough for the student's body to rotate to its normal (diagonal or vertical) floating position.
3. Cue student to recover to the standing position. He or she lifts the head, brings the knees toward the chest, presses the arms toward the bottom, and puts the feet on the bottom.

Prone Glide

1. Repeat Step 1 of prone float.
2. Student pushes up and forward from the pool bottom. (He or she may also use the pool wall.) Walk backward and gently guide the student in the glide. Student extends the hips and knees to streamline the body.
3. As momentum slows, cue the student to recover the same as in the prone float.

As students gain confidence they can glide without support.

TIPS for Prone Float and Prone Glide
■ Students may face the wall and stand submerged to the shoulders just out of reach of the wall. They push off gently on their own and reach for and grasp the wall. They recover by lifting the head, bringing the knees toward the chest, and returning the feet to the bottom.

- Students may also glide by pushing off from the wall with one or both feet.
- You can also use the jellyfish float to demonstrate buoyancy and increase the students' confidence in the water. From a vertical position, have students inhale deeply, lower the face into the water, and reach the hands to touch as far down the legs toward the toes as possible. Students bend the knees slightly so the feet leave the bottom. They should relax as much as possible.

Supine (Back) Float

1. Stand behind the participant, who is submerged to shoulder depth. Cue the participant to look up, slowly arch the back gently and lean back, and try to relax on the water. Place your hands, palms up, under the participant's back for support. (For more support, put both hands under the participant's shoulders and cradle the head. Use this position for extremely fearful participants.) Do not try to raise the participant to the floating position but let him or her rest on your hands. As the participant loses balance, the feet gently rise to their natural buoyant position.
2. As the participant experiences buoyancy, gradually decrease support by removing one hand and then the other until the participant is floating without assistance.
3. Cue the participant to recover. He or she raises the head, flexes the hips, scoops forward under the buttocks with the arms, places the feet on the pool bottom, and stands. Stay behind the participant to guide the head if needed.

Supine Glide

1. Repeat Step 1 of supine float.
2. Participant pushes off from the bottom or wall. Walk backward and gently guide the participant in the glide. Cue the participant to extend the hips and knees to streamline the body.
3. As momentum decreases, cue participant to recover the same as with the supine float.

TIPS for Supine Float and Supine Glide
- You should warn participants before you remove all support. Also warn them before you help them recover to the standing position. This prevents them from being startled or taking in water through the mouth and nose. Such an unpleasant experience could stall a participant's progress.
- To recover to a standing position, ask them to imagine sitting down in a chair, reaching back, and pulling the chair underneath them.
- Teach finning or sculling motions as needed to help less buoyant participants float and glide.

Finning

1. Demonstrate and explain finning.
2. On dry land, students extend arms and practice the finning motion.
3. With support, if needed, from an aide or partner, students glide supine in chest-deep water and do finning motion at hips. An aide's palms can support student's back as in the supine float.

TIPS for Finning
- Keep the arms and hands in the water.
- Avoid fast, jerky movement.

Sculling

1. Demonstrate and explain sculling.
2. On dry land, students imitate demonstration by extending arms and practicing the sculling motion.
3. In chest-deep water, students glide supine and do sculling motion at hips.

TIPS for Sculling
- Students stand against the wall and trace the figure-eight movement of the scull against the wall as if smoothing a pile of sand by sweeping the palms in and out. Palms never turn completely up, but point downward or sideways during the stroke.

ENTERING THE WATER

The following entries are taught in Levels II through VI.

Feet-First Entry

1. Participant jumps into chest-deep water unassisted. You should be in the water but to one side to help the participant, if needed, return to the surface and move to the side of the pool.
2. To jump into deep water, participant keeps the body as straight and vertical as possible. The hands and arms are along the sides of the body, stretched over the head, or holding the nose. When downward momentum slows, participant leans forward, opens the eyes, and either pushes off from the bottom or starts kicking and swimming diagonally to the surface. At the surface, participant levels off and swims to safety.

Long Shallow Dive

> **Safety note:**
> Be sure to teach this dive in water at least 9 feet deep. Tell participants not to dive in water less than 5 feet deep, once they have become proficient.

1. Participants use the teaching progression in Chapter 20 to learn a headfirst entry.
2. Demonstrate the long shallow dive.
3. Participants practice the long shallow dive, in deep water, from the deck.
4. When participants can safely dive from the deck, they may practice this dive from starting blocks located over deep water.

OPEN TURNS

This skill is first required in Level V, but those swimming for fitness even at lower levels may want to learn basic turns to reverse direction at the pool wall. You may teach open turns to these students. As their swimming skills improve, students learn flip turns and speed turns, covered in Chapter 21.

Open Turn on the Front

Explain to students that in this skill they turn in the direction *opposite* the hand that touches the wall. For example, if your right hand first touches the wall, you turn to your left.

1. Demonstrate the open turn on the front for the front crawl, using first one hand to turn in one direction and then the other hand to turn in the other direction.
2. In shallow water, students push off from the wall, glide in a streamlined position and start to stroke.
3. Students walk forward and grasp the gutter, turn in the opposite direction, inhale, submerge, push off, and start the stroke.
4. Students swim to the wall and do an open turn.

TIPS for The Open Turn on The Front
- Start slowly and gradually increase speed.
- Streamline body after pushing off.

Backstroke Spin Turn

Explain to students that in this skill they turn toward the hand that touches the wall. If your left hand touches the wall first, you rotate toward your left. Also point out that students may do this turn with the head out of the water but that submerging allows for a smoother, more efficient turn.

1. Demonstrate a backstroke spin turn in both directions.
2. Students push off on the back from the wall with hands overhead, glide in a streamlined position, and start the stroke.
3. Students glide backward to the wall with one hand extended. They do the spin turn when they touch the wall.
4. Students flutter kick to the wall with one hand extended forward of the head ready for a spin turn, then repeat with the other hand leading.
5. Students do the full backstroke spin turn.

TIPS for the Backstroke Spin Turn
- Teach students to watch a landmark on the ceiling or overhead to gauge the distance to the wall without looking back.
- In an outdoor pool, have a partner stand on the deck 3-4 feet from the wall to help students see when they are close to the wall to prepare for the turn.
- In some pools, backstroke flags are available as the landmark. Students should count the number of strokes from the time the head passes under the flags until the hand touches the wall. Flags are positioned at a consistent distance in pools used for competition.
- As a dry land drill to practice the spin, have students lie on their backs next to a wall and practice how to spin and plant the feet. Unless the deck is tile, it is a good idea for students to wear tee-shirts or practice on a towel to avoid scraping their backs.

Sidestroke Turn

1. Demonstrate the sidestroke turn.
2. Students walk through the water, touch the wall with the leading arm, place feet on the wall in a side-lying position, and push off into the side-lying glide position with opposite ear in water.
3. Students practice the full turn on both sides.

TIPS for the Sidestroke Turn
- After doing this turn, students can rotate to the other side if they prefer to sidestroke only on one side.

UNDERWATER SKILLS

These are taught at Levels V and VI.

Swimming Under Water

1. Demonstrate underwater swimming, emphasizing the arm stroke pattern.
2. Participants practice the arm stroke, first on dry land and then standing in chest-deep water.

3. In waist- to chest-deep water, demonstrate a porpoising action to submerge the body. Participants practice this.
4. Participants practice the full underwater stroke.

TIPS for Swimming Under Water
- Tell participants that their head and face position influences the depth they can maintain under water.
- Participants may also practice by submerging and pushing off in a prone glide under water.
- Emphasize slow exhalation under water.
- Buoyant persons will have to angle the head and the arm pull downward to stay under the surface.

Surface Diving

Feet-First Surface Dive
1. Demonstrate and explain the feet-first surface dive.
2. In deep water, students practice the full skill. After submerging, students tuck their knees to the chest, roll forward to a horizontal position, and swim under water.

Headfirst Surface Dives
1. Demonstrate and explain headfirst surface dives in the pike or tuck positions.
2. On dry land, demonstrate the arm and body action. Students practice.
3. In deep water, demonstrate the arm action from a front glide. Students practice.
4. Explain to students that as the hands press toward the bottom, they lift the legs overhead in either the pike or tuck position.
5. As students practice headfirst dives, they level off and swim under water.

TIPS for Surface Diving
- Use key words for headfirst surface dives: pull, flex, press, lift.
- Teach the pike or tuck position dive completely and then introduce the other position as an option.
- Have students practice in shallow water. Tell them to imagine reaching for the bottom as though they were doing a hand stand.

19 | teaching strokes

This chapter helps you apply the teaching principles discussed in Chapter 8. Below is a generic outline for teaching strokes in the American Red Cross Learn to Swim program. Use this outline to develop your lesson plans for each stroke. Refer to Chapter 6 of *Swimming and Diving* for stroke mechanics. (Use the chart in Appendix L to help set up the video.)

After the generic outline are TIPS (Tips to Insure Participants' Success) for teaching the individual strokes. As you gain experience,

you can develop your own TIPS. Included also are common errors in doing each stroke and ways to correct them.

With the generic outline, the TIPS, and the lists of common errors, you may use a movement-exploration approach, a whole approach, a part-whole approach, a progressive part approach, or a combination. For a discussion of these teaching approaches, see the *Instructor Candidate Training Participant's Manual.*

General Approach for Teaching All Strokes

1. Demonstrate and explain the stroke. Keep the demonstration slow and repeat it several times. Use the American Red Cross *Swimming and Diving Skills* video to reinforce your demonstration. If you can, have the video available on deck for students to view it as needed.
2. Conduct a movement-exploration drill or whole-approach drill.
3. Demonstrate and explain the kick while holding on to the wall or other support. You may also do a dry land demonstration if you can suspend your legs (such as by sitting on bleachers or benches).
4. Students practice the kick out of the water (dry land drill), if feasible. Students may sit on the edge of the pool or dock or lie down.
5. Students practice the kick in the water, holding on to the wall or other support (bracket drill). (See page 114.) Assist as needed by manipulating students' legs.
6. Demonstrate the kick using a kickboard.
7. Students practice the kick in the water, using a kickboard or similar aid. Assist as needed by manipulating students' legs.
8. Students practice the kick in the water, without support.
9. Demonstrate and explain the arm stroke—
   a. On land.

   b. In water, stationary.
   c. In water, moving.
10. Students practice the arm stroke out of the water. Assist as needed by manipulating students' arms.
11. Students practice the arm stroke in the water, but without moving (static drill). For face-down strokes, students bend at the waist to put the torso in correct body position. For the sidestroke and strokes on the back, students may be supported by aides or partners.
12. Students practice the arm stroke in the water (fluid drill). For face-down strokes, students walk on bottom, at first. Then, if needed, they may be supported horizontally by aides or partners. For the sidestroke and strokes on the back, use support as needed.
13. Demonstrate the whole stroke and explain its mechanics again. Focus on coordination between the kick and arm stroke.
14. Demonstrate and explain the breathing pattern and how to coordinate it with the kick and arm stroke.
15. Conduct dry land drills, static drills, and fluid drills of the full stroke and kick, as needed. These may involve mass practice and individual practice.

FRONT CRAWL

TIPS for Front Crawl

- Emphasize correct head position since it determines body position.
- Since students have been working with breath control since Level I, they may be able to integrate breathing with many of the activities.
- You may introduce rhythmic breathing in the kick demonstration.
- In drills for arm stroke, the face may be out of water at first, then submerged to practice breathing pattern. Putting the face in the water also teaches good body position.
- Emphasize head position and rotation for an effective breathing pattern. Have students practice rhythmic breathing on both sides before choosing the more comfortable side.
- Having one leg forward and one back in standing drills encourages correct body roll.
- In kickboard drills, students may keep head above water to work on the kick. If their shoulders bounce or rock, tell students to relax their thighs.
- Since students generally need a lot of time to learn smooth rhythmic breathing, devote part of each lesson to this. It may help them to walk through the water rotating the face in coordination with the arms. As they put the whole stroke together, they will benefit from this practice.

- Students may need to experience how each arm moves separately before coordinating the alternating movement pattern of both arms.
- Armstroke drill to improve technique: Students hold the edge of a kickboard in both hands and push off the wall in a front glide. Students do a complete stroke with one arm, hold the edge for a moment in both hands, then do a full stroke with the other arm. The hand holding the edge must stay extended in front of the head until the other hand grasps the edge.
- Hand touch drill (like the armstroke drill, but without the kickboard): Recovering hand touches other hand (extended in front of the head) before the other arm starts its pull.
- For correct arm recovery, students imagine they are pulling the hand out of their pants pocket, dragging the thumb up the side to the armpit, then extending the forearm.
- Finger tip drag (like previous drill, to practice recovery): Students relax and trail the finger tips through water but do not touch thumb to side.
- To learn high elbow recovery, have students swim close to a wall or lane line. If the hand strikes the wall or line, the student should lift the arm more by rolling the shoulders forward or bending the elbow more.

Common Errors in the Front Crawl

Error	Correction
■ Legs and hips too low.	Tell students to lower head position.
■ Arm recovery and breathing are difficult due to tucked chin, head drops down.	Have students raise head position.
■ Ineffective kick due to thighs not separating.	Tell students to kick at least 10 inches below the surface.
■ Head lifted up to breathe.	Tell students to keep chin to shoulder. Ear stays in water while inhaling.
■ Feet break the surface too much.	Have students lift head slightly to drop legs. Be sure kick starts from the hip.
■ Toes "hook" at end of downward beat because ankles are allowed to flex.	Have students keep toes relaxed and pointed. Have them practice with swim fins.
■ Arms lift out early.	Have students fully extend arms by pushing to thigh.
■ Arms sweep wide in recovery.	Practice high elbow recovery with relaxed forearm and wrist.
■ Hands, elbows, and arms drag through the water.	Have students lift elbow higher. They may also need more body roll.
■ Inefficient propulsion due to pulling with straight arms.	Stress the "S" pattern with high elbow as the arm pulls through. Have students practice arm pulls with support such as a pull buoy.
■ Inefficient stroke because of incorrect breathing.	Repeat learning drills for rotary breathing. See pages 117–118.

Back Crawl

TIPS for Back Crawl

- Emphasize body position since an efficient stroke depends on it.
- In dry land drill of kick, participants sit with legs in water to feel propulsive thrust of correct kick. Tell students to lift the water with the tops of their feet.
- It may be helpful for participants to experience how each arm moves separately with shoulder rotation before coordinating the alternating movement pattern of both arms.
- In static drills of the arm stroke, participants may grasp the gutter with one hand and in a back float position practice arm movement with the other arm.
- Since the face is out of the water, participants can breathe naturally in practice. Watch that participants do not hold their breath.
- As a fun activity to work on stable head position, participants place a cup half full of water on the forehead and swim without spilling the water.

- "Wall swimming" exercise: Participants float on back alongside the pool wall and reach one hand, elbow straight, above head to grasp the gutter. The other hand may be forward of the head or at the side. The hand grasping the gutter slowly pulls the body forward until the thigh reaches that hand, then lets go. Participants grasp the gutter again with the same hand and repeat the drill. This exercise focuses on the power of the inverted, bent-elbow pull and the push of the hand downward at the end of the pull.
- Modify the previous exercise by having participants grasp lane line discs from the underside with their fingertips and repeat the same motions with the lane disc instead of the gutter. More participants can do this exercise at the same time.

Common Errors in the Back Crawl

Error	Correction
■ Extreme arch in back; head too far back.	Tell participants to relax the back, tuck the chin in slightly, and keep ears in water.
■ Hips bend excessively.	Have participants practice flutter kick with arms extended behind the head. Have them focus on stretching the body and keeping kick lower than body line.
■ Torso bends side to side.	Check for proper body roll. Be sure head is aligned with spine and that hands enter the water at 11:00 and 1:00 o'clock.
■ Legs too deep.	Stress that toes should reach surface at end of each upward beat. The kick should churn the surface.
■ Knees bend too vigorously on downbeat.	Stress starting the leg movement from the hips.
■ Hips too low in water.	Emphasize body position, check head position.
■ Arm enters water with back of hand first.	Have participants overcorrect rotation. Emphasize little finger enters first.
■ "Splash entry." Bent arm recovery, elbow enters water first, forearm and hand are thrown into the water.	Have participants practice arm strokes with legs supported. Have them do one-arm drills.
■ Arms overreach on water entry and hands enter behind head or opposite shoulder.	Have participants overcorrect point of entry outside of shoulders.

SIDESTROKE

TIPS for Sidestroke

- Emphasize body position. Participants cannot do the stroke well if the body rotates from the side-lying position.
- Drills with arms alone may not work well since it is hard for participants to keep the body in position.
- To illustrate coordination, tell participants to imagine a string connecting the palm of their trailing arm and the knee of their top leg in the power phase.
- Land drills for the kick can help pattern the kick; explain that the scissors kick opens and closes much like a pair of scissors.
- Let participants learn the stroke on the side of their choice. Then encourage them to try the other side.
- Have participants hold a kickboard under their heads with the leading arm. This gives support while they practice the kick and trailing arm stroke.

Common Errors in the Sidestroke

Error	Correction
■ Body bent at hips or back severely arched; body almost turned onto stomach or back.	Tell participants to stretch the body from the head to the toes during the glide and relax neck and back muscles.
■ Head held too high, legs too low.	Have participants relax neck muscles and lay cheek in water.
■ Top and/or bottom knee drawn too far forward toward chest.	Have participants keep back straight. Emphasize relaxation and an easy recovery movement.
■ Top ankle not flexed during leg extension.	Tell participants to flex top ankle after extending the leg so big toe points toward head.
■ Ineffective glide.	Check whether kick and trailing arm pull are simultaneous. Have participants glide until momentum is almost lost.
■ Kick begins before trailing arm starts the power phase.	Be sure trailing palm faces the feet before doing the kick.
■ Legs drop too deep.	Have participants lower heads into water and start the next stroke sooner.
■ Legs open vertically on recovery.	Have participants practice kick lying on deck to simulate scissors action.
■ Breaststroke kick	Have participants practice extending top leg on land, in bracket drill, or with kickboard.

Elementary Backstroke

TIPS for Elementary Backstroke

- Have students "hug" kickboard, not put it under their heads, to ensure proper body position.
- Use dry land drill for kick only if students can suspend their legs. One option is to have students lie on their stomachs on benches.
- Have students practice the kick sitting on deck with legs extended into water. They bring their feet back until heels touch the wall, then kick.
- In bracket drill, aides or partners may help support students in correct body position.
- You may introduce the breathing pattern in the kickboard drill or during the demonstration of arm stroke.
- For the kick, explain how the knee acts like a hinge and that students should lift their thighs only slightly. Emphasize that students must rotate the thighs for correct motion of the legs.
- Have students do drills in the water with one foot on the bottom so they can more easily keep their balance.

Common Errors in the Elementary Backstroke

Error	Correction
■ Body bent downward at the middle; body sitting in the water.	Tell students to tilt head back, look directly overhead, and raise the hips toward the surface.
■ Extreme arch in back during arm thrust. Face may submerge.	Check head position. Stress keeping arms parallel to surface during thrust.
■ Knees break surface excessively during recovery.	Check body position. Students who are very buoyant should tilt the head forward slightly and round back and shoulders slightly. This lowers hips and legs. The feet should drop down rather than the knees pull up.
■ Hands reach too far forward of head.	Emphasize sliding hands away from the shoulders in a perpendicular line with the shoulders.
■ Water washes over face during arm recovery.	Check whether students are tilting head back, lifting the knees, or pushing water toward the face with the hands.
■ Water washes over face during pull.	Tell students to tilt chin downward slightly and pull parallel to the surface.
■ Hands recover from thighs or hips directly into extended position.	Emphasize dragging thumbs up sides of body to armpits.
■ Power phases of arms and legs not together.	Emphasize recovery of arms to armpits before legs start the power phase.

BREASTSTROKE

TIPS for Breaststroke

- This stroke requires separate arm and leg work.
- Students should practice the arm stroke before you introduce the breathing pattern, so they can focus on one thing at a time.
- In static drills, be sure students bend forward to put the torso in correct body position.
- Students may find it easier to practice the arm stroke alone if their feet do not sink. Students may use pull buoys, water wings, a rubber float, or just enough slow flutter kick to keep the feet up.
- To prevent reaching too far back with the arms, students can stand with the arms held over a pole placed against the chest at the armpits. As they pull the arms back, the pole prevents them from moving too far back.
- To practice correct pull if your deck is at water level, have students lie on deck with their arms over the water and their shoulders just clear of the pool wall. The wall prevents them from pulling too far back.
- You may cue the students when to start each stroke from the glide.
- Have students practice the kick sitting on deck with legs extended into water. They bring their feet back until heels touch wall, then kick.
- Leg recovery exercise: Students float face down with arms at sides and wrists extended, then touch feet to hands at the end of the recovery.
- Use dry land drill for kick only if students can suspend their legs. One option is to have students lie on their stomachs on benches.
- 3–1 drill: Execute 3 kicks (arms extended), 1 complete stroke, 3 kicks, 1 complete stroke, repeat. This promotes proper timing.
- 1–3 drill: Execute 1 kick, 3 arm pulls, repeat. This helps improve arm pull.
- Have students flex ankles and rotate feet, then walk around on deck. This helps them become familiar with proper foot position.
- Breaststroke hop (dry land exercise for kick): Students stand with feet spread outward 45 degrees and heels together or up to 1 foot apart. They squat, keeping knees in, and then *gently* bounce up and down. This exercise improves feet position and flexibility.

> **Safety note:**
> This exercise may be too strenuous for anyone who is just learning the breaststroke or for anyone with knee problems. Advise students that if they feel pain they should stop using the exercise.

Common Errors in the Breaststroke

Error	Correction
■ Ineffective kick.	Have students keep ankles flexed and feet rotated outward. They push around and back until the feet touch.
■ Scissors kick action.	Emphasize a narrow kick to avoid scissors action.
■ Trunk, legs, and feet too low; excessive arch in back.	Check head position. Emphasize making the body "long." Tell students to relax back muscles and tighten abdominal muscles.
■ Knees and thighs drawn too far under hips.	Have students practice with dolphin kick to develop correct "feel" of raising and keeping heels near surface during recovery.
■ Propulsion of kick is outward instead of to the rear.	Stress pressing feet around and back, not out. Emphasize a semicircular motion. Have students do the kick in two steps, recovery and propulsion, not slowing feet until they touch. Wall exercise: gently hold inside of feet during propulsion to add resistance and have student feel direction of power. Do this very gently to avoid injury to knees.
■ Knees move outside heels.	Stress proper alignment: knees in line with the hips and heels wider than the knees.
■ Elbows drop too soon during power phase.	Have students keep elbows high until hands align with them at the end of the downsweep.
■ Too much drag from leading with back of hand during recovery.	Be sure students lead with fingertips.
■ Arms pull all the way to the thigh.	Have students shorten the pull and end downward and outward sweep when hands are under the elbows with forearms vertical.
■ Faulty timing.	Have students practice sequence from glide: pull and breathe, kick and glide.

BUTTERFLY

TIPS for Butterfly

- The undulating movement of the body may be demonstrated and practiced standing out of water. Students can sit on edge of pool coping or other support, drop feet, and thrust to feel the propulsion of the correct dolphin kick.
- In kicking drills, swim fins may help students develop proper leg action.
- Demonstrations and drills of the arm stroke should emphasize a keyhole pattern.
- In moving water drills of arm stroke, legs may start a natural undulation.
- Butterfly wiggle: Students do a body wiggle under water, face down, on the right side, on the left side, then face up. Those with a "natural wiggle" should learn this stroke easily.

- Because of the strenuous nature of the full stroke, have students stroke with only one arm, keeping the other extended *forward* of the head. (The extended arm may hold a kickboard if needed.)
- Emphasize kicking *up,* not just kicking down.
- Emphasize accelerating hands through the finish and into recovery
- Have students practice the dolphin kick with a front crawl arm action. Have them work on a downward thrust in the kick each time a hand enters the water.

Common Errors in the Butterfly

Error	Correction
■ Weak arm propulsion. Hands enter water too wide or narrow.	Conduct arm strengthening drills.
■ Hands "slip" by entering water too flat.	Emphasize firm wrists, hands, and fingers; hands angled down and out; and thumbs rotated down.
■ Loss of propulsion due to dropped elbows.	Stress keeping elbows higher than hands but lower than shoulders.
■ Loss of propulsion due to pushing arms too wide during backward press under body.	Emphasize bending elbows and pressing arms backward with hands coming close together under body.
■ Body bobs because arm action stops at point of entry.	Be sure students continue momentum from arm recovery to carry the arms to a depth of at least 10 inches before the pull.
■ Ineffective kick because knees are not fully extended during downbeat.	Have students press feet down and use knees to snap lower legs to full extension. Conduct underwater dolphin kick drills.
■ Lack of continuous undulation due to over-emphasizing downward beat and pausing before lifting legs.	Have students practice kick on the side or back in the water. Conduct drills with fins.
■ Not enough breathing time due to narrow kick.	Check coordination of breathing and arm pull. Have students increase the size of the kick until it is about 2 feet from top to bottom.
■ Difficulty in getting arms out and around during recovery.	Emphasize accelerating hands through finish and into recovery.

20 | teaching diving

This chapter contains progressions for teaching diving as a safe and fun activity. The mechanics of each skill are discussed in Chapter 8 of *Swimming and Diving*. Also included here are lists of common errors and ways to correct them. Methods of manual assistance are described for helping students perform a dive without being injured. *Use manual assistance only when there is a chance a student may cause pain or injury to himself or herself.*

The students' safety is foremost when you teach diving. Before you try to teach these skills, review the safety precautions in Chapters 3 and 8 in *Swimming and Diving*. In addition, follow these guidelines:

- Water depth must be at least 9 feet (or deeper if state or local regulations require).
- Make sure students are physically and psychologically ready to do the skill. *Do not force a student to do a skill.* Students who seem very fearful about doing a step should practice the preceding step until they gain confidence.
- Be sure students can demonstrate correct hand, arm, and head position before trying to dive.
- Be sure students can jump into deep water, swim to the surface, turn around, level off, and swim 10 feet.
- Be sure students can hold the arms over the head and in line with the body on a forceful push and glide under water.
- Do not let students dive over stationary objects.
- Do not let students dive over any hard device, such as a pole.
- Do not let students dive through inner tubes or hoops.
- Be sure the deck is not slippery. If students slip during drills, check their foot position for correct push-off. You can put a wet towel on the deck and hang it over the pool edge to give better traction, especially on tile decks.

Safety note:
The springboard diving skills and progressions in this manual apply to beginning divers on 1-meter diving boards. Experienced and competitive divers may vary in the depth they need to maneuver safely under water. Standards for diving boards and diving towers used in competition are set by the National Collegiate Athletic Association (NCAA), the Federation Internationale de Natation Amateur (FINA), United States Diving, and other organizations that sponsor diving competition.

BODY ALIGNMENT

These skills help participants practice proper arm and head position for diving, reducing the risk of injury as they first learn.

Step 1. Torpedoing

1. Participants push forcefully from the wall and glide in a prone position in chest-deep water. They should keep their eyes open. Emphasize straight body alignment: arms straight and overhead, arms covering the ears, thumbs together or interlocked, body tense from arms to feet, toes pointed, legs together.
2. They hold the position until they almost stop.

Step 2. Step Dive

This skill is named from the former practice of using the steps of the pool ladder (or steps into water that is at least chest-deep) as the takeoff point. However, since participants' feet might slip from the step in this drill and be caught between the ladder and the pool wall, you should use this drill only from the pool steps or from a chair or bench firmly secured in the water.

1. Stabilize the chair or bench if necessary. You can put downward pressure on the back of a

chair or put one foot on top of a bench and press downward.
2. Participants aim toward a target on the surface 2 to 3 feet ahead.

3. Participants extend the arms over the head, bend the knees slightly, lean forward, then push forward into a prone glide. Emphasize proper arm and head position.

Step 3. Porpoising

1. Participants start as in Step 1, then angle the head and arms down, surface dive toward the bottom, level off, and glide to the surface. Emphasize body alignment.

2. As a variation, participants jump forward and slightly upward from a standing position.
3. Show participants how to change their body's angle in descent and ascent by raising and lowering the head and arms as a single unit.

Common Errors in Body Alignment Drills

Error	Correction
■ Lifting the head up and/ or letting the arms drop.	Have participants hold hands together, interlock the thumbs, and squeeze the arms against the ears.
■ Letting the arms drop toward or below the shoulders.	Have participants squeeze the arms against the ears.
■ Diving at too steep an angle.	Have participants imagine diving toward a target on the bottom 4 to 5 feet in front of them.

Instructor's note:
Participants may repeat these errors throughout the teaching progressions for diving. If participants continue to make an error such as raising the head in more advanced skills, have them practice body alignment drills to correct this error before they proceed to later steps. Do the same with any persistent error.

DIVING FROM THE DECK

Step 1. Kneeling Position

1. Make sure students position their legs and feet properly for pushing off the deck and that arms and head are aligned.
2. If the deck is within 8 inches of the surface, have the students touch the surface with their hands before pushing into the water. If the students cannot reach the surface, instruct them to *try* to touch the water before pushing from the deck.
3. Instruct students to aim downward, not outward.
4. Students dive toward a target on the surface or on the bottom. They should use the same target when they practice.
5. To use your hand as a target, place it on the surface at the right distance. Students dive toward your hand. Be sure to move your hand before the student enters the water.
6. Students keep the body aligned until the whole body is in the water, then lift the head and pull with arms to return to the surface.

Manual Assistance From the Deck
(For Those Having Trouble)
1. Kneel next to the student and place your hand just above his or her head. Your hand should not touch the head unless you need to help keep the head down (FIG. 20–1, *A)*.

FIG. 20–1, *A*

2. With your other hand, hold the student's ankle of the leg that is down on the deck.
3. As the student pushes toward the water, press down on the head and lift up on the leg, if necessary, to keep the student from doing a belly flop (Fig. 20–1, *B).*

FIG. 20–1, *B*

Manual Assistance From the Water
(For Those Having Trouble)
1. Position yourself in the water to the side of the student, who is on the deck. *Do not get directly in front of the student.*
2. Hold your hand out and have the student place his or her hands on your hand (Fig. 20–2, *A).*

FIG. 20–2, *A*

3. Direct student to keep the head down.
4. Student pushes toward the water, staying in contact with your hand.
5. Lower your hand down and away from the pool edge as the student pushes toward the water (Fig. 20–2, *B*).
6. When the student's head reaches the surface, quickly move your hand away.

Fig. 20–2, *B*

Common Errors in the Dive From Kneeling Position

Error	Correction
■ Lifting the head while pushing toward the water (causing a flat entry).	Use verbal cues; emphasize squeezing the head between the arms.
■ Aiming out instead of down (causing a flat entry).	Point out a specific target on the bottom to dive toward or place your hand as a target on the surface.
■ Somersaulting upon entry.	Emphasize keeping the head aligned with the arms. The head should be tilted back slightly so the students can look toward the hands; emphasize diving toward a target on the surface.

Step 2. Compact Position

1. Students assume the kneeling position as in Step 1.
2. Students lift the knee up off the deck, reach and push toward the water, then dive as in the kneeling position.

Manual Assistance From the Deck

■ Stand to the side of the student with your hands at the waist to help stabilize the body. As the student pushes toward the water, tell him or her to lift the back leg (Fig. 20–3).

■ Manual assistance from the water is the same as for the dive in the kneeling position.

■ The corrections for errors in dives from the kneeling position also apply here.

Fig. 20–3

Step 3. Stride Position

1. Students stand with one foot forward and the other back.
2. They focus on a target for this dive 1 to 2 feet farther out than for dives from the kneeling and compact positions.
3. Students lift the rear leg as they push toward the water.

Manual Assistance From the Deck
Stand to the side of the student with one hand around the waist and the other hand on the rear leg, just above the knee, to help stabilize the body. As the student falls toward the water, lift up on the rear leg and guide the student into the water (Fig. 20–4).

Fig. 20–4

Common Errors in the Dive From Stride Position

Error	Correction
■ Aiming out instead of down.	Emphasize reaching for the target and lifting leg high while falling toward the water.
■ Lifting head while falling toward the water.	Emphasize squeezing the head between the arms.

Step 4. Standing Dive

1. Students take the proper position.
2. Students use the same target for this dive as from the stride position.
3. Students lean forward toward the water before the push.
4. Students push the hips and legs up as the hands and head angle downward.

Manual Assistance From the Deck
Use this technique only for a student having difficulty lifting the legs during the dive.
1. Sit at the pool edge to one side of the student. Place one arm in front of the student midway between the feet and knees about 12 inches away from the legs (Fig. 20–5).
2. Student dives over your arm and pushes the legs up as he or she angles down toward the water.
3. Move your arm away as the student leaves the deck.

Fig. 20–5

Common Errors in the Standing Dive

Error	Correction
■ Diving too far out causing flat landing.	Tell students to dive toward same target as the dive from the stride position.
■ Lifting the head up causing flat landing.	Emphasize squeezing the head between the arms.
■ Falling into the water rather than pushing away from the side.	Have students practice torpedoing and porpoising in deep water. Emphasize pushing off the side of the pool.
■ Not lifting the legs high enough.	Have students push from the deck and kick the legs up and over the hips as the head and arms angle down toward the water.
■ Pushing too late in the dive, causing legs to flip over head in back arch or somersault.	Have students stretch the arms toward a target a little farther out and raise head to proper position between the arms.

SPRINGBOARD DIVING

Beginner Progression From Diving Board

Teaching diving from a springboard begins with the same progressions as diving from the deck. Start with the kneeling position and progress to the standing dive. When participants are doing the standing dive from the diving board, you can help them refine their entry position by introducing them to the forward dive fall-in (page 141).

Safety note:
- Move the fulcrum as far forward as possible to help stabilize the board.
- Put a wet towel on the end of the board for dives from the kneeling position to prevent knee abrasions.
- Participants must keep the head and arms aligned during all steps.
- Participants should use a target the same distance away from the end of the board as in the diving progressions from the deck.
- Do not use manual assistance for spring board dives. Make sure participants are proficient in diving from the deck before moving to the diving board.
- Participants should dive down, not out.
- You may be in the water with a flotation device, to the side of the tip of the board so participants won't hit you when they dive. Being close at hand may give participants more confidence.

Common Errors in the Beginner Progression From Diving Board

Participants make the same errors as in diving from the deck, but the added height of the board adds to the error. Be sure participants can do each step properly before progressing to the next.

Error	Correction
■ Lifting the head from between the arms.	Emphasize squeezing the head between the arms.
■ Letting the hands and arms split apart before and during water entry.	Have participants practice torpedoing and porpoising in deep water.
■ Not extending the legs before entry.	Emphasize straightening the body in torpedoing drills in deep water. Have participants practice the entry from the deck. Emphasize keeping the legs straight during entry.
■ Ducking the head at entry.	Emphasize squeezing the head between the arms. Tell participants to keep their eyes on the target until the hands hit the target. They should close eyes just before entry.

Forward Dive Fall-In

Be sure participants have practiced this skill thoroughly before doing headfirst dives.
1. Participants practice proper entry position while standing on the deck. Check for proper alignment.
2. Participants practice the forward dive fall-in from the diving board several times before you give feedback.

Approach and Hurdle

> **Safety note:**
> Before trying a forward approach, hurdle, and dive from the diving board, students must be able to—
> ■ Successfully do a standing dive from the diving board, swim to the surface, level off, and swim to the side.
> ■ Jump from the diving board with legs together, arms at the sides, and body tense; descend to the bottom or until momentum stops; and swim back to the surface.

The first four steps are dry land drills. Do these exercises only on a dry deck.

Step 1. Hurdle Leg and Arm Action
1. Students practice using each leg for the hurdle and decide which leg they prefer to lift.
2. Students stand with feet together and arms at the sides.
3. Students swing the arms slightly backward and then forward and upward above the head. They keep the hands and arms in line with or slightly outside and in front of the shoulders.
4. Students lift the hurdle leg while swinging the arms forward and upward.
5. Check for correct hurdle leg position.

Step 2. One-Step Approach
1. Students swing the arms back slightly to prepare for the swing forward and upward.
2. Students step forward with the push leg while swinging the arms backward.
3. Students lift the hurdle leg into position at the same time they swing the arms upward into position.

Step 3. One-Step Approach and Hurdle
1. Students do Step 2 and, as the hurdle leg and arms drive forward and upward, jump upward and forward 1 to 2 feet.
2. Watch carefully for problems of balance in the hurdle.

Step 4. Full Approach and Hurdle

1. Students take at least three normal walking steps before the hurdle, with the last step before the hurdle slightly longer than the others.
2. Students practice a few times, counting to determine how many steps they want to take.
3. Put two tape strips on the deck, one to simulate the end of the board and one to indicate the starting point.
4. Advise students to start walking with the push leg if they use an odd number of steps or to start with the hurdle leg if they use an even number of steps.
5. Students practice this step on deck, simulating a jump from the end of the diving board.

Step 5. Standing Jump

■ Students do a standing jump from the tip of the diving board. They should keep their arms at the sides and legs together and straight with the toes pointed downward for the feet-first entry.

Step 6. One-Step Approach and Hurdle From Board

■ Put a strip of tape on the board to indicate starting point.
■ Students do the one-step approach and hurdle from the diving board, jumping into the water each time.

Safety note:
Students should jump to the end of the board and spring upward, forward, and into the water. They *must not* bounce back onto the diving board.

Step 7. Full Approach and Hurdle From Board

1. Each student walks to the tip of the diving board, turns around, and puts the heels about 1 inch from the tip of the board. He or she then performs a full approach and hurdle back toward the anchored end of the board to note the proper starting point for the approach.
2. Student turns around and stands with the toes where the heels just landed.
3. Mark this position with tape so the student can adjust the starting place if needed.
4. Students practice the full approach and hurdle, jumping into the water each time after the spring from the end of the board. For beginners, the entry should be at least 5 feet from the tip of the board.

Common Errors in the Approach and Hurdle

> ***Safety note:***
> Any error that causes a student to miss the
> end of the board may cause serious injury.
> Make immediate and full corrections.

Error	Correction
■ Landing several inches back from the tip of the board after the hurdle.	Move the starting position forward a few inches at a time until students land 1 to 2 inches from the tip of the board.
■ Too much forward momentum. (Student may miss the end of the board, or trajectory is too far outward.)	Have students take normal walking steps in the approach.
■ Last step before the hurdle is at the end of the board. (Student may miss the board or not have enough momentum to clear the board.)	Place a strip of tape about 2 feet from the tip of the board. The students should step on the tape in the last step in the approach. Check whether the steps in the approach are too long.
■ Dropping the arms below the shoulders too soon while in the hurdle (downward press is out of timing).	This is usually a balance problem. Note whether the student is leaning backward or forward during the last step in the approach or kicking the hurdle leg forward at the beginning of the hurdle.
■ Kicking the lower part of the hurdle leg forward rather than keeping it perpendicular to the board (may affect balance).	Have the students practice the hurdle without a jump on dry land. Have the students hold the hurdle position in front of a mirror if possible.
■ Hurdle is too long, causing outward and low trajectory.	Shorten the approach by moving the starting position forward a few inches at a time.
■ Hurdle is too short. (Students enter too close to board.)	Shorten steps in the approach, if they are too long, or move starting position farther back. Be sure the forward jump gives enough momentum to project the students forward and away from the board.
■ Dropping the head to watch the end of the diving board while in the hurdle. (This may cause forward lean and loss of balance while pressing board).	Be sure students look at the end of the board during the hurdle while keeping the head erect. Have them practice proper head position in the dry land approach and hurdle. Have students look at the strip of tape on the deck with head erect while descending from the hurdle.

Forward Jump, Tuck Position

Treat each of the following skills as a separate step. Do not proceed to the next skill until participants are successful with the one before.

1. Participants get into a sitting tuck on the deck.
2. Participants do a standing jump tuck from the deck.
3. Participants do a standing jump tuck from the diving board.
4. Participants do a jump tuck with a one-step approach and hurdle.
5. Participants do a jump tuck with a full approach and hurdle.

Forward Dive, Tuck Position

Treat each of the following skills as a separate step. Do not proceed to the next skill until participants are successful with the one before.

1. Participants review the standing jump tuck as needed.
2. Participants perform the standing forward dive tuck from the diving board. Watch that they rotate properly. Remind participants to press the arms to the side (laterally) and overhead in the "come out."
3. Participants perform the forward dive tuck with a one-step approach and hurdle.
4. Participants perform the forward dive tuck with a full approach and hurdle. Advise participants not to take a full spring the first few times they practice this dive.

Forward Dive, Pike Position

Participants practice the forward dive pike using the same progressions as the forward dive tuck. These include:

- Standing forward dive pike
- Forward dive pike with one-step approach and hurdle
- Forward dive pike with full approach and hurdle

Common Errors in the Forward Dive Tuck and Pike

Error	Correction
■ Too much forward momentum.	Emphasize pushing the hips up and upper body down in flight.
■ Overrotating and passing vertical.	Check to see if participants are lowering the head too much in flight. If so, tell them to continue watching the entry point from the takeoff until they line up for the entry.
■ Swinging the arms directly forward in the "come out" (may cause rotation past vertical).	Have participants press the arms laterally and over head to prepare for the entry.

21 | teaching starts and turns

This chapter describes teaching progressions for the grab start, the backstroke start, the flip turn for the front crawl, the flip turn for the backstroke, and speed turns for the breaststroke and the butterfly. The mechanics of each skill are detailed in Chapter 7 of *Swimming and Diving*. Also included here are TIPS (Tips to Insure Participants' Success) and lists of common errors. Open turns are covered in Chapter 18.

GRAB START

> **Safety note:**
> Participants must be skilled in the long shallow dive before learning this technique. You should not teach this skill unless the water is at least 9 feet deep. Once learned, the start should not be done unless the water under the starting blocks is at least 5 feet deep. Be sure starting blocks are fastened securely.

The grab start is named from the way a swimmer grabs the front of the block, a position that allows the swimmer to push off quickly. With this start the swimmer generates a powerful push off the block, attains the proper direction of force, and keeps momentum with a smooth entry and streamlined glide.

Step 1. Jump From Deck

1. From a dry place on the deck, the participants practice jumping into the water. Remind them to be careful in these jumps.
2. Participants jump without using their arms. They start in a position with the same knee bend they will have in the grab start. On your signal, they increase the knee bend slightly and jump.

Step 2. Jump With Arm Swing

- Participants prepare to jump, as in Step 1, but with their arms pointed out in front at an angle toward the floor. On your signal, they bend slightly more at the knee, push off the deck, and throw their arms up in front of them. At the end of the push off the deck, the arm swing stops at an angle of about 45 degrees from the body.

Step 3. Start Position on Block

The participants can now try the grab start from the blocks. If the pool happens to have a place to grab at the side of the pool, they could first practice there. Explain that the angle of entry from the blocks is much steeper than from the deck.

- Participants get into the "ready position" several times on the blocks without actually diving. This helps them get used to the commands ("swimmers ready, take your mark") and the balance of the blocks and feel of the starting position. Participants keep the body relaxed, toes gripping the edge of the block, knees bent enough, and fingers grabbing the blocks. Be sure they balance on the balls of their feet, not leaning back or so far forward that they cannot return to a standing position. In the ready position, participants give all their attention to the starting signal.

Step 4. Full Start From Block

When the participants are used to the feel of the ready position, let them practice the whole grab start. Watch carefully for errors but let them practice a few times before giving corrective feedback. Often they recognize and correct their own errors. If you see a participant repeat a fault in several trials, make appropriate corrections and follow up on those corrections.

TIPS for the Grab Start

■ The goal of Step 1 is for participants to get as high off the ground as they can. As a variation, have participants jump using only their ankles and not the knees or only the knees and not the ankles. This helps them learn how the muscles work together to produce the greatest force.

Common Errors in the Grab Start

Ready position:
■ Not grabbing block forcefully
■ Not being balanced on balls of feet
■ Not being relaxed

Reaction phase:
■ Letting go of the block and doing an arm swing instead of pulling on the block
■ Not pulling hard enough on the block
■ Pulling too hard on the block

Power phase:
■ Not using the whole body for propulsion
■ Not extending the arms forward quickly enough
■ Not stopping arms at correct position, usually bringing them too far forward (If the hands go too far, the jump will be less powerful and the body will land too flat on the water.)
■ Not throwing the head forward as arms go forward
■ Incorrect angle of push (pushing too high or too quickly into water)

Entry and stroke:
■ Not entering the water smoothly
■ Landing too flat (because of either a poor angle or the participant not bending at their hips slightly on entry)
■ Not streamlining
■ Stroking too late or too early
■ Not holding hands together on entry

BACKSTROKE START

Your approach to teaching the backstroke start is like that for the grab start because the skills are similar.

Step 1. Tuck Position on Deck

This step reinforces the proper path of the hands and the change in the head position. You can also have the students press their hips forward in this drill to reinforce keeping the hips up in the start.

1. Students bend deeply at the knees and put their hands on the deck in front of them with the head tucked. From this position students simultaneously stand, raise their hands over-head along the side of the body, and lift the head to look at the ceiling. They should be fully extended, hands stretched overhead, heads looking up, and hips forward. This corresponds to the midair position in the backstroke start.
2. Students repeat the drill faster and faster. Have them start to push off the deck as they would push off the blocks in the actual start.

Safety note:
In this drill students tend to throw the upper body back. Tell them to be careful not to lose their balance backward. You might have students practice with a partner standing behind them.

Step 2. Full Start in Water

■ As with the grab start, you can have students repeat the ready position several times to get used to the commands and the pull to the tuck position. Emphasize a relaxed yet ready position; the tuck should be tight.
■ Remind the students of the key points of this skill and let them try it a few times before giving corrective feedback.

Common Errors in the Backstroke Start

Ready position:
- Not pulled tight enough in the ready position
- Feet in an incorrect position on wall (either too low or out of water)

Reaction phase:
- Not pushing against the block with the hands

Power phase:
- Poor extension of body; sitting down in water
- Not moving head back far enough
- Not swinging arms to side (The arm swing in the power phase is critical. If students throw the arms straight over the body, the hips are pushed down. If the arms travel in an arc to the sides outside the body, the hips more easily stay above the water, as is ideal.)
- Hips not coming out of water (If the hips stay high, the entry is much smoother and the person can enter the water through a narrow "hole.")

Entry and stroke:
- Not streamlining
- Pulling both hands down at same time
- Stroking too soon or too late (When they start to stroke, many inexperienced swimmers pull both hands down to their sides at the same time rather than starting the stroke one arm at a time.)
- Not exhaling continuously through the nose while under water.

FLIP TURN FOR FRONT CRAWL

Although it looks complicated, the flip turn is fairly easy to learn. Try to teach the whole progression in one session so students get the idea of the whole skill.

Step 1. Forward Roll in Shallow Water

This step simply gets students to do a forward roll and learn how to somersault in the water without becoming disoriented. Students should keep their eyes open and exhale continuously through the nose.

1. Students stand with their hands at their sides in waist-deep water, palms facing front.
2. Students bend slightly at the waist and push gently off the bottom while tucking the head (chin to chest) and tucking the legs. As the roll starts, they press the hands over the head to continue rotation. They should exhale through their nose during this step. When they complete the rotation, they should be able to stand up facing the way they began.

Step 2. Forward Roll From Glide

This step gets students used to doing the roll with some forward momentum. They will learn it is easier to do the roll when they are moving forward.

- Students repeat Step 1, except that they start the roll from a glide rather than standing. They can start the glide by pushing off the bottom or the wall.

Step 3. Forward Roll From Swimming

This step helps students work on going from the freestyle stroke to the preparatory position (hands down to side, palms facing down). Have them do this away from the wall.

- Students swim freestyle and after four or five strokes leave first one then the other hand down by their side. After a short glide, they do the same forward roll as in Steps 1 and 2. They should finish standing facing the way they started.

Step 4. Forward Roll at the Wall

This step adds three critical parts to the skill. First, students come out earlier from the forward roll; they end on the back rather than standing up. Second, they must start to gauge how far from the wall they must start the roll. Third, they must keep their hands forward of their heads as they plant the feet on the wall.

1. Students stand in the water facing the pool wall, one body length away from it.

2. Instruct them to come out of the roll earlier and to place their hands forward of their heads when they try to plant their feet.
3. Students repeat Step 3, adapted this way, several times, each time starting closer to the wall. (Because of the distance from the wall, they will not touch the wall with their feet the first several times they do this.)
4. Eventually students move close enough to the wall that their legs are bent about 90 degrees when their feet make contact. They plant their feet on the wall with their toes pointing up or slightly to the side.

Step 5. Forward Roll at the Wall With a Push

When the students succeed with Step 4, have them push off the wall while on the back or in a side-lying position. They should keep a stream-lined body position.

Step 6. Full Flip Turn

In this final step, the students simply roll or rotate into a prone position after pushing off the wall. They should stay in a streamlined position. When their speed slows to swim pace, they take one or two kicks and start to stroke.

TIPS for the Flip Turn
- Emphasize a tight tuck of the legs and head. The tighter the tuck, the quicker the roll. Students can repeat Step 3 several times in a single 25-yard length of the pool.
- Step 4 takes the most time of all the steps, so be sure to allow enough time for it.

Common Errors in the Flip Turn

Step 1:
- Not coming up facing in the same direction as at the start (This is caused by tucking the head under one shoulder or the other instead of straight down. A student is likely to have the same fault throughout the drill.)
- Not completing the roll (coming out of the tuck too early or not keeping chin tucked)

- Not tucking tight enough

Step 2:
- Not starting with the hands down at sides
- Doing several small circles with the hands wide instead of one pull to above the head with the arms close

Step 3:
- Starting the roll with one or both hands ahead of the head instead of at the side

Step 4:
- Misjudging the distance from the wall
- Rolling to one side (dropping the shoulder)
- Coming out of the roll too late (to a standing position instead of a supine position)
- Ending up with the hands down at the side rather than over the head
- Bringing the head out of the water to look at the wall instead of looking at it under water

Step 5:
- Not streamlining
- Not keeping body parallel to the surface (the push-off goes too deep or too shallow)

Step 6:
- Starting the rotation to the front in the roll instead of after the push
- Not streamlining

BACKSTROKE FLIP TURN

The backstroke flip turn is nearly identical to the front crawl flip turn. Participants who have learned the flip turn for the front crawl usually learn this skill easily. To teach this turn—
1. Have participants gauge their distance from the wall. Glancing to right or left while stroking helps them judge this.
2. Participants roll to a prone position about one stroke from wall.
3. Participants do the flip turn as for the front crawl, but in the push from the wall they stay on the back instead of rotating to the front. Be sure they stay streamlined.
4. Participants continue exhaling during the glide. They resume kicking after slowing to swimming speed.

5. Participants resume stroking when the raised arm breaks the surface.

SPEED TURNS FOR BREASTSTROKE AND BUTTERFLY

The turns for these two strokes are very similar. They differ only in the depth of the push. The push for the breaststroke is deeper to give a longer glide for the pullout. The push for the butterfly is shallower and adds a dolphin kick to the surface.

Step 1. Turn and Plant

1. Participants stand next to the end wall facing the side of the pool, with the hand of the trailing arm (in this example, the right hand) on the gutter. They crouch so that the head is just out of the water. They extend the hand of the leading arm (in this example, the left hand), palm up, toward the other end of the pool and about a foot under the surface.
2. Still holding onto the wall, participants put both feet parallel on the wall and pointing the same direction participants are facing.
3. Participants let go of the gutter as they drop the head under water. (The hand of the leading arm helps pull the head under.) As soon as the hand of the trailing arm lets go, it comes over the head and meets the hand of the leading arm forward of the head. At this point, both hands are forward of the head (arms slightly bent), the feet are planted on the end wall, and the whole body is in a side-lying position.
4. Have them repeat this step several times without pushing off.

Step 2. Plant and Push

Participants hold the gutter with the hand of the trailing arm and extend the leading arm toward the opposite end of the pool. They plant feet and push off. The key is for participants to stay in a side-lying position as they push off. They often have a tendency to rotate to a prone position before pushing off. As a drill you may have them push off on the side and glide on the side to reinforce this side-lying position. Eventually participants push off and rotate to a prone position after their feet leave the wall.

Step 3. Underwater Pullout
(For Breaststroke Turns)

1. Participants glide in prone streamlined position, arms forward of head, for 2 seconds. They perform an arm pull to the thighs, then glide with arms at sides for 2 seconds.
2. Participants recover arms with hands close to body as they recover legs.
3. As they kick, participants extend arms forward of head, breaking the surface.
4. Participants resume breaststroke.

Step 4. Full Turn

Doing the whole skill at this point adds the stretch to the wall and the tuck when participants plant their feet on the wall. Participants, thus, do the whole skill at this time. Once they can do the basic parts properly, they can practice to gain speed. As they increase their speed, encourage them to touch the flat of the wall (not grabbing the wall) when they make contact.

TIPS for the Speed Turns for Breaststroke and Butterfly
- If the participants are having difficulty when they practice the full turn, have them swim to the wall and tuck and plant without pushing off, to let you see if they are in the right position before they push.

Common Errors in the Speed Turns for the Breaststroke and Butterfly

Stretch and contact:
- Gliding too long or coming too close on the touch (Contact should come when the participant is fully extended. Both hands should touch at the same time and at the same level.)
- Not touching at the same time or the same level

Tuck and plant:

- Not dipping the shoulder of the leading arm after the touch
- Not staying in the side-lying position
- Not dropping under water (and pulling with hand of leading arm) before pushing off
- Pushing off before arms are fully extended
- Not returning the trailing arm over the surface

Push:

- Not streamlining
- Not maintaining proper depth (going too shallow or too deep)
- Not doing underwater pullout during turn for breaststroke
- Not gliding long enough before underwater pullout
- Not recovering hands close to body during underwater pullout

- customizing for disabilities
- customizing for adults
- customizing by integrating fitness components
- customizing with games and water activities

customizing the program

22 | customizing for disabilities

Mainstreaming, integration, inclusion—these words all mean the same thing: someone with a disability joining nondisabled people in an activity or program for the general population. While there will always be a need for a variety of programming opportunities, you should try to include people with disabilities and other conditions in regular programming whenever possible. Fewer and fewer people with disabilities want or need specialized aquatics courses.

Meeting the challenge of mainstreaming people with disabilities into your courses can be tremendously rewarding. Much of the reward comes from watching participants succeed and knowing that you, as instructor, are helping them learn and improve skills, maintain and increase their physical fitness, achieve success and recognition, and experience self-actualization in a regular aquatic environment. This chapter describes specific teaching methods for helping these participants reach their goals. If you are interested in working with individuals with more severe disabilities, you should seek more training. Some Red Cross units, colleges, universities and professional organizations offer specialized training.

ASSESSING PARTICIPANT NEEDS

Water Safety Instructors are trained to teach aquatics to the general population, including people with disabilities and other conditions. A regular swimming class might include participants with the conditions discussed in Chapter 9 of *Swimming and Diving*.

Note that having a particular medical condition does not automatically mean a person has an impairment. Having an impairment does not automatically mean a person is disabled. A person with impaired function or a disability might not need special or separate aquatics programming.

For example, a disability limiting a person's range of motion on land might not limit functions in the water.

As you plan your classes, pay attention to the needs of all your participants. Often you only have to modify your teaching a little to include people with disabilities or other conditions in your courses. Specific recommendations for such changes are discussed later in this chapter. Sometimes the program itself has to be modified. Whether you adjust your teaching style or change the program, you must be aware of the needs of people with disabilities or other conditions and the many ways you can meet those needs.

Needs of People With Disabilities

People with disabilities or other conditions have many of the same needs as everyone else. The most important concern for a person at any time depends on several factors, as discussed in Chapter 9 of *Swimming and Diving*. You must also consider the emotional comfort of people with disabilities. Two factors affect their emotional state:

- **Adjustment to their condition**. With most congenital impairments, the person is already adjusted to the condition before entering an aquatics program. If the impairment is acquired, however, consider how long the person has had to adjust to the condition and to learn to function with existing capabilities. A person with a progressively deteriorating condition needs to have accepted the ever-decreasing ability.

  You must accept the person as an individual. This will help you both adjust. Since both the situation and the person may change, you should continue to monitor the person's progress and adjust your teaching as needed.

- **Instructor-participant relationship**. Participants must be confident that you can provide emotional security as well as teach skills. All participants, regardless of their ability, need to feel your interest in them as individuals. A consistent, calm approach helps build their confidence.

The Range of Programming

Aquatics programming ranges from participation in regular programming ("mainstreaming") to one-to-one instruction in an adapted aquatics program given by a Water Safety Instructor trained to teach people with disabilities or other conditions. Between these extremes are many possibilities, summarized in Table 22–1.

Instructor Responsibility

Many factors affect how successful people with disabilities will be. When a person with a disability is interested in your program, you have a responsibility to provide him or her with the best possible opportunity. Meeting this responsibility may require you to—

- Give basic information about the program.
- Fairly and consistently screen all program participants. Any age or height requirements should apply to all participants. If there are no restrictions for applicants, a person with a disability should be able to apply.
- Discuss entry into the program with the person to determine program suitability.
- Get more information from the person to determine entry into the program and ensure the person's safety. This might include—
  - The specific nature of the disability.
  - Whether the person has seizures.
  - Whether the person can control the bladder.
  - If the person is on medication.
- Have the person get a doctor's statement about fitness to participate.
- Give a pretest or a trial lesson if the person has medical approval but you are unsure whether the program is appropriate.
- Consider all aspects of programming before making any final decision. These might include—

- Class size.
- Instructor-participant ratio.
- Size and depth of swimming area.
- Air and water temperature.
- The person's ability to control behavior.
- The person's previous aquatic experience.
- The person's degree of independent functioning.
- The person's mental level.
- Peer group sensitivity.
- Instructor training and background.
- Give the person the specific reasons if admission to a particular program must be denied.
- Help the person find a different suitable aquatics program if needed.

Designing the Right Program

There is no one method that is always successful for teaching aquatic activities to people with disabilities. However, you can use many different methods singly or in combination. Keep in mind three points when working with anyone in an aquatics program:

1. **The need to individualize the approach**. Regardless of the grouping of participants or the approach you use, your teaching should focus on individual performance standards and should emphasize individual abilities. When working with people with disabilities, remember that *the best programs do not label and restrict but meet individual needs and focus on all participants' ability, not disability.* The following section, "Techniques to Enhance Learning," presents ways to vary your teaching style. You can use these techniques with people with disabilities in any setting, including regular aquatics programs.
2. **The need to modify the program**. In addition to teaching techniques, you sometimes have to modify the program itself. A later section in this chapter discusses how to change the program to accommodate participant needs. These methods apply mostly to the third column in Table 22–1.

TABLE 22–1. RANGE OF PROGRAMMING IN AQUATICS

	Regular Program	Regular Program With Modification	Adapted Program
Taught by:	Water Safety Instructor	Water Safety Instructor	Water Safety Instructor specially trained to teach people with disabilitiess
Participants:	Nondisabled People with mild to moderate disabilities	Nondisabled People with mild to moderate disabilities	People with moderate to severe disabilitie
Location:	Any aquatic facility	Any accessible aquatic facility	Any accessible aquatic facility Any facility specially designed for use by people with disabilities
Adaptations needed:	Possible modification of strokes for maximum efficiency	Possible modification of strokes for maximum efficiency Small instructional group Peer assistance of swimmers	Stroke modification Small instructional group, individual attention Instructor aide assistance One-to-one instruction
Instructional support needed:	Consultation with Water Safety Instructor trained to teach aquatics to people with disabilities	Consultation with Water Safety Instructor trained to teach aquatics to people with disabilities	Consultation with other Water Safety Instructors trained to teach aquatics to people with disabilities Medical professionals

3. **The need to adjust expectations**. The mainstream is not always the best place to be. While most people with disabilities are successful in regular programs, some are not. Sometimes you can predict lack of success; sometimes you cannot. When adaptations to mainstream programming fail to meet the needs of some people, these individuals should be referred to an adapted aquatics program. The final section of this chapter, "Exploring Alternative Programs," discusses related issues and resources.

TECHNIQUES TO ENHANCE LEARNING

No two individuals with the same type of disability function exactly the same. For one person, a medical condition may result in severely restricted functioning. For another, the same condition may have no disabling effect at all. Your sensitivity to individual differences is the key to helping each person succeed.

- Do not hesitate to ask participants, in an appropriate, considerate manner, about their capabilities, range of movements, and ways of doing motor tasks.
- Give people with disabilities as much independence as possible. Do not do anything for them that they are able to do. Often, just giving people a few extra minutes lets them do the skill independently.
- Make sure to read the medical clearance sheet, if one exists, for each participant, noting any special conditions.

Factors That Affect Learning

The factors affecting learning are discussed in Chapters 6–8. The environment, the participant, and the instructor all interact in the learning process. Some factors influence learning for all participants in varying degrees. Other influences can affect—positively or negatively—learning by people with disabilities. These include—

- The degree to which the disability inhibits mental, motor, and/or sensory function.

- The degree to which the individual has adjusted to the impairment and/or disability.
- The instructor's acceptance of the individual.
- The group's acceptance of the individual.
- The individual's prior experience.
- The accessibility of the environment.

Sensory Impairment

People with impairment in one sense do most of their sensory learning through the other senses. You must try to capitalize on the senses that give the most information to the individual. Examples are given in the following sections.

Hearing Impairment

A person with a hearing impairment usually has no observable characteristics. A person may seem inattentive if she or he cannot hear. Be careful not to mistake a hearing impairment for lower intelligence. People with hearing impairment usually have normal intelligence and are very attentive, especially visually. Most people with hearing impairments are quite successful in a regular aquatics program.

For people with a hearing impairment, you can improve learning in these ways:

- Give most information visually. Increase demonstrations.
- Decrease auditory distractions.
- Be sure the area is well lighted.
- Minimize glare on the water.
- Give clear verbal directions. Do not exaggerate your speech. Be sure participants can see your face when you are speaking, since many people with hearing impairment can read lips.
- Move the participant's arms or legs in the desired pattern of movement. This enhances kinesthetic awareness.
- Use pictures and charts as tools to reinforce a demonstration. You may use the American Red Cross *Swimming and Diving Wall Charts* to do this.
- Supplement your instruction with the American Red Cross *Swimming and Diving Skills* video, which is closed captioned.

- Be aware that a person with a hearing impairment who wears a hearing aid is at a disadvantage in the water, since hearing aids cannot be worn in the water.
- Remember that wearing a swimming cap and/or putting the head under water decreases hearing ability.
- If possible, learn to sign the terms used in aquatics instruction, so you can communicate with participants who use signing. Consistent, clear gestures also aid communication.
- Use an interpreter, if possible, in classes that require a lot of verbal information, such as lessons on safety.
- Be aware that a person with a hearing impairment may also have impaired speech. Impaired speech does not indicate impairment in intelligence.
- Listen attentively to participants who can speak (most people with hearing impairment can), so you learn to understand the person's speech. Do not pretend to understand when you do not.
- Advise participants to keep their eyes open to stay in visual contact with their environment.

> **Safety note:**
> Establish clear gestures for emergency situations. Use printed material to add to verbal information, particularly information related to safety.

Some individuals may need additional specialized instruction. People with profound hearing impairment combined with severe communication impairment may need instruction from someone skilled in signing. People with multiple disabilities, such as someone who is deaf and blind, may need specialized one-to-one instruction.

Vision Impairment

People with a vision impairment may be either blind or partially sighted. Most people with a vision impairment are quite successful in a regular aquatics program. For a person with vision impairment, you can improve learning in these ways:

- Give most information through hearing and touch.
- Decrease auditory distractions.
- Be sure the area is well lighted.
- Minimize glare on the water.
- Give clear verbal directions.
- Before the lessons, give an orientation to the environment.
- Let participants with vision impairment be directly in front when you demonstrate skills. Having them touch your body while you demonstrate the skill can also aid understanding.
- Let participants with a vision impairment keep their faces out of the water in early learning phases so that they can hear better and ask questions.
- Let participants with vision impairment wear goggles if pool water is an eye irritant or if they wish to wear contact lenses.
- Let participants with vision impairment wear plastic glasses with plastic lenses in the water. (Diving or jumping into the water is not permitted with glasses on.)

> **Safety note:**
> Keep decks free of clutter. Be sure safety lines are in place. Have an auditory signal that means "stop, stand still, danger." Have large-print copies of facility rules available.

Some people with a vision impairment may need specialized instruction. People with a severe visual impairment may need instruction from someone skilled in mobility training. People with multiple disabilities may need specialized one-on-one instruction.

Kinesthetic Impairment

For a person with kinesthetic impairment, you can improve learning in these ways:

- Be aware that the person will have problems orientating the body in water since he or she cannot feel where body parts are. Adding weights to the ankles reduces the effect of buoyancy and helps the individual orient to up and down in the water.

157 ◀

- Use your hands to move a participant's body parts through the desired skill.

Tactile Impairment

If an individual has a tactile impairment, its severity will determine how successful the person will be in a regular aquatics program. You can improve learning in these ways:

- Control the temperature of shower water. Not having feeling in the arms or legs can lead to burns unknown to the person.
- Check legs and feet for abrasions. Plan activities to avoid scraping feet and legs. The person might not feel pain and thus not notice abrasions and cuts.
- Let participants who lack feeling in their legs wear socks or water shoes to minimize abrasions from underwater surfaces.

Mental Impairment

People with mental impairments process information differently. A functional impairment can be so slight that the individuals themselves and others might not notice it. Mental functioning can also be so severely impaired that a person needs custodial care for his or her whole life.

Impairment in Intelligence

If a person has an impairment in intelligence, development may be delayed and maximum potential may be decreased. Individuals with mild cognitive disability usually are successful in a regular aquatics program with little or no adaptation. Some individuals with moderate cognitive impairment are successful in regular programs while others may need a more specialized setting. Individuals who need on-going assistance with daily living, who are totally dependent, and who need consistent supervision are considered to have a severe disability. Specialized programming is needed for these individuals even to enter the water and to learn any skills.

For a person with mental impairment, you can improve learning in these ways:

- Be sensitive to the extra time the person may need to learn information and master skills.
- Use various ways to practice skills, since participants are sensitive about having to repeat practice. Variety improves learning.
- Break skills down into component parts.
- Use the progressive part and part-whole methods to teach skills. Using the whole method can be very confusing for someone with impairment in intelligence.
- Keep verbal directions clear and concise.

Learning Disabilities

A person with an impairment in information processing is often diagnosed as learning disabled. (Do not confuse a learning disability with intellectual impairment.) Information processing is the brain's ability to integrate information received through the senses and to direct motor activity. Characteristics such as hyperactivity, distractibility, and emotional instability may interfere with a person's ability to understand and follow directions and learn motor skills.

For a person with a learning disability, you can improve learning in these ways:

- Eliminate distractions.
- Try to keep the same general format and organization for each lesson.
- Provide structure for skill learning and practice.
- Be ready to change activities frequently because the person's attention span may be short.

- Emphasize common elements between skills already learned and new skills you are introducing.
- Have clear expectations for the person's behavior. Keep the rules simple and penalties appropriate. Enforce policies uniformly and consistently.

Behavior or Emotional Disturbance

People with a behavior or emotional disturbance may have difficulty relating to the aquatic environment. For a person with a behavior or emotional disturbance, you can improve learning in these ways:

- Be sure you clearly state and discuss the rules.
- Be sure participants understand clearly the consequences for inappropriate behavior and displays of emotion.
- Consistently enforce all rules and safety procedures.
- Praise appropriate behavior.
- Plan all parts of the lesson to prevent unoccupied time.

Safety note:
Do not hesitate to use time-out procedures or to stop the class for the day if participants cannot control their behavior.

Most people with mental impairments can be successful in regular programs. However, if the participant does not progress in learning aquatic skills, if his or her behavior jeopardizes the safety of other participants or peers, or if instruction of the whole class is inhibited, the person may need a more specialized adapted aquatics program.

Motor Impairment

When a person with a motor impairment is in water, increased buoyancy can make mobility easier than on land. People with limited movement are more comfortable and more mobile in the water than anywhere else. Many disabilities are less obvious when the body is in water. A person with a degenerative condition can still function in water long after motor function on land is severely diminished.

For a person who has an impairment in motor function, you can improve learning aquatic skills in these ways:

- Teach recovery to a stand or pool side as a part of all activities.
- Do not assume what the person can do in terms of motor function.
- At first teach the strokes without modifying them.
- Emphasize stroke pull along the midline of the body to decrease body roll for students with balance problems.
- Avoid activities that involve dragging body parts on the deck or underwater solid surfaces. Abrasion injuries can result.
- Encourage participants to use their full range of motion in all joints.
- Use a hands-on approach to move a participant's limbs through desired motor patterns. Be careful not to force any movement against joint resistance.
- Avoid letting the person get chilled, to decrease the risk of cramping.
- Stop the activity when participants become tired. This is particularly important for someone with a degenerative condition.
- Be sure the person can independently access the aquatic area.

Safety note:
Avoid activities causing skin abrasions. If a person has lower back instability (such as paralysis or spina bifida), prohibit diving and any other activity that could twist the spine.

A person who walks unaided and has good communication and breathing skills should have little difficulty in a regular aquatics program. Using a wheelchair or crutches and braces on land does not mean a person cannot succeed in a regular program. However, the more body parts affected by disability, the more likely the person is to need specialized instruction. A person disabled in all four extremities (quadriplegia), using an electric wheelchair, or communicating with a conversation board needs specialized, one-to-one instruction to be successful or receive rehabilitative benefit.

Other Physical Conditions

Several medical conditions demand special attention in aquatics programs. These are discussed in Chapter 9 of *Swimming and Diving*. People with these conditions should consult their health care provider before joining any aquatics program.

> **Safety note:**
> Do not let participants become chilled or fatigued. Let each person's comfort guide his or her participation. If a person has a seizure while in the water, help the person immediately. (For more information on seizures, see Chapter 13 of *Swimming and Diving*.) Participants who have seizures that are not under medical control need close supervision and should probably swim only in an adapted program with specially trained personnel.

MODIFICATIONS

If a participant is not successful in learning skills, you may need to change the skills. The sections that follow discuss several ways to do this. As a general rule, modify a skill only as much as needed to help the participant succeed.

Modifying Skills

Not all individuals perform skills exactly the same way. People have their own center of buoyancy, percentage of body fat, lung capacity, range of joint motion, height, and weight. No two bodies float or move identically in water. It is up to you to help each individual develop the most efficient stroke possible.

Having a person with a disability in class does not mean you *automatically* modify skills or

strokes. Give people with disabilities the same instruction you give all other participants.

Make modifications only after the initial teaching of a skill. Once you see how participants perform skills, you can provide coaching, make corrections, and try modifications. Don't be too quick to decide something is too hard for a person. Give participants time to practice positive and corrective feedback on how to improve in doing the skill. Then make changes to improve the person's performance.

Some people with disabilities find certain skills impossible. A person with complete paralysis will never be able to do a kick. A person with only one arm must pull close to the midline of the body to move forward in a straight line.

Some people with disabilities find certain skills difficult. A person with loss of some motor function may have problems balancing on one side for the side stroke. The elementary backstroke might not be comfortable for a person with a visual impairment because the person would be gliding headfirst with no way of telling where he or she is. Difficult skills may take much longer to learn. Use verbal cues as needed for safety. With time and patience, most participants can meet the course requirements. See pages 91–92 for information on applying performance standards for strokes.

When considering modification of a skill or stroke—

■ Let the participants try the skill or stroke several times before you consider modifying it. They will get the feel for the activity, and you can identify particular problem areas.

■ Change only one part of the skill at a time. Trying to do too many changes at one time may be confusing.

■ Let participants try several alternatives. Swimming on each side in the side stroke, for example, may help identify which side is more efficient.

■ Discuss modifications with participants. They know best how their bodies feel and move.

■ Do not make assumptions about what is or is not possible for any participant. Try everything.

■ Allow for practice time before deciding something does not work. Breaking old habits and learning new skills always takes time.

Other Modifications

Use the following guidelines to help ensure participant success:

■ Give additional instruction time. Extra practice, more feedback, and individual attention often increase learning. Scheduling practice time outside of lessons and/or arranging for additional instruction may improve learning.

■ Adjust the instructor-participant ratio. With more severe disabilities or a greater number of individuals who need more attention, more staff are needed. This might include assistant instructors or Water Safety Instructor Aides. Those who have had experience or training with people with disabilities can give the most support.

■ Change class placement. Some class groupings are more conducive to learning than others. It is hard to mainstream a person with a disability into a large class, a class with several participants with behavior problems, a class of participants with a higher or lower skill level, and/or a class in which the person with a disability is not accepted by peers. Try to find an appropriate class setting.

■ Change instructors. Some Water Safety Instructors have had additional training in adapted aquatics. Other instructors have had more experience in teaching classes with mainstreamed participants. Some instructors let their own fears and insecurities interfere with their teaching. Sometimes a participant and an instructor are simply not compatible. For any of these reasons it is acceptable to change instructors.

EXPLORING ALTERNATIVE PROGRAMS

If placement in a regular aquatics program does not seem to be working, you have several alternatives. You should explore these alternatives to find an appropriate solution to the problem. Simply removing the participant from the course is not usually an appropriate solution. A person should be excluded only on the basis of medical advice or when there are no alternatives to an exceptionally bad situation.

The following are signs that the program placement is not appropriate:

■ The participant expresses unhappiness, frustration, and/or anger toward self or others.

■ The person is not making progress in learning skills, even with extra time, help, practice, and skill modification.

■ The person is in conflict with other participants in class.

■ The person is frequently absent.

■ The person has frequent illness and/or injuries during the course.

■ There is a large gap between the person's functional ability and that of the rest of the class.

You might find it useful to consult with others about how to make aquatics more successful for all your participants. Seeking advice from Water Safety Instructors trained to teach aquatics to people with disabilities can be very helpful. Physical therapists, occupational therapists, teachers in exceptional education, recreation therapy professionals, and other Water Safety Instructors who have people with disabilities in their courses are excellent resources. Parents also can give valuable information. People with disabilities know themselves best and often can give you insight. Your local Red Cross unit may provide or help you locate specialized training. Appendix A of *Swimming and Diving* lists resources for teaching people with disabilities.

For a very small group of people, mainstream aquatics programming is not appropriate. Individuals with severe, multiple disabilities, who are deaf and blind, who are quadriplegic and nonverbal, or who are so severely mentally impaired that they need continual supervision on a one-to-one basis should be referred to an adapted aquatics program. The characteristics of specialized, adapted aquatics, described earlier, make it a suitable alternative for people with severe disabilities.

No matter what class placement is made, remember that placement can always be changed. Placement should be flexible, allowing people with disabilities access to the aquatics programs most appropriate to their needs at the time. As needs change, placement should change.

SUMMARY

The American Red Cross Swimming and Water Safety program means opportunity for all. Whether this means adjusting your teaching style, modifying expectations, or referring participants to an adapted aquatics program, you can help people with disabilities or other conditions get full benefit from their time in the water.

23 | customizing for adults

Adults differ from children and teens in their attitudes, values, aspirations, anxieties, self-regard, and responsibilities, as well as physical characteristics. Adults also differ from children and teens in their approach to learning. When children learn a skill, they are also learning *how to learn* the skill. Adults already have many learning strategies they rely on when learning new things. Adults have more extensive learning histories: a combination of past experiences, what has been learned, and how information and skills have been acquired. Thus, even though children and teens may learn motor skills faster because of their physical ability, adults bring more developed learning strategies to what they want to accomplish.

Besides being different from younger participants, those over 18 are also often very different from each other. They enter the learning environment with an incredible diversity of interests, needs, concerns, and habits. These characteristics of adult participants can influence what you teach and how you teach it. Moreover, because adults often differ from one another in strength, size, functional ability, and general health and fitness, teaching them is an exciting challenge.

CHARACTERISTICS OF ADULT LEARNERS

Chronological Age Versus Physiological Age

Aging is truly a highly individualized process. We mark our progress through life by counting the years we have lived (chronological age). However, chronological aging by itself rarely produces a dramatic physical change. Most of what affects the ability to learn results from changes in physiological function. The extent of these changes depends greatly on how active people stay throughout adulthood. Current research suggests that as much as 50 percent of the physiological changes attributed to the aging process actually result from inactive lifestyles. Therefore, do not consider chronological age the primary factor when you assess the needs of adults. Instead, classify both young and old adults in terms of physiological function. The participants' age might only remind you that disease or dysfunction might be present; do not use it to categorize a segment of the population.

Physiological Changes

Most people reach physical maturity by age 18, when many physiological functions (strength, physical ability, motor control, reaction time) are near peak levels. By age 30, physical capacity has begun a slow decline that continues through the rest of life.

During most of adulthood, the percentage of body fat gradually increases and lean body mass decreases. This is especially true for inactive adults. With advanced age (over 70), this trend is likely to reverse. Although adults in middle years may be quite buoyant due to their percentage of body fat, people of advanced age tend to be thinner and less buoyant.

Overall strength drops little throughout life, especially in muscle groups used in daily activities. This means that most people have enough strength for aquatic skills. However, inactive individuals of advanced age may have much less strength, especially in the legs.

One of the greatest changes from the aging process is the gradual loss of flexibility, especially in joints and muscle groups not used regularly. The saying, "move it or lose it," has great meaning as we grow older. Stretching and range of motion are important for acquiring skills as we age.

Most adults are affected to some extent by gradual degeneration in the joints. Healthy, active adults at any age may also have an injury, from sports or some other cause, that affects their mobility. Joint pain and swelling may limit the person's ability to swim certain strokes. For example, the breaststroke kick might not be possible or desirable for a person who has undergone knee surgery.

The older the person, the more likely it is that other changes will influence the person's ability to learn new tasks. The ability to process information changes with age. The speed of the nerve impulse as it conducts a message from one point to another is slowed. This affects the speed of problem solving and may lead to slower response or reaction times. As a result, the person may need more time to plan and start actions. Past learning also affects the way adults process information. One's learning history may inhibit learning or make a task easier to learn. Sometimes adults take longer to start an action because they are trying to take advantage of past learning.

With age comes the increased chance that hearing, vision, and thermoregulatory responses (how the body regulates its temperature) may be impaired. (Suggestions for teaching people with a hearing or vision impairment are in Chapter 22.) Older adults are particularly susceptible to heat illnesses, requiring attention to safe exercise programming for later adulthood. Adults may chill easily in average water temperatures and be unable to generate enough heat to stay comfortable through a lesson.

As they age, adults become more vulnerable to heart disease, osteoarthritis, diabetes, hypertension, and osteoporosis. These diseases may seem to speed up the aging process, limit functional ability, and reduce the ability to learn motor skills. It is often hard to draw a line between the normal aging process and a chronic degenerative disease. You should not keep adults from a program just because of their age. Age should only remind you to make a few adjustments if needed in your teaching approach.

Psychological Changes

Healthy, active adults have psychological needs just as younger people do. They need security, recognition, a sense of accomplishment, and a feeling of belonging. However, self-confidence and perceptions of self may change through the aging process. Some adults want to succeed in new tasks but lack the self-confidence to do so. They learn best in a nonthreatening learning environment that promotes trust and a sense of accomplishment and self-worth.

Reasons for Participating in Aquatics

A very important benefit you have when working with adults is that nearly all adults take swimming lessons because they want to. Most often they want to learn or improve aquatic skills. Perhaps they did not have the time or opportunity to learn to swim when they were younger. Perhaps they want to join their children in aquatic activities. Many adults pursue new activities to help stay functionally independent as long as possible, and regular physical activity has quite an impact on lifestyle. Some adults may have strong skills but desire certification. Others may want to improve their skills to compete.

Adults frequently learn to swim to improve their health and fitness. Those with an injury may need swimming for rehabilitation. Their doctors or physical therapists may have advised them to take up aquatics as therapy. Older adults often take an aquatics course for reasons of health and rehabilitation. In your planning, consider fitness swimming alternatives such as lap swimming and the Swim and Stay Fit program. (For more information on adding fitness components to your courses, see Chapter 24.)

Another reason adults give for joining an aquatics program is enjoyment and social contact. Swimming attracts adults because it feels good and is good for the body while helping one meet new friends and have social contact during the day. Thus, you should include recreational aquatic games in your program. (For more information on water activities, see Chapter 25.)

Finally, don't overlook the importance of safety. Adults who own a home pool or who plan aquatic activity with family, especially children, want safety information to help them prevent aquatic emergencies and to respond to them if necessary. Make information on water safety an integral part of each program. You may want to arrange a showing of the American Red Cross video, *Home Pool Safety: It Only Takes a Minute.*

For many reasons, adults are determined to learn. Understanding their motivation helps you establish objectives and plan lessons that address their needs.

TECHNIQUES TO ENHANCE LEARNING

Planning With the Participants

The most significant benefit to working with adults is that you can enlist then in the planning process. All adults like to pursue their own interests and make their own decisions about what they want to learn or accomplish. By discussing their motivations, interests, and needs with the participants, you can make lesson time as productive as possible. You *plan with* them, rather than *plan for* them. By involving them in this way, you also help ensure their motivation to follow the mutually designed plan of learning.

The critical step in planning is to consider the participants' past experiences, current goals, and physical characteristics. Ask yourself the following questions:

■ **"What do they know?"**
(Past experience)
Participants with experience may want just a few "coaching" tips to help them improve. In this case it is easy to analyze their existing skills and work toward more efficient movement. Many participants have no past experience in the water. They may have the same fears and anxieties as youngsters who are learning to swim. In this case you may want to reorder your usual progressions to teach strokes that let the person keep the face out of the water, such as the sidestroke, elementary backstroke, or a modified breaststroke. Then slowly work on submersion and rhythmic breathing.

■ **"What do they want to know?"**
(Current goals)
When working with adults you should not have rigid rules. Consider each participant's needs and desires. Stroke choices should reflect their wants. If an apprehensive adult wants to learn only the front crawl, plan an approach that sets up small successes along the way. Encourage participants to try all strokes to learn which they do best, but remember that personal desires are often very strong motivation to learn. Never underestimate the ability of older adults to learn what they have set out to learn. You need to be flexible in your lesson plans regardless of the course you are teaching. Plan to introduce all the required skills but customize to meet the goals of your participants as well as the objectives of the course.

■ **"What are they able to do?"**
(Physical capability)
Since physical abilities change with age, physical characteristics and abilities may determine how successful participants are in learning certain strokes. One objective of your planning should be to help the participants adapt strokes to their physical capabilities.

Individualizing the Approach

The ideal teaching situation for any activity is to be able to work with a group that is completely alike in interests, previous experience, physical characteristics, goals, and motivation to learn. Unfortunately, limitations in programming, facility, or staff may not permit scheduling separate classes for such homogeneous groups.

As mentioned earlier, the most important characteristic of adults is how much they differ from each other. These differences may require an individualized plan. Thus, within a single group, you may have as many lesson plans as you have participants. Although this may seem a complicated task, certain learning characteristics of adults actually help this style of teaching.

- Adults want a lot of freedom. They like to practice on their own with minimal interruption. A combination of a carefully chosen, logical teaching progression and a less formal approach in organizing and conducting the class can make learning as self-directed as possible.
- Adults, regardless of age, can learn new motor skills. However, the pace at which they learn may be faster or slower than that of young people. Some adults can use their past learning strategies to learn skills quickly. Others need more trials for mastery and may improve more slowly than younger learners. Allow participants the freedom to try new skills their own way first.
- Most adults in an aquatics class are eager to be there. However, some may have serious doubts about their abilities to succeed at new tasks. Some may also suffer from perfectionism and be impatient to learn. They have a tendency to worry more about the accuracy of a skill than the speed with which it is performed. Whereas a young participant may work quickly through a drill just to get it finished, an adult may take time to do each part correctly. Be sure to allow adequate practice time and give positive corrective feedback.

Adapting Teaching Methods

The Instructor Candidate Training course introduced you to several teaching methods for motor skills. The following guidelines may help you adapt these methods for adult participants.
- The *whole approach* works well with skills that are simple and for which the individual can transfer past experience, i.e., relate existing skills to the new learning. Even though adults may need to practice skills in parts, they are interested in the final "product," not the parts. They often want to try the "whole" on their own first.
- The *part-whole approach* may be better when you want to focus the attention of the adult on a key concept rather than the whole skill. It

gives an opportunity for many small successes. Since in the early stages of learning one often forgets some information, one might otherwise forget the parts before combining them to make the whole.
- The *progressive-part approach* limits some of the forgetting that can occur in the part-whole approach. This approach provides more trials from the start to finish of the skill and may minimize the frustration of trying to master a more complex stroke or activity.

Other teaching methods are reviewed in the *Instructor Candidate Training Participant's Manual* and in Chapter 6–8. Remember always to give positive corrective feedback to your adult participants. A person can improve a skill only with feedback. Adults need to know how they are doing and are just as affected by feedback in the learning process as younger participants.

ADJUSTING THE LEARNING ENVIRONMENT

Physical Elements

Several aspects of the learning environment may affect adults more than children or teens. Adults are more sensitive to the whole physical environment. Children might not notice a dirty locker room or swimming area because of their excitement to get into the water. An adult, on the other hand, may react to dirty locker rooms, cold showers, or a cluttered swimming area as reasons to stop coming to lessons. Locker rooms and swimming areas should be checked regularly for cleanliness and safe conditions. Adults may also have concerns about getting a foot infection from the locker rooms or deck. Refer any potential problems to the facility management.

Another issue is safe access to the water. Adults with a physical disability cannot participate in a program if they cannot safely enter and exit the buildings or the swimming area. You should know how to use any access equipment in your facility.

Water temperature may also be a key issue for your program. Most adults are relatively comfortable learning in water of 82–85 degrees F (28–29 degrees C) if they are kept on task. This temperature is only slightly above that enjoyed by serious lap swimmers. Older adults may have difficulty regulating their body temperature and may become easily chilled. If the water temperature cannot be adjusted to accommodate them, you may have to keep the lessons to 20–30 minutes to reduce discomfort. You may want to let participants wear additional clothes for warmth as long as it does not interfere with learning the skills. For instance, a sweatshirt is too heavy in the water but a tee-shirt might help. A swim cap may also minimize heat loss. You should be alert to the early signs of hypothermia and take precautions to prevent it.

Most adults who can stay focused on a task will not be bothered by minor distractions. Older adults may be more easily distracted by background noise than younger participants. Be alert to any distractions in the setting. Follow these guidelines:

- Minimize interfering background noise. This may be especially critical if any participant has a hearing impairment.
- Move the class to a quiet area or offer the course at a time when there is less activity in the facility.
- Minimize interruptions in the learning process by being prepared and having equipment ready before the lesson starts.

Psychological Elements

Everyone needs a relaxing, positive environment for learning. The following are ways to prepare the psychological environment to give the best opportunities for success:

- Start practice sessions with a good review that includes some previously learned skills, especially those related to skills in that day's lesson.
- In each lesson, include skills that participants can do reasonably well.

- Remind participants that few people do everything right the first time.
- Take breaks from hard and/or complex skills before participants become frustrated.
- Create an atmosphere where participants are not ridiculed and are not afraid to make mistakes.
- Provide privacy as much as possible. Even curious onlookers can seem threatening.
- Be enthusiastic and reward each step toward success. Let participants feel your desire to be there or you will lose the interest and respect of the group.
- Develop trust by always being prepared, organizing the course effectively so participants do not feel that their time is being wasted, and preparing participants for each new experience.
- Provide a social atmosphere.
- Give participants more time to respond to the information you give them. You can help them be more successful by slowing down the presentation of skills and giving them enough freedom to work at their own pace.
- Do not over-explain a skill. Most adults can understand the principles involved in aquatic skills. You should know and be able to explain the various physical laws and how they apply to swimming. Use vocabulary appropriate for the age and capabilities of the adults in the courses.

Working With Apprehensive Beginners

A certain amount of fear and anxiety is normal among people who cannot swim or who swim poorly. However, intense fear can keep someone from learning a new skill or make someone reluctant to try it.

Adults in your courses may have avoided learning to swim for some reason. The most common fears are fear of losing control, fear of drowning, anxiety about not being able to breathe, and fear of not being able to get back to safety. Adult beginners may fear deep water or they may fear being forced to do something that they perceive to be personally threatening. They may simply be afraid of failure. Fear may be strongest when a person has seen or experienced a near-drowning. Apprehensive beginners often exhibit the avoidance behaviors listed on page 30.

Issues of Scheduling

A program orientation helps prepare participants for the program. This is critical for an apprehensive beginner. Orientation reduces the frustration of the first lesson because adults know where to go, how to find the swimming area, what the first-day procedures are, and whom to ask for help. Even if they are rushing from a job, they may arrive for the lesson more relaxed because they are familiar with the setup of the program.

Schedule the orientation at a separate time and publicize it well. Make the orientation meaningful. If possible, invite former or current participants to share success stories. The orientation may seem like a waste of time unless you treat it as an important part of the program.

A typical lesson lasts about 45 minutes, but this depends on the needs and comfort of the participants. Older adults need warmer water; their lessons may have to be shortened if the water is too cold for them. For some adults, there never seems to be enough practice time. You might schedule a course before a recreational swim time so that the participants can stay as long as they want after the lessons.

Another scheduling issue is the number of lessons per course. It may be useful to give an "ongoing" program and let adults participate until their needs are satisfied. If a course offers a set number of lessons, individual planning and goal setting in the first lesson should help you determine whether certification is the goal of any participants. Determine how much material is to be covered in each lesson to meet group and individual needs. You may find yourself with many goals within the same course. Capitalize on the learning characteristics of adults to help you plan your lessons.

You may find that participants respond better when you give more individual practice time and less guided group practice. When incorporating more individualized practice in your lesson plan, follow these guidelines:
- Plan for frequent rest periods throughout the lesson.
- Watch for signs of fatigue—
    - Making more rather than fewer mistakes in a new skill.
    - Having difficulty with a skill that had been mastered. (This means that it is time to rest or change to a different skill.)
- People often practice only those skills at which they are successful. When you plan for individualized practice, include skills that need additional work for mastery.
- For each lesson, prepare more material than you think you will need. This helps you to accommodate differences in the speed of learning.

SUMMARY

The primary objective of aquatics courses for adults is to give safe, enjoyable aquatic activities that enhance the participants' quality of life. Fun, fitness, and social interaction should be included in each course. Courses should be designed around desires of the participants and address a wide variety of interests. They should provide maximum success in a relaxed social setting.

24 customizing by integrating fitness components

As an American Red Cross Water Safety Instructor, you can help your students become aware of the role that fitness swimming and aquatic exercise can play in a healthy lifestyle. With a little planning, you can easily introduce fitness concepts in your courses and help your students use swimming and/or aquatic exercise for fitness.

As you plan your lessons, review the concepts in Chapters 10 and 11 of *Swimming and Diving* to remind yourself of basics such as the importance of the warm-up, stretching, and safety considerations. Also consider using Appendix C of *Swimming and Diving* as a resource for helping students calculate the target heart rate range. You will probably want to teach your students the following fitness concepts and techniques.

- The F.I.T. principle
- How to adjust the workout to help improve cardiovascular fitness
- How to figure the target heart rate range
- How to monitor the intensity of the workout by checking the pulse
- How to do a fitness workout when learning to swim
- How to use a pace clock to mark time and monitor pulse

With careful planning, you can include fitness in your courses at almost every level of the American Red Cross Learn to Swim program. As students become self-confident in swimming and aquatic skills, fitness can become a part of each lesson. Remember that it takes *at least* 15 minutes of continuous rhythmic movement with the heart rate in the target range for the exercise to provide cardiovascular improvement. Your students might not be able to reach and maintain this minimum intensity at the beginning of the course, but you can help them move gradually toward fitness as you teach them to swim. For instance, you may have students whose goal is to learn to swim to become more fit. In the beginning, they need only be able to stand with their faces out of the water. Before they learn the first complete swim stroke, they can be working toward fitness by doing aerobic exercise in the water.

PROVIDING FITNESS OPPORTUNITIES WITHIN THE LESSON

You can provide a fitness workout with the same stroke and learning drills you use in your lesson plan. You already have the tools. You need only plan correctly, and you can work fitness into any or all of your courses. The following sections show how to plan for fitness within your lesson.

At the Beginning of the Lesson

After an opening segment, you may introduce an aerobic set. If your students cannot move continuously for 15 minutes, you can use the progression on pages 237–238 of *Swimming and Diving* to start them toward fitness. Then follow the aerobic set with the new skill sequence and the practice session.

You may also use the aerobic set to start your lesson. Start slowly with easy swims or movements and then gradually increase the intensity. A good example for Level V and above in the Learn to Swim program is to start with elementary backstroke (or back float with flutter kick and finning), switch to sidestroke, and finish with front crawl or stroke drills.

Follow the opening with a stretch and then continue the lesson or continue with a new skill sequence and finish the practice session with a stretch. Be sure to have students check their heart rates during and after the exercises.

To conduct an aerobic set at the beginning of a lesson, you may—
- Use any combination of walking, jogging, running, jumping, skipping or hopping to get from place to place in the water.

- Teach correct arm stroking patterns or other activities chosen from Chapter 10 or Appendix B of *Swimming and Diving*.
- Review lap swimming etiquette and then let students swim continuously in a circle using any combination of strokes. If they need to rest, limit them to 30-second rest breaks. Encourage them to decrease their rest breaks in each successive lesson.

The benefit of having the aerobic set at the beginning of the lesson is that students warm up and thus can sit longer while you explain and demonstrate a new skill. Students get a rest during your explanation and demonstration so they can catch their breath for the practice session. One disadvantage is that they may be too tired to practice the new skill well. After an aerobic set, do not teach something like the butterfly, which requires much energy for the practice session. Sidestroke or dive entries are better choices. Be sure to monitor your class so they do not overexert themselves. You may want to give students a longer rest period before or during the new skill practice.

In the Middle of the Lesson

Use the review or new skill practice session as a fitness opportunity. Plan to teach several drills for variety and have the students swim stroke drills for a set time.
- Let students do a continuous circle swim. Change stroke drills at the end of each lap. You can let students rest as long as 30 seconds. Use this time for individual feedback.
- Use a wave drill. Organize students into two or three groups. Group 1 starts the drill. Group 2 follows after 5 seconds. Group 3 follows Group 2 by 5 seconds. After all groups reach the wall or other designated point, Group 1 starts the next lap. The rest time per student is the time it takes for the other groups to complete the lap. As students learn the drills they complete them faster; this decreases the rest break.

- If you have a rectangular area to work with, have students swim the perimeter. This is a line drill. Students swim the perimeter of the area in single file. The first student swims a stroke drill from one corner to the next. The next student takes off 5 seconds later. You can have students start a different stroke drill at each corner. They can alternate swimming or jogging, or they can alternate stroke drills with a resting stroke as they work from corner to corner. Encourage each student to work at his or her own level and rest or change the drill as needed.

One advantage of incorporating a fitness segment into the middle of the lesson is that you can use the rest breaks to give individual feedback. If students are practicing a new skill, you may give them a break by alternating the drill with other activities. You can easily adjust the intensity of the skill practice to meet the needs of your students. If you are using the fitness activity as a review session, you may spend some time working with students who are having trouble with a skill.

The drills you select may be too easy for some and too hard for others. Monitor your class. Watch to see if students are too red in the face or breathing too hard. Then adjust the intensity of the practice session by including rest breaks for some students and continuous swimming or additional stroke drills for others.

At the End of the Lesson

This may be the most convenient time to add an aerobic set to your lesson. The students practiced while they were fresh and they can use the rest of the lesson to work on things that they enjoy.

Choose any combination of exercises from Chapter 10 or Appendix B of *Swimming and Diving*. For variety, use activities in Chapter 11 of *Swimming and Diving*. With highly motivated students you can turn the last minutes of the lesson over to them and let them choose an activity with your guidance.

Most younger students need more direction. Plan the fitness segment for them because they might not use their free time well. Include activities that most of the group has mastered so that they can enjoy the exercise. Do not use stroke drills at this time. Often they take more energy than stroking, and students may be too fatigued to do them correctly.

Putting the fitness segment at the end of the lesson gives you time to work with students who are having difficulty with a given skill while the rest of your class is doing a constructive aerobic activity. This time is also good for students who need to practice skills they enjoy but did not have a chance to practice during the lesson.

MAKING SUGGESTIONS FOR BETWEEN LESSONS

Emphasize the importance of a lifetime fitness program. Many adults choose swimming as their fitness activity. Help your students learn how to develop an aquatic fitness program of their own. Include optional activities at any level when time allows. Levels V to VII of the Learn to Swim program are ideal for teaching fitness principles. However, since lesson time is limited, students may be eager to swim between lessons and to continue swimming when lessons end.

Refer your students to Chapters 10 and 11 of *Swimming and Diving* for a discussion of fitness and training. Chapter 12 of *Swimming and Diving* gives information on various competitive programs, synchronized swimming, water polo, and triathlons.

The American Red Cross Swim and Stay Fit program may be a good way for students to maintain and improve their fitness. The *Swim and Stay Fit Program: Information for Chapters and the Monitor,* available through your local Red Cross unit, explains how to implement and report the program. The *Swim and Stay Fit Wall Charts* can be used to track an individual's progress. The *Swim and Stay Fit Individual Record* allows each student to track each quarter mile swum. At the completion of each 10-mile increment, students are eligible to receive a certificate to attest to their accomplishment.

The goal of the program is to complete 50 miles. A person can repeat the program and be awarded for total miles swum. You can proctor and report this at any facility, since it does not require a Water Safety Instructor as monitor.

SUMMARY

Adding a fitness element into your courses requires flexibility. For your participants to improve, follow the F.I.T. (frequency, intensity, and time) principle described in Chapter 10 of *Swimming and Diving.* Appendix B of *Swimming and Diving* has excellent warm-up, aerobic set, and cool-down activities for the upper, middle, and lower body. You can use these activities at the beginning, middle, or end of a lesson, depending on the energy level, size, and goals of your students.

When you plan your courses, decide how you want to work a fitness segment into your lessons. This may vary from course to course but it does not require extra time in the water. Your attitude and instruction may encourage your students to spend more time exercising on their own. Fitness activity is not just a program that can be used for a lifetime; it may lengthen that lifetime as well.

25 customizing with games and water activities

Everyone needs to play. This seems obvious when we watch young children. Their play is their life, the way they grow and learn. Play and joyful experiences are essential for a child to develop a positive attitude toward self and the world. However, this principle might not seem as important for adolescents and adults. Our days are so filled with work, study, social contacts, and home and family obligations that we often do not take the time for recreation. Most of us have trouble fitting in a daily run, a fitness class, or a swimming lesson. Even when we do find the time, taking care of our bodies and staying in shape can be a source of even more stress and work. We set goals for ourselves, monitor our progress, and work hard to attain our fitness goals. We feel good when we're finished, but we can't wait to hit the shower. We succeed or fail, depending on how hard we push ourselves.

We're all aware that water is an excellent place to play. What infant doesn't reach for and swat the bar of soap or the washcloth around in the bathtub if nothing else is at hand? What preschooler doesn't bring a bag full of floating, pouring, scooping, and sinking objects to the beach? What school-aged child hasn't adapted playground games in the water, with or without a ball?

This chapter discusses ways to make the learning process fun for participants of all ages. It describes suggested games, relays, and activities in detail. You are encouraged to adapt favorite games and activities for water fun throughout your program. Many of the games and activities were designed for use in a pool. Most can be easily modified for use in other aquatic settings.

Be sure to choose games and activities with care, so you ensure the safety of the participants. Most activities can be made safe and suitable for everyone by adding rules or changing the game as needed, but you should plan ahead. If you need any special equipment, keep it in a secure place until it is used. Choose games appropriate for the swimming ability and social level of the participants. This helps make the games functional and fun. Even people who cannot swim can enjoy many simple water games and activities.

When you choose a game or activity, be clear about the purpose you want it to serve. Is the goal primarily instructional, to practice and help master skills already learned? Is it mostly recreational, to help cool down and ease stress and tension built up after a lesson or workout? Is it social, to provide an atmosphere where participants can converse with one another in an aquatic setting? Whatever your goal, you can find a fun way to achieve it.

A Word About Children

Because much of a child's early learning results from play, the knowledgeable instructor takes advantage of images, games, and rhymes to enhance the child's natural ability to imagine and pretend while learning skills. You may be familiar with games from your own childhood such as "Simon Says," "Mother May I," "Red Light/ Green Light," and "Follow the Leader," and songs such as "Ring Around the Rosie," "Itsy Bitsy Spider," and "Pop Goes the Weasel." It's not too hard to imagine using these games and activities in the water with children to ease their fears and help them get used to moving in the water. Rely on your own experience, use your imagination, and watch the children themselves for more ideas. Check out one of the many children's song and/or game books from the library for more creative ideas. Try to make the activity fun for everyone.

WATER ADJUSTMENT

In addition to being fun, water games and activities help promote water adjustment. Children will do many things in the context of a game that they will not try in a "lesson." As they focus on the activity, you can divert their attention from any fear or anxiety they may have about getting into the water.

Water adjustment activities for young children may be as simple as playing with favorite toys in a restricted area or a wading pool. Children seem to be able to play with all sorts of objects: floatable toys (boats, animals, etc.), sponges, washcloths, ping pong balls, weighted plastic flowers, hula hoops. *Guided* play with these toys helps the child become adjusted to the water. A child can fill a sponge, for instance, and squeeze it out on his or her parent's head. You might then encourage the child to try it on his or her own head, as a natural progression toward going under water. You might have the children blow ping pong balls or plastic boats across the water, first with their *faces close* to the water, then with their *chins in* the water. Then have a relay race with the children blowing the ping pong balls or boats across the water.

You should also ask parents to help children prepare at home for their first swimming lesson or water experience. Parents can help their children adjust to the water before they even get to the aquatic facility. For example, parents and children can take turns singing "It's Raining, It's Pouring" and dribbling water over each other with plastic cups or sponges. The children's book, *Waddles Presents AQUACKtic Safety,* features Waddles the Duck and his friends at their first lesson and is available for purchase from your local Red Cross unit. Parents and children can read together about what to expect in swimming lessons.

Children aren't the only ones who need to adjust to the water. Many adults cannot swim and are afraid to submerge. Aquatic exercises such as walking or running in the water, jumping jacks, or practicing arm strokes without putting the face in the water may make adjustment easier. These activities, as well as the exercises in Appendix B of *Swimming and Diving*, can help participants prepare for exercise in the water. The more they focus on the task at hand, the less they attend to their fears. Chapter 24 discusses ways to customize your courses with additional fitness activities.

The following are sample activities you can use to help the timid child or adult adjust to the water. Consider the maturity, age, and experience of your participants when choosing an activity. You can modify some children's games so adults can enjoy them as well.

Motorboat, Motorboat

Equipment: None

Number of players: Any number

Strategy: Players hold hands and walk clockwise in shallow water singing, "Motorboat, motorboat, go so slow; motorboat, motorboat, go so fast; motorboat, motorboat blow bubbles as fast as you go." Then they submerge and blow bubbles.

Electricity

Equipment: None

Number of players: Any number

Strategy: Players hold hands and stand in a circle in shallow water. The instructor squeezes the hand of his or her neighbor, who submerges and then passes the squeeze to the next player's hand, and so on, back to the instructor. After everyone is submerged, the instructor starts the "electric current" again, and when a player's hand is squeezed this time he or she stands back up. You can substitute other skills to suit all levels, such as squatting on one foot or submerging deeper.

> *Safety note:*
> Play this game in small groups to control the amount of time a player is under water.

Tommy Over the Water

Equipment: None

Number of players: At least four

Strategy: Players hold hands and stand in a circle. One player is "Tommy," who stands in the center of the circle. The other players walk around the circle, chanting:

> Tommy over the water,
>
> Tommy over the sea;
>
> Tommy caught the blackbird,
>
> But he can't catch me!

As they say "me," the players squat quickly, or submerge if they have mastered that skill. Tommy tries to tag a player before the player gets into a squatting position. If Tommy is successful, the player tagged changes places with him or her and the game is repeated with the new "Tommy" in the center.

Monkeys in Trees

Equipment: None

Number of players: Any number, in groups of three

Strategy: Two participants in each group form a "tree" by joining hands while the third participant (monkey) stands encircled by the arms of the tree. On the signal, the partners briefly release hands and the monkeys leave trees. All the monkeys then move around in the water along with one or two monkeys who have no home trees. On the next signal, each monkey must try to get inside any tree. Those who do not must move through the water until the next signal, when the process is repeated. Rotate monkeys and trees periodically so everyone gets to be in each role. The way monkeys travel can be varied to match the skill levels of participants.

Cake Pan Race

Equipment: One pan per person

Number of players: Any number

Strategy: Float a cake pan on the water. On the signal, players walk across the shallow end, pushing the pan with the chin or nose. The first one to reach the other side of the pool wins. If the pan sinks the player must start over.

Cork Game Race

Equipment: Several dozen corks, ping pong balls, or other small floating objects

Number of players: Any number, in two or more teams

Strategy: The teams line up on opposite sides of the swimming area, and dozens of corks, ping pong balls, etc., are thrown into the water. On the signal, the teams try to get as many of the objects as possible. The team collecting the greatest number in a given time wins.

GAMES AND CONTESTS

> *Safety note:*
> Be sure participants are in water of appropriate depth for their ability.

Games and Contests for Levels I–IV

Anagrams

Equipment: Two sets of nonfloating alphabet letters with extra vowels

Number of players: Any number, in two teams

Strategy: Put letters in shallow water. On the signal, some players from each team wade in to recover the letters. Players take them to the side of the swimming area while other teammates compose words of more than 3 letters. When time is up, the team with the most words wins. For more advanced swimmers, players can surface dive into deep water for the letters.

Coin Wish-Pond

Equipment: Pennies

Number of players: Any Number, in two teams

Strategy: Both teams stand to the side of the swimming area. On the signal, players wade in or surface dive for pennies on the bottom and return them to a set place at the water's edge. The team finding the most pennies wins.

Variation for better swimmers or larger teams: One player is designated to dive. When he or she returns to the surface, the remaining teammates form a line from the diver to the deck and hand the pennies down the line to reach the side. No player may swim with the penny. Be careful that participants do not become fatigued.

Duck In, Duck Out

Equipment: Lane lines and a whistle or music

Number of players: Any number

Strategy: Make a loop of lane lines or string rope around posts. Adjust the size of the loop to accommodate the number of players. Start all players outside the loop. On a double blast of the whistle (or start of the music), players start swimming around the outside of the loop. When the whistle blows once (or the music stops), each player ducks under the loop without touching it and moves to the inside of the circle. The last one into the circle drops out. The whistle blows twice again (or the music starts) and the players start swimming around the inside of the circle. (Different strokes may be used as directed by the instructor.) When the whistle blows once (or the music stops), each player ducks under the loop, going outside, without touching it. The last one outside the circle drops out. The last player left is the winner. You can adapt this game to any ability level.

Variations: The lane line can be placed in shallow water to help accustom beginners to putting their faces in the water and help them learn to swim under water. The lane line can be used to practice different strokes and to build endurance. It can be placed in shoulder-deep water for participants of moderate ability and in deep water to provide endurance practice for more advanced participants. Played with music, the game can be used at Levels V–VII to incorporate rhythm and synchronized swimming strokes or sculls.

Floating News Report

Equipment: One sheet of newspaper for each player

Number of players: Any number

Strategy: Players line up at the starting line with their backs to the finish line. Each takes a newspaper. On the signal, each player glides on the back, kicks, and reads aloud from the newspaper. The player must try to keep the newspaper above water at all times. The player crossing the finish line first wins. A player who drops the newspaper or stops reading aloud has to drop out. You can adapt this game into a relay race for more advanced swimmers, who may use various kicks.

Stroke Fun

Equipment: None

Number of players: Any number

Strategy: All players start at the same starting point. The finish line is about 25 yards away. The group starts by treading water. One whistle blast means "swim the elementary backstroke," two short blasts mean "change direction," and three short blasts, "tread water." This game is lots of fun, especially if the players end where they started instead of at the finish line. This can also be adapted for more advanced swimmers by substituting more difficult skills for treading water and the elementary backstroke.

Whistle Mixer

Equipment: Whistle

Number of players: Any number

Strategy: Players swim according to the instructor's directions (crawl, floating, bobbing, etc.). When the whistle blows, players stop swimming and form a circle. The number of whistle blasts indicates the number of people in each circle. Extra players, or players in circles of an incorrect number, are eliminated. The instructor can even blow the whistle just one time. The variations of single circles (if players think fast enough to form them) are creative and amusing. This game can be used as a practice for skills previously learned or to begin a lesson. It is like musical chairs.

Variation: If the game is played in deep water, scatter kickboards in the area. Players must form circles by towing the kickboards.

Games and Contests for Level IV

Aquatic Steeple Chase

Equipment: Hula hoop, kickboards

Number of players: Any number

Strategy: A player starts at Station 1 and swims a designated stroke to Station 2. At Station 2, the player performs a skill such as treading water and does sidestroke to Station 3. At Station 3, player does a surface dive through a hula hoop, then proceeds to Station 4 doing the front crawl. At Station 4, player receives a kickboard and does a designated kick to Station 5. From Station 5, the player does a different stroke to finish at Station 6. The next player starts at Station 1 when the previous player reaches Station 3. Vary the skills and number of stations depending on space and time.

Water Poison

Equipment: Floating object, such as kickboard

Number of players: Six or more

Strategy: Players join hands around a floating object. On the signal, all try to pull the others into the "poison" and avoid touching it themselves. Any player who touches it is eliminated. If two players break their grip, both are eliminated. The last player is the winner.

Pigeon Cross-Over

Equipment: None

Number of players: 10 or more

Strategy: Players are split into two groups at opposite sides of the swimming area. On the signal, "Pigeon," all players swim across the pool and get out as fast as possible. The last players getting out on each side are eliminated. The last player remaining is the winner. This game develops participants' stamina, endurance, and speed.

Games and Contests for Levels V–VII

Find Your Man

Equipment: None

Number of players: Any number, in two teams

Strategy: Teams line up on opposite sides of the swimming area. On the signal, members of Team A do feet-first surface dives and swim along the bottom toward the other side. Members of Team B swim the breaststroke, dive and try to find members of Team A. If a Team B player finds a Team A player, he or she must try to tag that player and they return to the surface together. This discovered player from Team A must help the Team B player search for other members of Team A until they have been found or have reached the other side. Then Team B has a turn under water. Each team member who reaches the other side scores 1 point. The first team to get 20 points wins.

Snake

Equipment: None, full length of the swimming area works best

Number of players: Any number

Strategy: All players line up according to ability, with the slowest in front and the fastest at the rear. Players start every 10 seconds. All players swim the same stroke up one lane and back another for a designated number of lengths. If a player catches up to the player in front of him or

177

her, the front player is tagged and must stop and tread water until everyone is finished. Players reaching the goal form another line and repeat the game. Those who make it to the end without being tagged are the winners.

Variations:
1. Use various strokes.
2. Slower players swim the front crawl while faster ones swim the breaststroke.
3. Change the time delay between players.

Inner Tube Water Polo

Equipment: Water Polo or similar ball, one inner tube per player, something to serve as a goal

Number of players: 10 or more, in two teams

Strategy: Players wear swim caps color-keyed for their team. All players sit in inner tubes. They may not play the ball unless they are in their tubes. Both teams line up in front of the goal they defend. When the whistle blows, the ball is thrown into the water. There are no time outs. The object is to pass the ball to your teammates and to score goals. You can use floating goals or mark gutter areas. Make rules to suit the ability of the players and ensure safe play.

Fouls may include pushing off the wall, punching the ball, and rough play. The penalty for a foul is to give the other team the ball. The team scoring the most goals wins.

TAG GAMES

Any form of tag is popular and fun as long as not too many players are involved. Larger classes should be divided by skill level into groups of about six. Use your imagination and modify games such Freeze Tag, Partner Tag, and Marco Polo by substituting simple rules like, "floating on your back is the base" to add skill practice and variety to the fun. Tag games and ball tag games can be adapted to any level of ability simply by moving the game to deep or shallow water. Always remember safety precautions. Here are a few examples to get you started:

Sharks and Minnows

Equipment: None

Number of players: Any number, in two teams

Strategy: Teams are called "sharks" and "minnows." In shallow water, the teams line up opposite each other, across the width of the playing area, on a line set by the instructor. Players stand in a stride position facing the instructor with one foot on the line and ready to run toward either goal line, which is their "safety zone." The instructor stands at one end of the two lines and calls either "sharks" or "minnows." If the instructor calls "sharks," they run and chase the minnows. If a shark tags a minnow before the minnow reaches the safety zone, the minnow becomes a shark. The sharks are chased by the minnows when the instructor calls out "minnows." After each chase, the players resume their starting positions on the line again unless they were tagged onto the opposite team. The team with more players at the end of the game wins. The teams must be given equal opportunities to chase.

Tag for Couples

Equipment: None

Number of players: Any even number of eight or more

Strategy: All participants are paired and must hold hands throughout the game. The couple designated as "it" tries to tag another couple without releasing each other's hand. If a couple breaks hands to keep from being "it" they are caught immediately and become "it".

Drop the Puck

Equipment: A rubber puck or other weighted object

Number of players: Any number

Strategy: Players stand in a circle in shallow water. The player who is "it" swims around them outside the circle with a puck in hand. The puck is dropped behind one of the players who must recover it and chase "it" around the circle, trying to catch him or her before he or she takes the player's place. If the player chasing "it" fails to catch him or her, that player becomes "it".

Variation: The game can be played by participants at all levels by changing the water depth and putting in a specific stroke that "it" or the player giving chase must do.

Cat, Bird, Dog Triangle

Equipment: None

Number of players: 15 to 18

Strategy: The instructor assigns one player as the cat, one as the bird, and one as the dog. The remaining players form three circles of equal numbers, arranged as a triangle in the water. The cat, bird, and dog each has his or her own circle, which is a safety zone. The game is played like tag; the cat tries to catch the bird and the dog tries to catch the cat. If the cat, bird, or dog gets tired, he or she can tag someone in his or her circle. If the bird or cat gets caught, the roles are reversed (the bird becomes the cat and the cat becomes the bird or the dog becomes the cat and the cat becomes the dog). As the game goes on, it gets confusing, which adds to the fun.

Dog Kennel

Equipment: None

Number of players: 12 to 18

Strategy: Players line up on the edge of the swimming area and are given the name of a dog (spaniel, lab, beagle, etc.). One player is the kennel owner and another is the customer. Players keep their dog names secret at the beginning. The customer comes to the kennel. "What kind of dog do you want?" asks the owner. "I'm looking for a poodle" may be the reply. Immediately the poodle swims away toward a safety zone with the customer in pursuit. If caught before reaching the safety zone, the "dog" becomes the customer and the former customer takes his or her place in the kennel and is given a different dog name.

Marco Polo

Equipment: Blindfold

Number of players: Any number

Strategy: "It" wears a blindfold or keeps eyes closed. Players scatter in a designated area of water. "It" must tag one of the players by using the senses of hearing and touch. "It" locates the other players by calling out "Marco" and all others must immediately answer "Polo." When a player is tagged, he or she becomes "it."

Variations:
1. Play the game in pairs or threesomes.
2. Use underwater swimming with eyes open to locate players rather than blindfold
3. With small classes, reverse process by having players shut eyes and have "Marco" with vision.

Whirlpool Stunt

Equipment: Whistle

Number of players: Large number

Strategy: Players stand in a circle. On the signal, players start running around a designated area in shallow water, creating a "whirlpool." On a whistle blast, they start doing the front crawl in the same pattern. On the second blast, they float supine in place.

BALL GAMES

Ball games are easily adapted to the water and can lead to more complex activities like water polo. Tag is good preparation for more complex ball games. Be especially careful when players throw a ball at, rather than to, another player. A large, soft rubber ball is better for developing ball control without risking injury. (A water polo ball is too firm to be thrown directly at another player.) Use your imagination to adapt variations of Dodge Ball, such as Center Dodge Ball or Prison Dodge, for use in the water. Other examples are as follows.

179

Seven-Up

Equipment: Playground ball

Number of players: 6 to 10, in two teams

Strategy: Teams face each other. Each team member counts off consecutively. The leader calls out a number and throws the ball into the water between the teams. As the number is called, the two opponents whose number has been called swim to the ball. The first one there grasps it and swims back to place while the opponent pursues. If the player is tagged while carrying the ball, the opposing team scores one point. If the player reaches home safely, that player's team scores and the process is repeated with another number called. The team that scores the most points wins.

Octopus

Equipment: Soft foam ball

Number of players: 10 to 13

Strategy: On the signal from "it," all players try to swim to the deep end. "It" tries to hit any of the players with the ball. When a player is hit with the ball, he or she becomes part of "it's" team, trying to tag others by hand while treading water in the area where he or she was tagged. Players who are tagged by one of "it's" team must also tread water and try to tag other players. Only "it" can throw the ball and move through the water. Each time the players swim from one end to the other, there are fewer players swimming and more tagging. The last player to be tagged is "it" for the next game. To ensure practice treading water, all players must swim or tread water. No standing allowed! This is also a good lead-up game for water polo, since it helps develop endurance.

Water Spud

Equipment: Soft foam ball

Number of players: Any number

Strategy: Players stand in a circle in shallow water and count off consecutively. The leader stands in the center of the group holding the ball and calls out a number. The player whose number is called swims into the center for the ball while the other players swim away from the ball until the person grasps the ball and calls "stop." The player then tries to hit one of the other players with the ball. Anyone hit with the ball has one "spud" counted against him. Players are eliminated when they accumulate three spuds. The last player left is the winner.

Adapting Land-Based Ball Games for the Water

It isn't hard to adapt basketball, volleyball, or baseball for the water. Floating backboards and baskets are available. A volleyball net can be strung so that the bottom of the net is 2 or 3 feet above the surface. You can use land rules in shallow or deep water depending on the abilities of your participants, or adapt the rules to incorporate some skill practice. In baseball, for example, have the participants swim under water to first base, breaststroke to second, etc. For basketball, try having the participants play basketball while sitting in inner tubes, tossing the ball up in the air for every stroke instead of dribbling. Some other ball games you can play in the water are as follows.

Keep Away

Equipment: Large water ball

Number of players: Any number, in two teams

Strategy: One team has possession of the ball and tries to keep it among its players while the other team tries to capture the ball and pass it among its players. The ball must be kept moving, the players tossing it to one other. This is a good training game for water polo.

Push or Cage Ball

Equipment: Water ball

Number of players: Any number, in two teams

Strategy: Teams push ball in opposite directions using hands or feet. They cannot hold or throw the ball. The first team to reach the goal (such as reaching a wall) scores.

Tadpole

Equipment: Playground ball

Number of players: Up to 12, in two teams

Strategy: Teams stand in shallow water. One team forms a circle, and the other forms a line. The first teammate in the line is about 3 feet from the circle team. The player in the circle standing nearest the line holds the ball. On the signal, the player holding the ball hops on both feet, carrying the ball in both hands over the head, and passes the ball to the next player in the circle. After passing the ball, the player returns to his or her original position. The ball must make as many trips around the circle as there are players on the circle team. At the same time, the players in the line must swim around the circle once, each player touching off the next. The line team is racing the ball as it is being passed around the circle. The team that finishes its assigned task first wins the match. Teams should be reversed after each match. Vary the size of the circle to keep teams evenly matched.

RELAYS AND RACES

Relay races are yet another way to improve skills and stroke technique and can provide a welcome diversion from routine swimming. You can build any aspect of skill practice into your races, or just for fun you can have participants race with hats or clothes on. You are limited only by your imagination. Aside from practicing and perfecting skills and having a good time, relay races let you match teams evenly. In this way you can put a less skilled person on a team with fairly strong competitors to give him or her a better chance of succeeding and build self-esteem. Everyone on the team is a winner!

Relays and Races for All Levels

Arch Relay

Equipment: None

Number of players: 10 or more, in two or more teams

Strategy: Teams line up parallel to each other in shallow water, standing with legs astride. Rear player swims through arched legs of all team members and the whole line keeps moving back to make room for him or her at the front. When the player surfaces at the front of the line, the new rear player starts. The first team to restore the original order wins.

Baton Race

Equipment: One baton per team

Number of players: Any number, in two or more teams

Strategy: The starting player of each team has a baton. He or she swims to the wall, touches it with the baton, then swims back to the team and hands the baton to the second person on the team. The relay continues until all team members have completed the course. The team that finishes first wins. Vary the skill to suit the players' abilities.

Paddle Boat Race

Equipment: One kickboard for each team

Number of players: Any number, in two or more teams

Strategy: Teams stand in lines on one side of the shallow end. The first member of each team has a kickboard. On the signal, the first player of each team climbs onto the kickboard, paddles to the other side of the swimming area, turns around, and comes back the same way. If they fall off the kickboard, they must go back to the beginning and start again. The team that finishes first wins.

Ping Pong Relay

Equipment: One ping pong ball per team, one spoon for each team member.

Number of players: Any number, in two or more teams

Strategy: Players line up behind their leader in a straight line. Each player has a spoon, and the first player on each team also has a ping pong ball. The object is for the players to walk across the swimming area and back with the spoon in their mouths and the ping pong ball in the spoon. If they lose the ball on their way, they may put it back where it was dropped.

Variation: If players can walk across the swimming area easily, they can try swimming across.

Seal Show Relay

Equipment: One beach ball per team

Number of players: Any number, in two or more teams

Strategy: The first player of each team slips into shallow water with the team ball. This player travels across the swimming area skipping and bouncing the ball off his or her head. On the return, the player treads water while pushing the ball with the nose. The next player repeats the cycle until all have had a turn.

Variation: Change strokes and depth.

Relays and Races for Levels V–VII

Button-Unbutton Relay

Equipment: One large shirt with buttons and one pair of large pants for each team

Number of players: Any number, in two or more teams

Strategy: Divide players so half of each team is on the deck at opposite sides of the swimming area. On the signal, the first player on each team puts on his or her set of clothes (making sure all buttons are buttoned). The player jumps in, swims to the other side, gets out of the water, takes off the shirt and pants. The next player on each team then puts on the clothes, jumps in and swims to the starting point. The relay continues until the last person has taken off the clothes.

Variations: Use kicks or arm strokes only to reach the other side. Add a pair of sneakers to the clothing used. Have players dress and undress in the water.

Fill the Donut Hole

Equipment: One inner tube and ball for each team, floating near the starting point

Number of players: Any even number, in two or more teams

Strategy: Half of each team is on the deck at opposite sides of the swimming area. On the signal, the first player on each team enters the water, places the ball inside the tube and swims to the opposite side without touching the ball with the hands. Once there, the player knocks the ball out of the tube without using the hands. As soon as the ball is out, the next team member starts. The first team to have all its members exchange sides wins.

Floating Obstacle Course

Equipment: Three or more inner tubes per team (you may want to anchor the tubes)

Number of players: Any number, in two teams

Strategy: Teams line up at one side of the swimming area. On the signal, the first player in each team pushes off the wall and swims to the first inner tube. Then the player surface dives and comes up in the center. Pushing himself or herself up through the inner tube and over the edge, the player then swims to the next tube, and so on until he or she completes the whole course. Then the next player on each team begins the course. The team that finishes first wins.

Kickboard Relay

Equipment: Kickboards

Number of players: Any number, in two or more teams

Strategy: Half of each team is at opposite sides of the swimming area. On the signal, the first player from each team kicks across the swimming area and hands the kickboard to his or her partner, who proceeds to kick back to the next team member, and so on. The team that finishes first wins.

Variation: Designate different kicks and distances.

Mermaid Croquet

Equipment: None

Number of players: Any number, in three teams

Strategy: Two teams line up at one end, while members of the third team position themselves as croquet wickets and stand or tread water. On the signal, the first player on each of the competing teams pushes off the wall and swims to the first wicket and surface dives under it. He or she repeats the process for all the wickets. The first player reaches the end, touches the wall, swims back to the start, and tags the next player on the team. The first team to finish is the winner. This game is good for practicing strokes and building endurance.

Variations: Use different strokes, or walk, hop or skip in shallow water.

Ping Pong Number Relay

Equipment: Ping pong balls, slips of paper, waterproof marking pen, plastic bag

Number of players: Any even number

Strategy: Place ping pong balls, with numbers on them, in the water. Place numbered slips of paper corresponding to the ping pong balls in a plastic bag. Players are in two even lines. On the signal, the first player from each team takes a number from the bag, pushes off the wall, and looks for the ball with the corresponding number on it. When they find it, they return to the starting point and the next team member begins. The first team to find its ping pong balls wins. (Suggestion: To make the game more difficult and a lot more fun, have more balls and numbers than players.)

Variation: To play as a game instead of a relay, all players pick numbers and search for the corresponding ping pong balls at the same time.

Split Stroke Relay

Equipment: None

Number of players: Any even number, in two teams

Strategy: Players choose partners and divide into teams. Half of each team is at the shallow end and the other half is at the deep end. The first set of partners of each team gets into the water at the shallow end. One player in each pair floats on the back, placing the feet on the shoulders of the partner, who is also floating on the back. The first player in each pair does the arm stroke of the elementary backstroke while the partner does the kick. The partner doing the kick may hold the partner's feet if needed. They swim the length of the swimming area. The partners may keep their rhythm by talking to each other. The partners at the deep end repeat the process to return to the starting point. When all members of the team have finished, the game continues again with the partners switching places. The team that finishes first is the winner. This game helps strengthen and coordinate the arm stroke and the kick of the elementary backstroke and can be used as an initial exercise for synchronized swimming.

Straw Hat Race

Equipment: One Straw hat for each team

Number of players: Any number, in two or more teams

Strategy: Teams line up at the deep end of the swimming area, the first player in each team wearing a hat. On the signal, they jump into the water and completely submerge. Leveling off, they recover their hats (without using hands), swim to a designated point, and return. The hat is handed off to the next team member who repeats the stunt. The team that finishes first wins.

The Swimming Waiter/Waitress

Equipment: Aluminum pie plate and plastic champagne glass for each team

Number of players: Any number, in two or more teams

Strategy: One half of each team stands at each end of the swimming area. On the signal, the first player on each team pushes off the wall holding the pie plate as a tray with a water-filled champagne glass balanced on it. The player swims to the opposite end of the swimming area, holding the tray out of the water. If the glass topples over, the player must stop and set it upright. When the player reaches the opposite end, he or she hands the tray to a teammate who swims back to the other side in the same manner. The first team to return to its starting position wins.

Two-Person Underwater Race

Equipment: None

Number of players: Any number, in pairs

Strategy: Pairs of players line up along side of swimming area. The objective is for both players to swim under water as one person. The partner in the back may only kick and the partner in the front may use arm strokes only. The player in back holds onto the partner's ankles. The pair that reaches the goal line first wins.

Variation: Less skilled players can swim on the surface and use other strokes on the surface.

Wheelbarrow Race

Equipment: None

Number of players: Any number, in pairs

Strategy: One player in each pair floats supine, legs spread, while his or her partner stands holding the teammate's ankles. On the signal, the partner races to the other side, pushing the teammate, who may paddle with hands. When they reach a designated spot, they switch positions for the return. The pair that finishes first wins.

Relays and Races for Levels VI and VII

Passing the Puck

Equipment: One puck per team

Number of players: Any number, in two or more teams

Strategy: Half of each team is at each end of the swimming area. On the signal, the first player on each team pushes off from the wall holding a puck with hands out of the water. They swim on their backs, using a designated kick, to the other end of the swimming area. There they pass the puck to a teammate who is already in the water. The first team to finish the relay wins.

Variation: Use a heavier object, such as a diving brick, to increase the challenge and build endurance.

Coin Dive

Equipment: Whistle. For each player, 10 coins of various sizes, painted different colors with waterproof paint (3 yellow coins, 3 red coins, 4 black coins) and a waterproof container to store coins.

Number of players: Any number, in two teams

Strategy: Teams line up at the wall in the deep end of the swimming area about 10 feet apart. The instructor blows the whistle and throws 10 coins (3 yellow, 3 red, 4 black) into the water. One player from each team pushes off the wall under water and tries to catch as many coins as possible before they touch the bottom. The players may not take more than one breath or pick coins off the bottom. After the players surface, they swim to the side of the pool and return to their line. The procedure is repeated for the remaining players. Yellow coins count three points, red coins two points, and black coins one point. The team with the highest score wins.

Variation: Teach money counting skills by using coins of different denominations and adding their values.

SYNCHRONIZED SWIMMING

Synchronized swimming is a creative way to teach body awareness in the water and let participants enhance their aquatic skills. It can be fun if your participants can combine standard skills, strokes, and figures to gain an appreciation of this sport. To make it challenging, have participants develop their own routines to music of their choice. Besides the fitness benefits of synchronized swimming, participants learn to cooperate, develop rhythmic awareness, and exercise their imagination.

The only equipment you need to start is a cassette tape player and music, as well as nose clips for each participant. To develop a sense of competition, you can divide your class in half or have one class compete against another. Each team can develop a routine according to the guidelines you set.

Review or teach basic sculling hand motion, front crawl with face out of water, sculling techniques on pages 99 and 277–278 of *Swimming and Diving*, and floating patterns. The following activities are examples of aquatic formations that may stimulate participants' interest in synchronized swimming. You can also consult synchronized swimming publications for other figures, patterns, and activities.

Shadow Swimming

One participant swims under water while another participant on the surface synchronizes his or her stroke with the one under water. This gives the illusion of a shadow on the bottom. The breaststroke is the simplest stroke to work with.

Butterfly Floating

Two participants float supine next to each other with the feet of each one next to the head of the other. Partners grasp each other on the underside of the nearer ankle. The pair can turn themselves around by slowly and gently spreading and closing their arm and legs.

Tub Float

Each participant floats supine and assumes a position like a tub by slowly drawing the knees toward the chest, keeping the knees and feet together and on the surface. The participant stays in a stationary position by sculling. To turn to the right, the participant sculls with the right wrist flexed and the left wrist hyperextended. After they master the figure, have participants try it in pairs or combine it with other figures or stroking.

The Foursome

Two participants swim on their backs side by side using the flutter kick and join inside hands with arms stretched to the side. With their free hands, they pull two other participants who are also using the flutter kick but swimming on their stomachs, keeping their heads up. They also join inside hands with arms stretched to the side.

Supine Floating Patterns

Having your participants create floating patterns at the surface is a fun and challenging activity. Six or more participants make the most interesting patterns, but encourage your group to use their imaginations. Some participants may need to scull to stay afloat. In other formations, additional participants can support the floaters by treading water. You can also try these in shallow water where some can stand to provide support. Suggestions for supine floating patterns include—
- A circle with toes to the center.
- A circle with heads in the center and hands held.
- A circle with alternate participants facing in and out.
- A straight line of participants connected.
- Two or more participants with heads facing the same direction and floating with sides touching and holding inside hands.
- Two or more participants with heads facing alternating directions floating with sides touching and holding inside hands.

Changing or moving the float provides additional variety. Have floaters open or close their legs, bend a knee, or otherwise change body positions. Additional participants can move the pattern by walking or treading water while supporting one or more floaters. Have participants in the pattern experiment with kicking or stroking.

SUMMARY

A creative instructor can incorporate games, stunts, and activities into swimming lessons to make learning fun for participants of all ages. You can use games to reinforce specific skills or increase a participant's endurance or comfort in the water. Be sure to include games that are just plain fun. When your participants learn how playful aquatics can be, they may adopt swimming as their sport of choice and have many years of enjoyment.

- the basic water safety course
- the emergency water safety course

basic water safety and emergency water safety

26 the basic water safety course

T he purpose of the American Red Cross Basic Water Safety and Emergency Water Safety courses is to provide individuals, groups, and families with general water safety information. This chapter contains a course outline and lesson plans for the Basic Water Safety course. Chapter 27 contains a course outline and lesson plans for the Emergency Water Safety course.

> **Instructor's note:**
> Taking the Basic Water Safety course or the Emergency Water Safety course, or both, does not qualify a participant to be a lifeguard. For information on lifeguarding courses, contact your local Red Cross unit.

The objective of the Basic Water Safety course is to create an awareness of causes and prevention of water accidents, to develop a desire to be safe, and to encourage health and safe water recreation. The course focuses on personal and community water safety and is ideal for families, scout troops, and other community groups or individuals interested in general water safety.

ADMINISTRATIVE NOTES

The following points apply to the Basic Water Safety course.

Prerequisites

The course may be taken by people of any age, regardless of swimming ability. This includes both swimmers and nonswimmers. Participants must attend all sessions; however, their level of participation in water activities may vary. There are three levels of participation:
1. Observers—those who do not wish to enter the water and want to observe and participate in all activities that take place on land.

Listening to the instructor and observing the practice sessions increases an awareness and understanding of water safety.
2. Life-jacket wearers or novice swimmers—those who do not feel totally comfortable in the water yet wish to participate in water activities while wearing a life jacket. They must wear a Coast Guard-approved life jacket for all water activities. These participants practice in water up to chest-deep.
3. Swimmers—those who feel comfortable in deep water without a life jacket and who have passed the skills pretest for water activities.

> **Instructor's note:**
> Observers may change to Level Two for the second or third session if they want.

Course Length

This course is designed to be taught in a minimum of 9 hours. The course content is presented in three 3-hour sessions. Each session includes a classroom discussion followed by a 15-minute break. You demonstrate and explain water skills or show a video and then participants practice them. If a boat (small craft) is not available for use in Session 3, course length may be shortened by as much as 40 minutes.

Class Size

It is recommended that there be one instructor for every 10 participants in the course. If there are more than 10 participants, there should be a co-instructor or aide. Close supervision is required to ensure effective practice and the safety of participants. Furthermore, if you keep the class reasonably small, you can run sessions more efficiently and you are less likely to exceed the allotted time periods for various activities.

Facilities

The course includes classroom activities requiring dry land space with a writing surface for each participant and water activities requiring a swimming facility such as a pool or lake. For scheduling purposes, it may be necessary to rearrange the sequence of sessions or to devote an entire session to classroom activities and another to water activities. Breaks are scheduled so participants can change into swimsuits and go to the swimming area.

Equipment and Supplies

At the beginning of each session is a list of required equipment and supplies. A master list of equipment for the course can be found in Appendix A. Make sure all the equipment is ready and in working order before you teach the course.

All participants should have a copy of *American Red Cross Basic Water Safety* or *American Red Cross Swimming and Diving*.

Evaluation

There is no test, either written or of skills, at the end of this course. However, you may use the Basic Water Safety Skills Checklist in Appendix M to check off the skills completed.

Certificates

Students who complete the course, whether observers or in-water participants, are eligible to receive a course-completion certificate (Cert. 3411). (For more information on awarding certificates, completing records, and conducting course evaluations, see Chapter 5.)

COURSE ACTIVITIES

Skills Pretest

During Session 1, conduct the skills pretest for those who wish to participate without a life jacket. To pass the pretest, participants must—

1. Enter shallow water; swim into deep water next to the edge of pool, dock, or lifeline for 10 yards; float or tread water for 1 minute; and return to shallow water on the back.
2. Jump into deep water, level off, and swim 10 yards to safety.

Explanation and Demonstration

Demonstrate each water skill slowly and correctly, with an accompanying explanation, before participants attempt the skill. You may use the suggested audiovisuals to supplement or replace your demonstration.

Water Activities

Safety is an extremely important aspect of practice sessions. Every effort must be made to prevent accidents. In addition to regular precautions, you must be sure that participants who do not pass the skills pretest wear Coast Guard-approved life jackets anytime they are engaged in water activities.

All water activities include explanation and demonstration of the skill, followed by participant practice. In general, the participants practice on land, then in shallow water, and then in deep water when it is appropriate.

Practice

Design practice sessions so that each participant has maximum opportunity and ample space for practice. Make sure participants receive feedback on their efforts and offer suggestions for improvement, when necessary.

Organize water activities so participants do not have to enter and leave the water more often than necessary. Becoming chilled can be distracting and can interfere with the learning process.

COURSE OUTLINES

BASIC WATER SAFETY COURSE OUTLINE

SESSION 1

Activity	Approximate Time	Method	References*
Introductions and discussion of objectives	20 minutes	L/D	
Prevention	15 minutes	L/D	*BWS*, p. 2; *S&D*, p. 27
Emergency action plans	10 minutes	L/D	*BWS*, pp. 3–6; *S&D*, p. 27
Choosing a safe place to swim	10 minutes	L/D	*BWS*, pp. 6, 20–22; *S&D*, p. 28
Hazards	15 minutes	L/D	*BWS*, pp. 8–19; *S&D*, pp. 27–28, 34–42
Safety tips for other water activities	5 minutes	L/D	*BWS*, pp. 23–29; *S&D*, pp. 42–51, 51–66
Self-help in a water emergency	10 minutes	L/D	*BWS*, pp. 36–37; *S&D*, pp. 29–30, 32, 39–42
Optional audiovisual: *Survival Swimming*	(8 minutes)	AV	
Assignment and Break	15 minutes		
Water activities practice: Skills pretest	30 minutes	Demo/P	
Personal flotation devices	15 minutes	Demo/P	
Sudden immersion skills	35 minutes	Demo/P	
SESSION 1, TOTAL TIME	**3 HOURS** (add 8 minutes for optional video)		

*BWS = Basic Water Safety   AV = Audiovisual   D = Discussion   L = Lecture
S&D = Swimming and Diving   P = Practice   Demo = Demonstration

Basic Water Safety Course Outline

Session 2

Activity	Approximate Time	Method	References*
Review of Session 1 and discussion of objectives	15 minutes	L/D	
Emergency response: helping others	15 minutes	L/D	*BWS*, pp. 43–54; *S&D*, p. 287
Optional audiovisual: *Nonswimming Rescues*	(8 minutes)	AV	
Spinal injury management Audiovisual: *Spinal Injury Management*	50 minutes, including video	L/D/AV	*BWS*, pp. 30–34; *S&D*, pp. 302–309
Assignment and Break	15 minutes		
Water activities practice: Spinal injury	20 minutes	Demo/P	*BWS*, p. 31; *S&D*, p. 306
Water assists	45 minutes	Demo/P	*BWS*, pp. 44–55; *S&D*, pp. 288–291
Swimming clothed and inflating clothes for flotation	20 minutes	Demo/P	*BWS*, pp. 37–39; *S&D*, p. 32
Session 2, Total Time	**3 hours** (includes 25-minute video; add 8 minutes for optional video)		

*BWS = Basic Water Safety   AV = Audiovisual   D = Discussion   L = Lecture
S&D = Swimming and Diving   P = Practice   Demo = Demonstration

BASIC WATER SAFETY COURSE OUTLINE

SESSION 3

Activity	Approximate Time	Method	References*
Review of Session 2 and discussion of objectives	15 minutes	L/D	
Exposure to cold water	20 minutes	L/D	*BWS,* pp. 58–63; *S&D,* pp. 38–41
Ice safety	10 minutes	L/D	*BWS,* pp. 64–66; *S&D,* pp. 41–42
Boating safety	15 minutes	L/D	*BWS,* pp. 68–78; *S&D,* pp. 42–49
Optional audiovisual: *Boating Safety and Rescues*	(11 minutes)	AV	
Final review	15 minutes	L/D	
Break	15 minutes		
Water activities practice: H.E.L.P. position/huddle position	15 minutes	Demo/P	*BWS,* p. 61; *S&D,* p. 42
Introduction to rescue breathing	25 minutes	Demo/P	*BWS,* p. 85; *S&D,* pp. 300–301
Boating safety	40 minutes	Demo/P	*BWS,* pp. 71–78; *S&D,* pp. 46–49
Course review and wrap-up	10 minutes	L/D	
SESSION 3, TOTAL TIME	**3 HOURS** (add 11 minutes for optional video)		

*BWS = Basic Water Safety   AV = Audiovisual   D = Discussion   L = Lecture
S&D = Swimming and Diving   P = Practice   Demo = Demonstration

Lesson Plan

Session 1 3 hours

Equipment

- Enrollment and registration materials
- Chalkboard and chalk or flip chart and markers
- *Basic Water Safety* textbook, 1 per participant
- Coast Guard-approved life jackets in good condition, 1 per participant
- Five types of personal flotation devices for display
- Audiovisual: *Survival Swimming* (8 minutes) (optional)
- Video cassette recorder (VCR) and monitor
- Basic Water Safety Skills Checklist from Appendix M

Objectives

At the end of Session 1, participants should be able to—

- Identify major causes of water accidents.
- Identify measures for preventing water accidents.
- Develop an emergency plan for a given aquatic situation.
- Identify safe responses to a sudden immersion.
- Demonstrate the proper way to put on a life jacket.
- Perform survival floating.
- Tread water.

Participants who do not enter the water will describe rather than demonstrate the water skills.

INTRODUCTIONS AND DISCUSSION OF OBJECTIVES (20 minutes)

Welcome participants and introduce all teaching staff. Briefly point out the role and history of the Red Cross in water safety education. Ask participants to explain their reasons for taking the course and their expectations. Explain whether or not this course will meet their expectations.

Review with participants the purposes of the course:

- To provide individuals and families with general water safety information in order to create an awareness of the causes and prevention of aquatic emergencies.
- To develop a desire to be safe in, on, and around the water.
- To contribute to safe and healthy aquatic recreation.

Emphasize the importance of being prepared in water safety. Explain that by knowing how to respond to potential dangers in, on, and around the water, participants may prevent tragedy.

Describe course format and length:

- Meeting time and breaks.
- Attendance. To receive a course participation certificate, participants must attend all sessions. They must either observe or participate in the water activities.
- Clothing for water activities. Inform participants when they must bring or wear clothes for going in the water.
- Facility rules and regulations, such as about smoking and eating.
- Textbook requirements and homework assignments.
- Describe the three levels of participation listed on page 189. Remind participants that course emphasis is on aquatic emergency responses that can be safely performed by nonswimmers and novice swimmers.

Discuss the objectives for Session 1.

PREVENTION (15 minutes)
BWS, p. 2; S&D, p. 27

Cite statistics about the severity and extent of the water safety problem. Some things to point out include—

- About 4,600 Americans drown every year.
- Only motor vehicle collisions and falls cause more accidental deaths than drowning.
- Well over half of the drowning victims were doing something other than swimming or playing in the water when they drowned.
- Diving into shallow water results in the greatest number of serious spinal cord injuries of all sports.
- Diving into shallow water and striking the bottom can result in complete paralysis from the neck down.

Point out that many of these deaths and serious injuries could be prevented if people would take a few simple precautions *before* swimming, diving, or playing in the water.

Major Causes of Water Emergencies and Injuries

Ask participants what they think are the causes of most aquatic injuries. List all the responses on the left side of the chalkboard or flip chart (leave room to add information on the right side of the list), finishing the list yourself, if necessary. Then discuss how and why each item listed presents danger. Your completed list should include—
- Diving into water of unknown depth or water that is too shallow.
- Overestimating ability and stamina.
- Sudden immersion.
- Incidents involving small craft.
- Medical emergencies.

Discuss how to prevent aquatic emergencies. Ask participants how each cause listed could be prevented and write their responses on the right side of the list.

Point out that when an emergency happens, there is little time to analyze all the alternatives and decide what to do. A person who has thought in advance about what to do in case of an emergency—even if that person is a nonswimmer—has the greatest chance of averting tragedy. The best way to be prepared for an emergency is to have a plan.

EMERGENCY ACTION PLANS (10 minutes)
BWS, pp. 3–6; S&D, p. 27

Discuss the elements of an emergency action plan.
- A system of signals
- Safety equipment
- Development of site procedures

Also discuss the Emergency Medical Services (EMS) system in your community and how to access the system. (See the appendix on EMS on pages 79–82 in *Basic Water Safety* or page 286 in *Swimming and Diving.*) Explain how to make an emergency telephone call and tell participants what information the dispatcher will need. It is important to post emergency information, such as telephone numbers and directions to the facility, near the phone because in a crisis it can be difficult to remember important details. Refer participants to the sample tear-out form, "Instructions for Emergency Telephone Calls," on page 83 in *Basic Water Safety* or page 339 in *Swimming and Diving.*

Explain the emergency action plan for the facility you are using. Explain the differences between the emergency action plans for an indoor facility and for areas such as a beach or lake front.

Give a local example of an area not supervised by a lifeguard, such as a pond, private pool, quarry, or lake. Ask participants to analyze what type of emergencies could happen and to develop an appropriate emergency action plan for such an area.

CHOOSING A SAFE PLACE TO SWIM (10 minutes)
BWS, pp. 6, 20–22; S&D, p. 28

Discuss characteristics of a safe place to swim and explain why each characteristic is important. Use the following situations and write participants' responses on the chalkboard or flip chart.

You arrive at an unfamiliar pool (public or private). What are the safety conditions and characteristics to look for before you swim?

Your completed list should include these characteristics of a safe pool:
- Lifeguards
- Clean water
- Clean and well-maintained deck areas
- Nonslip surfaces
- Free of electrical equipment or power lines
- Emergency communications to get help
- Safety equipment
- Water-depth markings
- Buoyed lines separating shallow and deep water
- Supervision for children and nonswimmers

You are going swimming at a beach, lake, river, or ocean. What safety characteristics should you look for there?

Your completed list should include these characteristics of a safe beach:
- Lifeguards
- Clean water
- Clean and well-maintained beach
- Sturdy docks, piers, and rafts with nonslip surfaces
- Water-depth markings
- Firm, gently sloping bottom
- Free of electrical equipment or power lines
- Emergency communication equipment
- Safety equipment
- Supervision for children and nonswimmers

HAZARDS (15 minutes)
BWS, pp. 8–19; S&D, pp. 27–28, 34–42

Discuss potential hazards at waterfront facilities (beaches, lakes, rivers). Note that hazards differ around the country. Tell participants always to check out a new area before swimming. Emphasize hazards common to your area and briefly summarize other hazards.

Discuss each of the following hazards: waves, currents, dams, aquatic plants and animals, bottom hazards, bad weather, signs of danger (flags, audible signals, absence of other swimmers). Explain what they are, how and why they are dangerous, and what to do if you encounter them.

Describe and diagram appropriate hazards. (Don't label diagrams, so you can use them later to check participants' knowledge.) Show pictures or samples of various hazards. Consult with fish, wildlife, or water recreation agencies for supporting information and materials.

Discuss the causes, prevention, and treatment of each of the following hazards—
- Panic
- Cramps
- Exhaustion
- Hyperventilation
- Sunburn, heat stroke, heat exhaustion
- Hypothermia (you will discuss this in detail later)

SAFETY TIPS FOR OTHER WATER ACTIVITIES (5 minutes)
BWS, pp. 23–29; S&D, pp. 42–51, 56–66

Review the safety tips for swimming, diving, and other recreational activities, as appropriate for the group. Focus on those that pertain to the interests of the participants in your class (for example, infant and preschool swimming would be of greater interest to parents of toddlers than to teens or sports enthusiasts).

SELF-HELP IN A WATER EMERGENCY (10 minutes)
BWS, pp. 36–37; S&D, pp. 29–30, 32, 39–42

Define sudden immersion and discuss situations that might lead to suddenly finding yourself in the water. Explain that being near water is potentially dangerous whether you plan to swim or not. Explain that it is especially dangerous when people do not plan to swim because they tend to be less prepared.

Remind participants that—
- Unintentional falls into water cause many of the 4,600 drownings in the United States each year.
- People are usually unprepared for such falls, and they often panic if they are not good swimmers.

- Wearing a Coast Guard-approved life jacket around water is the most effective way to prevent drowning.
- Even if people fall into water without a life jacket and are not strong swimmers, they have a good chance to save themselves by staying calm and using the survival techniques taught in this session.

Cite one or more examples of immersion situations in which safety precautions were not followed, using local examples where possible.

Optional Audiovisual

American Red Cross *Survival Swimming*

Discuss safe responses to sudden immersion, including when to wait for help, when to try to reach safety, and what self-help techniques to use.

ASSIGNMENT

Ask participants to read Chapters 1 and 2 in *Basic Water Safety,* or pages 22–67, 286–287, and 300–301 in *Swimming and Diving,* for the next session. Tell them to bring clothes to wear in the water, including a long-sleeved, button down shirt or blouse.

BREAK (15 minutes)

Participants change into swimsuits.

WATER ACTIVITIES PRACTICE

> *Instructor's note:*
> Use the Basic Water Safety Skills Checklist in Appendix M to keep a record of participants' progress.

SKILLS PRETEST (30 minutes)

Determine how participants wish to participate in the water sessions. There may be three levels (see page 189):
- Observers
- Life-jacket wearers
- Swimmers

Before any participants enter the water, discuss facility rules. Point out the locations of shallow and deep areas. Have participants enter shallow water, not deep water, until you feel comfortable with their abilities.

Conduct a skills pretest. Participants who wish to engage in the water activities without wearing life jackets must perform the skills listed on page 190. Participants who cannot perform these skills must wear a Coast Guard-approved life jacket for all water activities.

Participants who do not want to enter the water may observe, join the discussion, take part in land activities, and practice water activities on land. If they are going to be near the water's edge, they must wear a Coast Guard-approved life jacket.

> *Instructor's note:*
> Before all practice sessions in the water, you must make sure that participants requiring a life jacket have put one on and fastened it properly. Remind participants wearing life jackets that they must not go into water deeper than chest-level.

PERSONAL FLOTATION DEVICES (PFDs)
(15 minutes)
BWS, pp. 7–8; S&D, p. 29

Display 5 types of PFDs, if available, and explain their differences and specific uses. Provide Coast Guard-approved life jackets to all participants and provide demonstration and practice time for the following activities:
- Putting on a life jacket
- Checking for proper fit and fastening
- Easing into the water wearing a life jacket
- Swimming in both prone and supine positions

SUDDEN IMMERSION SKILLS (35 minutes)
BWS, pp. 39–40; S&D, pp. 32, 39–42

> *Instructor's note:*
> See Chapter 18 for more information on teaching these skills.

Breath Control and Bobbing

Demonstrate breath control and bobbing in shallow water. Have participants enter shallow water and practice breath control and bobbing along with you. As participants become comfortable with the skill, progress to deeper water. Those wearing life jackets can practice by holding onto edge of pool or dock and pushing themselves under water.

Floating on Back

Demonstrate floating on the back then add a finning motion. Have swimmers practice floating on their backs and then add finning and kicking in deeper water. Participants wearing a life jacket can perform the exercise in shallow water.

Survival Floating

Survival floating utilizes the body's natural tendency to swing down into a semivertical position with the head at or just below the surface. It can be used to help conserve energy while waiting for rescue. Movements should be slow and easy.

> ***Instructor's note:***
> Since face-down floating causes the body to cool very quickly, this skill should be used in warm water only.
>   Demonstrate survival (face-down) floating. Have swimmers practice survival floating in deep water. Those wearing life jackets can simulate the exercise in chest-deep water. Observers can demonstrate the procedures on land.

Treading Water

Treading water is a skill that expends little energy when done properly and that helps swimmers stay afloat in an emergency situation. Have swimmers practice treading water in deep water. Participants wearing a life jacket should practice in water that is no more than chest-deep.

Releasing a Cramp

Demonstrate on the deck or land and in deep water how to work out a leg cramp. Have participants practice the technique on land and in shallower water.

SESSION 2 {3 hours}

Equipment

- Chalkboard and chalk or flip chart and markers
- *Basic Water Safety* textbook, 1 per participant
- Shepherd's crook
- Heaving line
- Throw bag
- Improvised reaching assist equipment
- Life jackets as required for water activities
- *Spinal Injury Management* video (optional but strongly recommended)
- Optional *Nonswimming Rescues* video (8 minutes)
- VCR and monitor
- Basic Water Safety Skills Checklist from Appendix M

Objectives

At the end of Session 2, participants should be able to—
- Recognize and identify signs of a person in trouble in the water.
- Demonstrate safe assists for use by people who are not trained lifeguards.
- Analyze a water emergency situation, select a safe and effective method of assisting, and activate the EMS System.
- Identify signs and symptoms of a spinal injury.
- Swim fully clothed.
- Use clothes for flotation.
- Demonstrate the hip and shoulder support technique for a victim of a suspected spinal injury.

Review of Session 1 and Discussion of Objectives (15 minutes)

Use some of the following questions to review Session 1 and introduce Session 2.

■ How do alcohol and drug use affect water safety?

■ What are some ways people push their limits in and around the water?

■ How can you avoid diving-related injuries?

■ Why do activities around water sometimes end in tragedy? How can such tragedies be avoided?

■ If you were invited to go out in a boat, how could you make sure the outing was as safe as possible?

■ What does education have to do with water safety?

■ What precautions should you take before you and your friends go swimming in an unsupervised area?

■ What should you do if you begin to feel panicky in the water?

■ When you find yourself suddenly and unexpectedly in water, what influences whether you stay and wait for rescue or try to reach safety?

■ How do you perform survival (face-down) floating?

Discuss the objectives for Session 2.

Emergency Response: Helping Others (15 minutes)
BWS, pp. 43–44, 54; S&D, pp. 286–288

Emphasize the importance of being alert to signs that someone may be in trouble.

Discuss what a person should do when helping someone in trouble in the water.

Display as many of the following rescue devices as possible, giving the name and purpose of each. Tell participants they will be practicing with them in the next water activities session.

■ Shepherd's crook or reaching pole
■ Heaving line

■ Throw bag
■ Ring buoy
■ Rescue tube
■ Improvised equipment, such as a jug on a line, beach towel, belt, or oar

Optional Audiovisual

American Red Cross *Nonswimming Rescues*

Spinal Injury Management
(50 minutes—including a 25-minute video)
BWS, pp. 30–34; S&D, pp. 302–309

Optional Audiovisual

Showing the American Red Cross *Spinal Injury Management* video is recommended because it demonstrates and clarifies the technical maneuvers described in *Basic Water Safety* and *Swimming and Diving.*

After the video, have participants refer to the illustrations on pages 30–34 in *Basic Water Safety* or the photographs on pages 303, 306–308 in *Swimming and Diving* as you reinforce the key points. Briefly discuss the anatomy and function of the spine and describe situations that may indicate spinal injury.

Explain and discuss the general procedures for handling a suspected spinal injury in the water.

Assignment

Ask participants to read Chapters 3 and 4 in *Basic Water Safety,* or pages 38–49 in *Swimming and Diving,* for the next session.

Break (15 minutes)

Participants change into swimsuits.

Water Activities Practice

Instructor's note:
Use the Basic Water Safety Skills Checklist in Appendix M to keep a record of participants' progress.

Have participants prepare to go into the water. Check to ensure that participants who are required to wear life jackets for water activities have put them on and fastened them correctly. Instruction for skills can be found in *Swimming and Diving*.

Spinal Injury (20 minutes)
BWS, p. 31; S&D, p. 306

Demonstrate the hip and shoulder support technique. Emphasize that it is used in calm, shallow water only for face-up victims of suspected spinal injury when no help is immediately available to assist in placing the victim on a backboard. Have participants practice the skill with a partner. If time allows, switch partners so that rescuers can experience handling different body types.

Water Assists (45 minutes)
BWS, pp. 44–55; S&D, pp. 287–291

Discuss the guidelines for making water assists to someone in trouble.

Reaching the Conscious Victim
BWS, pp. 44–54; S&D, pp. 287–291

Describe and demonstrate the following reaching assists. Allow ample practice time for participation.
- A reaching assist from the deck.
- A reaching assist from the water while firmly grasping a secure object such as a ladder or piling.
- A reaching assist using a towel or other improvised equipment to extend reach from the deck and in the water while grasping a secure object such as the pool wall.

Instructor's note:
Have participants practice water skills in depths in which they are comfortable and competent. Participants must be carefully supervised in the water.

Assisting a Submerged Victim
BWS, p. 47; S&D, p. 288

Point out that if a drowning victim is lying on the bottom and can be seen, a long reaching device can be used to recover the person. For example, use a shepherd's crook to encircle the victim or a boat hook to snag the victim's clothing. Instruct participants that if victim cannot be seen or reached under water, they will have to direct the lifeguard or rescuers to the victim's position. If possible, sink an object (for example, knotted, weighted beach towels) to the bottom and demonstrate use of the shepherd's crook to recover it. Have participants practice recovering the sunken object with the shepherd's crook.

Throwing Assists
BWS, pp. 49–54; S&D, pp. 288–290

Describe and demonstrate throwing assists. Have all participants practice throwing a variety of devices to victims. Participants who are observing should wear a Coast Guard-approved life jacket when practicing this skill.

Wading Assists
BWS, pp. 52–53; S&D, pp. 289–291

Describe and demonstrate wading assists. Review the techniques for making wading assists in shallow water with a flotation device. Review how to make a wading assist while remaining in contact with a stable object. Have participants practice making wading assists.

Swimming in Clothes and Inflating Clothes for Flotation (20 minutes)
BWS, pp. 37–39; S&D, p. 32

Demonstrate swimming with clothes on and demonstrate how to inflate a shirt by blowing and by splashing. Have participants enter shallow water with clothing over bathing suits and practice the skills listed below under close supervision.

- Swimming (using any combination of strokes that enables them to progress in the water and keep their faces out of the water)
- Inflating shirts by blowing
- Inflating shirts by splashing

Session 3   3 hours

Equipment

- Chalkboard and chalk or flip chart and markers
- *Basic Water Safety* textbook, 1 per participant
- *Boating Safety and Rescues* video (11 minutes) (optional)
- VCR and monitor
- Throw bag or heaving jug
- Extra line
- Sound-signaling device—whistle, horn, or bell
- Visual distress signaling devices—flares or flags for day, flares or electric lights for night
- Anchor
- First aid kit
- Bailing device
- Copies of local, state, and federal boating regulations
- Life jackets, 1 per participant
- *Rescue Breathing and Choking Supplement* for instructor reference
- One or more small craft, such as a rowboat or canoe (optional)
- Basic Water Safety Skills Checklist from Appendix M

Objectives

At the end of this session, participants should be able to—
- Identify the problems and preventive measures associated with exposure to cold water.
- Discuss how to prevent ice emergencies.
- Describe self-rescue procedures for falling through the ice or into cold water.
- Describe measures for preventing and treating hypothermia.
- Describe safe methods for assisting a person in a boating accident.
- Describe how to board and debark a small craft safely.
- Describe how to change positions in a small craft.
- Use the H.E.L.P. and huddle positions.
- Describe how to use an overturned boat for flotation.
- Describe how to reenter and hand-paddle a swamped boat.
- Position a victim for rescue breathing and maintain an open airway on land and in shallow water.

> **Instructor's note:**
> The water practice for boating safety section is optional, depending on the availability of small craft for practice. However, boating safety must be discussed and can be simulated in dry land drills.

Review of Session 2 and Discussion of Objectives (15 minutes)

Use some of the following questions to review Session 2 and introduce Session 3.
- What are signs that a person is in distress in the water?
- What should you do when you see that someone needs help?

- What devices can be used to help someone in trouble in the water?
- Why is it important to talk to a person in trouble in the water?
- How can you maintain your own safety when helping someone else?
- Where should you aim when throwing a rescue device?
- How would you use a support if you were wading out to assist someone?
- What should you remember when making reaching assists?
- What objects can be used for a reaching assist?
- Why is checking water depth before entering the water so important?
- When should you suspect a spinal injury?
- What general rescue procedures apply to all spinal injury rescue techniques?
- When do you use the hip and shoulder support?
- What should you do if you fall into water?
- Why should you keep your clothes on after you fall into cold water?

Discuss the objectives for Session 3.

EXPOSURE TO COLD WATER (20 minutes)
BWS, pp. 58–63; S&D, pp. 38–41

Point out that knowing what to do for someone who falls into cold or icy water is vital because there is very little time to act. The cold very quickly reduces a person's ability to respond. Cite an example of an accident of falling into cold water or falling through ice.

Discuss hypothermia, including what happens when hypothermia occurs. Mention that a victim of hypothermia may become unconscious or may die of heart failure. Explain that the amount of time a person can survive hypothermia without help depends on clothing, age, size, and body type. People with more body fat may survive longer than children or elderly people.

Discuss actions that can help prevent a cold water emergency:
- Have Coast Guard-approved life jackets and rescue devices in boats and around water or ice.
- Wear rain gear or warm clothing in cool weather.
- Don't drink alcohol to warm yourself.
- Carry matches in waterproof container.
- Never go near the water alone.

Discuss cold water self-help survival techniques for falling into cold water with and without a life jacket.

Be sure that the participants understand that even after a person gets out of cold water, danger is not past; it is important to act immediately to avoid hypothermia. Review first aid procedures for helping conscious and unconscious victims.

ICE SAFETY (10 minutes)
BWS, pp. 64–66; S&D, pp. 41–42

Discuss how to tell when ice is safe. Include characteristics of safe ice and conditions that weaken ice. Discuss guidelines for preventing ice emergencies or minimizing their severity.

Explain safe responses to cracking ice:
1. Lie down immediately.
2. Spread arms and legs out to distribute weight evenly.
3. Crawl or roll to safety.

Explain that a standing person puts full weight on one spot, but when a person lies down, a larger area of ice supports that weight. Discuss what to do if you fall through ice. Explain that while a natural response is to climb out, the ice might be weak around the edges and break off. Describe the correct procedures. Discuss safe and unsafe action to take when someone else falls through ice. Remind participants not to go on the ice themselves when making a rescue. Ask participants to identify the assists they would use and why.

BOATING SAFETY (15 minutes)
BWS, pp. 68–78; S&D, pp. 42–49

Point out that United States waterways are second only to highways as the scene of transportation deaths. Determine how many in the class have been on or around small craft (20 feet or less) and ask—
- Have you witnessed any dangerous situations?
- What happened and what were the outcomes?
- What might have caused the situation?
- How could the danger have been prevented?

Describe a boating emergency. Discuss causes and prevention measures. Note courses offered by local organizations. (Examples include the American Red Cross, U.S. Coast Guard Auxiliary, U.S. Power Squadron, U.S. Sailing, American Canoe Association. For more information on these organizations, see Appendix A of *Swimming and Diving.*)

Discuss the dangers of drinking and using drugs while boating. Review safe locations and conditions for boating.

Discuss and display, if possible, the minimum safety equipment for small craft. (See the section, Equipping Your Boat, on page 69 in *Basic Water Safety* or page 43 in *Swimming and Diving.*) If available, give participants local, state, or federal boating requirements or explain how participants can get copies.

Optional Audiovisual

American Red Cross *Boating Safety and Rescues*

FINAL REVIEW (15 minutes)

> **Instructor's note:**
> This is the last review in the Basic Water Safety course. It is placed here so participants can review the material before they change into swimsuits and go to the water activities.

Use the following review questions, and any other review questions you wish, to recap the entire course.
- What safety precautions can help prevent or minimize effects of cold water exposure?
- What should you do if you fall into cold water?
- How can you help someone who has fallen into cold water?
- How can you prevent ice emergencies?
- What should you do if you fall through the ice?
- How can you help someone who has fallen through the ice?
- Why is it important to act very quickly in a cold water or ice emergency?
- How does using alcohol increase the risk of boating accidents?
- Who should wear life jackets when in a boat?
- Under what conditions is it safe to drive or ride in small craft?
- What are the basic navigation "rules" for boating?
- What does it mean to trim a boat, and why is it important?
- Under what conditions would you leave a capsized craft and swim to shore?
- Of the assists you have learned, which can you use from a small craft?

BREAK (15 minutes)

Participants change into swimsuits. Check that participants who are required to wear life jackets for water activities have put them on and fastened them correctly.

H.E.L.P. POSITION AND HUDDLE POSITION (15 minutes)
BWS, p. 61; S&D, p. 42

Wearing a life jacket, explain and demonstrate the H.E.L.P. (Heat Escape Lessening Posture) and huddle positions. Have all participants wear a Coast Guard-approved life jacket and practice the H.E.L.P. and huddle positions in warm, chest-deep water.

Introduction to Rescue Breathing
(25 minutes)
BWS, p. 85; S&D, pp. 300–301

Use this opportunity to encourage participants to take a first aid or CPR course. Guide the participants through the steps of rescue breathing on land. Explain that rescue breathing can be done in shallow water but only with great difficulty, and only if the victim cannot be removed from the water immediately. Encourage participants to take the Emergency Water Safety course to learn how to do rescue breathing in water.

Boating Safety (40 minutes)
BWS, pp. 71–78; S&D, pp. 46–49

> **Instructor's note:**
> Use a small boat or canoe if available for these activities. However, if no small craft is available, the procedures can be explained and demonstrated using whatever props are handy. For example, a beach towel can serve as the boat bottom and a kickboard held on edge as the side of the boat. Simulate the activities in a land drill.

Skills to be learned can be found in Chapters 2 and 13 of *Swimming and Diving.* The following skills are to be included:
- Identifying and naming the main parts of a boat, using a boat or canoe, or a picture or diagram.
- Listing preparations and procedures for boarding and debarking a boat.
- Changing positions in a boat.
- Stating what to do if a boat capsizes or is swamped.
- Reentering a swamped boat.
- Hand-paddling a swamped boat while wearing a life jacket.
- Explaining what to do from a boat to assist a victim in the water.

- Reviewing precautions to take when making an assist from a boat.
- Throwing assist from a boat.

  Demonstrate, then have participants practice—
- Reaching from a boat.
- Throwing a device on a line.
- Helping a victim aboard.

  Refer participants to American Red Cross boating safety textbooks for additional suggestions on safe procedures for small craft.

27 the emergency water safety course

The objective of the American Red Cross Emergency Water Safety course is to help participants become familiar with potential hazards of water activities, to prevent accidents, and to respond effectively if an emergency does occur. The course builds on the goals and shares the objectives of the Basic Water Safety course, but it provides participants with additional skills.

The Emergency Water Safety course is intended for people who know how to swim well and want to know how to respond in an aquatic emergency. These include—

- People who participate in water recreation.
- People who enjoy hunting and fishing.
- Clubs and organizations interested in water activities.
- Police, fire fighters, and emergency personnel who may work around water.
- Scout leaders.
- Industrial workers at water sites.
- Youth groups.
- Young people who wish to build a foundation for future courses in lifeguarding and aquatics.
- Owners of private ponds and swimming pools.

ADMINISTRATIVE NOTES

The following points apply to the Emergency Water Safety course.

Prerequisites

To be eligible for the Emergency Water Safety course, the candidate must present a certificate from Level IV of the American Red Cross Learn to Swim program or successfully pass a skills pretest (see page 206). The candidate must also demonstrate competency in Basic Water Safety skills, including the following sudden immersion skills and water assists:

- Reaching assist
- Throwing assist
- Wading assist
- Survival (face-down) floating

It is strongly recommended that participants complete the Basic Water Safety course before they take the Emergency Water Safety course.

Course Length

This course is designed to be taught in 9 hours or less. This time includes the showing of one video. The course is presented in three 3-hour sessions. The unit on masks, fins, and snorkels at the end of Session 3 is optional depending on the needs of participants and has not been included in the total course times.

Although the Basic Water Safety course is not a prerequisite for this course, the skills taught there are the foundation of the Emergency Water Safety course. If participants have not completed, or have never taken, a Basic Water Safety course, you may have to build more time into the Emergency Water Safety course to teach and review elementary rescue skills and water safety.

Class Size

It is recommended that there be one instructor for every 10 participants in the course. If there are more than 10 participants, there should be a co-instructor or aide. Close supervision is required to ensure effective practice and the safety of participants. Furthermore, if you keep the class reasonably small, you can run sessions more efficiently and you are less likely to exceed the allotted time periods for various activities.

Facilities

The course includes classroom activities requiring dry land space with a writing surface for each participant and water activities requiring a swimming facility such as a pool or lake. For scheduling purposes, it may be necessary to rearrange the sequence of sessions or to devote an entire session to classroom activities and another to water activities. Breaks are scheduled so participants can change into swimsuits and go to the swimming area.

Equipment and Supplies

At the beginning of each session is a list of required equipment and supplies. A master list of equipment for the course can be found in Appendix A. Make sure all the equipment is ready and in working order before you teach the course.

All participants should have a copy of *American Red Cross Basic Water Safety, American Red Cross Emergency Water Safety,* and *American Red Cross Rescue Breathing and Choking Supplement.* As an alternative they may use *American Red Cross Swimming and Diving.*

Testing and Certificates

To be eligible for a course completion certificate, participants must score at least 80 percent on the written test consisting of 25 questions and successfully perform the four combined skills in the water skills test. Participants who pass the final skills test and the written test may receive an *American Red Cross Course Completion Certificate* (Cert. 3413). (For more information on awarding certificates, completing records, and conducting course evaluations, see Chapter 5.)

> **Instructor's note:**
> Exam security is your responsibility. Do not allow participants to see any test materials before you distribute the exam. You should retain both the answer sheets and the exam after the participants take the test. Under certain circumstances, you may administer a retest. If the problem is related to a reading or language difficulty, you may test the participant by reading the questions aloud. Since this should be done without disturbing the other participants, oral tests should not be administered until all other participants have completed the written test.

COURSE ACTIVITIES

Skills Pretest (30 minutes)

If participants do not have a certificate for Level IV of the American Red Cross Learn to Swim program, you must test their ability to do the following:

1. Swim continuously for 5 minutes while performing the front crawl and sidestroke for a minimum of 50 yards each.
2. Jump into deep water, swim approximately four body lengths under water, surface, and tread water for 1 minute.

In addition, participants, must demonstrate their competency in the following Basic Water Safety skills:

1. Make a reaching assist from land by extending one hand.
2. Make a throwing assist using a ring buoy with a line.
3. Make a wading assist using a ring buoy or a rescue tube as a supporting device.

Explanation and Demonstration

Demonstrate each water skill slowly and correctly, with an accompanying explanation, before participants attempt the skill. You may use the suggested audiovisuals to supplement or replace your demonstration.

Water Activities

Safety is an extremely important aspect of practice sessions. Every effort must be made to prevent accidents. All water activities include explanation and demonstration of the skill, followed by participant practice. In general, the participants practice on land, then in shallow water, and then in deep water when it is appropriate.

Practice

Design practice sessions so that each participant has maximum opportunity and ample space for practice. Make sure participants receive feedback on their efforts and offer suggestions for improvement, when necessary.

Organize water activities so participants do not have to enter and leave the water more often than necessary. Becoming chilled can be distracting and can interfere with the learning process.

COURSE OUTLINES

EMERGENCY WATER SAFETY COURSE OUTLINE

SESSION 1

Activity	Approximate Time	Method	References*
Skills pretest	30 minutes	P	
Introduction and discussion of objectives	20 minutes	L/D	
Understanding drowning	10 minutes	L/D	*EWS*, pp. 5–6; *S&D*, p. 287
Water assists	5 minutes	L/D	*EWS*, pp. 7–9
Assignment and break	15 minutes		
Water activities practice: Human chain	15 minutes	Demo/P	*EWS*, pp. 6–7; *S&D*, p. 291
Water entries	20 minutes	Demo/P	*EWS*, pp. 8–9; *S&D, 292*
Positioning	15 minutes	Demo/P	*EWS*, p. 9; *S&D*, p. 293
Tows	50 minutes	Demo/P	*EWS*, pp. 9–13; *S&D*, pp. 298–299
SESSION 1, TOTAL TIME	**3 HOURS**		

* *EWS = Emergency Water Safety*   AV = Audiovisual   D = Discussion   L = Lecture
  S&D = Swimming and Diving   P = Practice   Demo = Demonstration

Emergency Water Safety Course Outline
Session 2

Activity	Approximate Time	Method	References*
Review of Session 1 and discussion of objectives	10 minutes	L/D	
Rescue breathing segment, "What to Do When Breathing Stops"	70 minutes including video	AV	*Supplement*, pp. 1–19 *S&D*, pp. 300–301
Assignment and Break	15 minutes		
Water activities practice: Rescue breathing in shallow and deep water	20 minutes	Demo/P	*S&D*, p. 301
Recovery of submerged victim: Surface diving Swimming under water Recovery	25 minutes	Demo/P	*EWS*, pp. 14–15; *S&D*, p. 299
Escapes	20 minutes	Demo/P	*EWS*, pp. 19–21; *S&D*, 295–297
Removal from water	20 minutes	Demo/P	*EWS*, pp. 15–19; *S&D*, pp. 299–301
SESSION 2, TOTAL TIME	**3 HOURS** (includes 10-minute video)		

* *EWS = Emergency Water Safety*   AV = Audiovisual   D = Discussion   L = Lecture
  S&D = Swimming and Diving   P = Practice   Demo = Demonstration

EMERGENCY WATER SAFETY COURSE OUTLINE

SESSION 3

Activity	Approximate Time	Method	References*
Review of Session 2 and discussion of objectives	5 minutes	L/D	
Spinal injury — Audiovisual: *Spinal Injury Management*	35 minutes, including video	L/AV	*EWS,* pp. 24–32; *S&D,* pp. 302–305
Break	15 minutes		
Water activities practice: Spinal injury management	60 minutes	Demo/P	*EWS,* pp. 33–44; *S&D,* pp. 306–309
Testing			
Skills test	35 minutes	T	
Written test	20 minutes	T	
Evaluation, administration, and closing	10 minutes	L/D	
SESSION 3, TOTAL TIME	**3 HOURS** (includes 25-minute video)		

OPTIONAL SESSION

Activity	Approximate Time	Method	References*
Optional audiovisual: *Snorkeling Skills and Rescue Techniques*	(13 minutes)	AV	
Mask, fins, and snorkel	15 minutes		*EWS,* pp. 49–59
Break	15 minutes		
Water activities practice:			
Mask and snorkel	10 minutes	Demo/P	*EWS,* pp. 51–52, 56–57
Fins	10 minutes	Demo/P	*EWS,* pp. 53–55
Water entries with equipment	10 minutes	Demo/P	*EWS,* pp. 57–58
Swimming with equipment	15 minutes	Demo/P	*EWS,* pp. 58–59
SESSION 3, TOTAL TIME	**3 HOURS** (add 13 minutes for audiovideo)		

* *EWS = Emergency Water Safety*   AV = Audiovisual   D = Discussion   L = Lecture
   S&D = Swimming and Diving   P = Practice   Demo = Demonstration   T = Test

LESSON PLAN

SESSION 1   3 hours

Equipment

- Enrollment and registration materials
- Chalkboard and chalk or flip chart and markers
- *Basic Water Safety* textbook, 1 per participant
- *Emergency Water Safety* textbook, 1 per participant
- Rescue tubes and ring buoys, 1 per every 3 participants

Objectives

At the end of Session 1, participants will be able to describe the difference between an active and passive drowning victim and be able to describe or demonstrate various techniques for assisting or rescuing a passive victim.

SKILLS PRETEST (30 minutes)

If participants do not have a certificate for Level IV of the American Red Cross Learn to Swim program, you must test their ability to do the skills listed on page 206. Anybody who cannot pass the skills pretest may not take part in the course. Suggest that these candidates enroll in a course in the Learn to Swim program.

INTRODUCTIONS AND DISCUSSION OF OBJECTIVES (20 minutes)

Welcome participants and introduce all teaching staff. Briefly point out the role and history of the Red Cross in water safety education. Ask participants to explain briefly their reasons for taking the course and their expectations.

Explain the purpose of the course:
- To help participants become fully familiar with potential hazards of water activities
- To prevent water emergencies
- To respond effectively in an emergency

Emphasize that although participants will learn how to assist passive victims and tired swimmers, *this course does not teach lifeguarding skills.*

Refer those who are interested in a lifeguarding course to the local Red Cross unit.

UNDERSTANDING DROWNING (10 minutes)
EWS, pp. 5–6; S&D, pp. 286–288

Review how to help others: reach, throw, and wade. Lead a discussion that covers the following topics:
- Asphyxiation.
- Description of an active drowning victim.
- Description of a passive drowning victim.

Point out that knowing how to assist a passive victim or a tired swimmer can make the difference between life and death. To perform a water assist you must—
- Be a strong swimmer.
- Have skills acquired through training and practice.
- Be able to judge when to try a water assist and when to get emergency assistance.

Remind participants that in this course they will be learning assists for passive victims. They are not learning lifeguarding skills in this class.

Have participants evaluate the following situation:

> *You are a strong swimmer. You notice that someone who was just thrashing about in the water is now oddly still and floating face down. No lifeguard is nearby.*

Ask participants what factors would influence how they help the victim. Write their ideas on the chalkboard or flip chart.

Discuss the factors to consider in helping someone in an emergency situation:
- Condition of victim, active or passive
- Distance of victim
- Available equipment
- Available lifeguards and bystanders

▶ 210

- Water depth
- Weather and water conditions

Refer back to the situation described above and add any other factors to the list on the chalkboard or flip chart.

Have participants evaluate the next situation:

You are a strong swimmer. You notice that someone about 20 feet from the dock is thrashing about and has a panicked expression. No lifeguard is nearby.

Ask participants what factors influence how to help the person. Emphasize that to assist an active victim, you need strong, well-practiced skills. Remind participants to summon lifeguards or activate the EMS System. Tell them that rescuers must fix (sight) the position of the victim.

WATER ASSISTS (5 minutes)
EWS, pp. 7–9; S&D, pp. 288–293

Discuss using a water assist to help a passive victim and a tired swimmer. Explain that it is important always to use a flotation device while making a rescue. A rescuer must evaluate the situation and know what conditions would make it dangerous to attempt an assist such as:
- Bad weather
- Poor water conditions
- Too great a distance to victim

Remind participants again that the best decision may be for someone to call a lifeguard or activate the EMS System while another person keeps watching the person in trouble to report where the victim was last seen.

ASSIGNMENT

Give the assignment for the next class: Read Chapter 1 in *Emergency Water Safety,* as well as the *American Red Cross Rescue Breathing and Choking Supplement* and review Chapters 1 and 2 in *Basic Water Safety.* As an alternative, students may read pages 88–107 and 286–301 in *American Red Cross Swimming and Diving* and review pages 22–67 and 302–312.

Review the skills to be taught in the water activities.

BREAK (15 minutes)

WATER ACTIVITIES PRACTICE

> **Instructor's note:**
> Use the Emergency Water Safety Skills Checklist in Appendix M to keep a record of participants' progress. A description of the skills can be found in Chapter 13 of *Swimming and Diving.*

HUMAN CHAIN (15 minutes)
EWS, pp. 6–7; S&D, p. 291

Explain that the human chain can be used when enough people are available to help form a chain and when the water is not more than chest-deep or if it is fast moving. Have participants form a human chain.

WATER ENTRIES (20 minutes)
EWS, pp. 8–9; S&D, pp. 292–295

Explain and demonstrate three entries:
- Ease into the water
- Stride-jump entry
- Feet-first entry (compact jump)

Have participants practice each of the these entries.

POSITIONING (15 minutes)
EWS, p. 9; S&D, p. 293

Explain and demonstrate how to swim to a victim and how to move into position of safety to help a passive victim. Have participants walk through positioning on land first, then have participants wearing Coast Guard-approved life jackets position themselves as victims in the water. Have other participants (as rescuers) approach them from different directions and practice moving into a safe position. Reverse victim and rescuer roles.

Tows (50 minutes)
EWS, pp. 9–13; S&D, pp. 289–299

Describe and demonstrate the following tows:
- Wrist tow
- Single armpit tow
- Rescue tube tow

Have participants practice doing all the tows with different partners. Encourage participants to use the practice session to judge the effectiveness of the various tows with victims of different sizes. If necessary, work with participants individually to determine pulls and kicks they can use effectively.

> ***Instructor's note:***
> The collar tow and the technique for changing tows also may be taught if time allows.

SESSION 2   3 hours

Equipment

- *Basic Water Safety* text, 1 per participant
- *Emergency Water Safety* textbook, 1 per participant
- *American Red Cross Rescue Breathing and Choking Supplement,* 1 per participant
- Strongly recommended video: *American Red Cross Adult CPR* or *American Red Cross Community CPR*
- VCR and monitor
- Manikins, 1 per 2 to 3 participants, and manikin cleaning materials (see Appendix K)

Objectives

When they finish this session, participants will be able to describe when rescue breathing is necessary, position a victim for rescue breathing in shallow and deep water, describe how to perform rescue breathing, perform surface dives and swim under water, and remove a victim from the water.

REVIEW OF SESSION 1 AND DISCUSSION OF OBJECTIVES (10 minutes)

Use some of the following questions to review Session 1 and introduce Session 2.
- What factors should you consider when evaluating a water emergency? Why is each factor important?
- What are the steps in a water assist?

- Under what conditions should you NOT try a water assist?
- What are the advantages of a stride-jump entry?
- In what situation would a feet-first entry be a good choice?
- When should you enter the water by easing in?
- How would you position yourself to assist a passive victim?
- Why should towing a victim to safety be attempted only by a strong swimmer?

RESCUE BREATHING
(70 minutes—including a 10-minute video)
Supplement, pp. 1–19; S&D, pp. 300–301

Optional Audiovisual

The segment, "What to Do When Breathing Stops" in *American Red Cross Adult CPR* video or *American Red Cross Community CPR* is optional but strongly recommended because it demonstrates and clarifies rescue breathing. Discuss the EMS system in your community and how to make an emergency telephone call (see *Swimming and Diving,* page 339).

Demonstrate the proper way to decontaminate manikins after each use. (See Appendix K, Manikin Use and Decontamination.)

Introduce rescue breathing practice. Explain that one person will be a victim and one person will be a rescuer. After they practice the skill once, they will change places so that they each have a chance to be a rescuer. Remind them that, when practicing with a partner, they should not make mouth-to-mouth contact and should not give breaths.

Practice on a Partner

Lead participants through a practice as follows:
1. Move participants into a suitable practice area.
2. Assign partners or tell them to choose partners.
3. Tell the victims to lie on their stomachs. Their heads should all be pointed in the same direction, for example, toward the wall or toward the water.
4. Using the steps on pages 300–301 in *Swimming and Diving,* guide the rescuers through the steps for rescue breathing.

After you have completed this practice, have the participants reverse roles. Lead the new rescuers through the same steps.

Practice on a Manikin

Lead participants through a practice as follows:
1. Take the manikins out of their cases. The manikins should be placed on their backs. Tell the participants not to practice "positioning the victim" with a manikin. They should leave the manikins on their backs in order to keep the faces clean. Tell them to check for unresponsiveness and then open the airway.

2. Before participants start practicing on the manikins, demonstrate the correct way to clean the manikin's face each time a different person starts to practice on the manikin.
3. Lead participants through rescue breathing practice as described on pages 300–301 in *Swimming and Diving.*

At the end of practice on a partner or a manikin, check to make sure each participant knows how to do the rescue breathing skills.

ASSIGNMENT

Ask participants to read Chapter 3 in *Emergency Water Safety* and review pages 57–77 in *Basic Water Safety.* As an alternative, they may read page 41 and review pages 38–49 in *Swimming and Diving.*

BREAK (15 minutes)

Participants change into swimsuits.

WATER ACTIVITIES PRACTICE

RESCUE BREATHING IN SHALLOW AND DEEP WATER (20 minutes)
BWS, p. 5; EWS, p. 19; S&D, p. 301

Demonstrate the technique for rescue breathing in shallow water. Have participants practice rescue breathing in shallow water. They should simulate rescue breaths and not make mouth-to-mouth contact.

To help keep the victim's head above the surface of the water, have participants practice using a solid support by holding onto the dock or edge of the pool. Have them practice without the support so they can learn how difficult it is to keep the victim's head above water.

Move participants and victims to deep water and have them practice holding on to the deck or edge of the pool. Supervise this practice very closely.

RECOVERY OF SUBMERGED VICTIM
(25 minutes)
EWS, pp. 14–15; S&D, p. 299

Review the methods of recovering a submerged victim:
- Standing on land or deck, use a reaching device to encircle the victim's body or snag the victim's clothing and pull the victim to the surface.
- If the victim cannot be seen or reached, determine the exact location where victim went under water and direct rescuers to that place.
- Explain how to determine a victim's location and illustrate the technique by using objects in your facility or a chalkboard diagram.

To practice rescue sighting, position participants or floating objects at various locations to represent places where victims submerged. Ask participants to use fixed objects in the surroundings to practice single-rescuer sightings and two-rescuer sightings (also called a cross-bearing).

Surface Diving

Explain the procedures for recovering a submerged victim by surface diving.

Describe the three types of surface dives:
- Feet-first
- Pike
- Tuck

Note that surface diving to recover a victim is best done with mask and fins, if available. The mask enhances visibility, and fins increase speed. Explain that the feet-first dive is best for murky water or unknown water depths. Explain and demonstrate the feet-first surface dive. Explain that the pike dive is best for diving deeply and explain and demonstrate the pike surface dive. Explain and demonstrate the tuck surface dive. Have participants practice all three surface dives.

Swimming Under Water

Explain and demonstrate swimming under water. After a surface dive, level off in a horizontal position under water and swim forward.

Recovery

Use a 10-pound diving brick, other weighted objects, or a training manikin designed for water use to simulate a victim.

Explain and demonstrate how to recover a submerged victim by surface diving at the spot where the victim was last seen. Have participants practice in shoulder-deep water and then in deep water.

ESCAPES (20 minutes)
EWS, pp. 19–21; S&D, pp. 295–297

Discuss and review the guidelines for protecting yourself while making assists, and provide an overview of escape techniques. Have participants walk through the steps of the escapes on land while you check various parts of each skill. Then have participants practice escapes in shallow water before going in deep water.

To ensure safety, instruct participants in the "Let Go!" signal. Three taps anywhere on the body, whether they are taps or light pinches, are standard practice "Let Go!" signals. Discuss, demonstrate, and have participants practice the following defenses:
- Blocking
- Submerging
- Front head-hold escape
- Rear head-hold escape
- Wrist/arm escape

Removal From Water (20 minutes)
EWS, pp. 15–19; S&D, pp. 293–295

Explain and demonstrate methods of removing victims from the water.

- A *shallow water assist* is used for a swimmer who needs some support walking.
- A *drag assist* is used at a sloping beach. It is particularly useful for heavy victims.

- The *lift* is used when it is necessary to get a victim out of the water and onto a dock or pier. Do not use the lift for victims of suspected spinal injury.

Have participants practice removing partners of varying sizes and weights from the water.

Session 3

Equipment

- *Emergency Water Safety* textbook, 1 per participant
- Audiovisual: *Spinal Injury Management*
- Backboard, 1 for every 5 participants
- Rigid cervical collar, 1 for every backboard
- Velcro straps, cravats, or ties for use with backboard
- Pencils
- Written tests answer sheets (photocopy from Appendix N) 1 per participant
- Mask, snorkel, and fins, 1 set per 1 to 3 participants (optional)
- Optional audiovisual: American Red Cross *Snorkeling Skills and Rescue Techniques*
- Mask-defogging solution (optional)

Objectives

At the end of this session, participants will be able to describe the signs of a spinal injury and describe and demonstrate the general rescue procedures for the victim of a suspected spinal injury in the water.

Review of Session 2 (5 minutes)

Use some of the following questions to review Session 2 and introduce Session 3.

- What should you do if a drowning victim lies submerged on the bottom? What if you can't see or reach the victim?
- How can you protect yourself from injury when removing a victim from the water?

- In what situation would a drag assist be useful?
- In what situation would a lift be necessary?
- If you are unable to lift a victim from the water at poolside, what should you do?
- How can you protect yourself from being grabbed by a panicky victim?
- Why is it important to know how to escape from a victim's grasp?
- What are the steps in rescue breathing?
- How do you check for responsiveness if the victim is not moving?
- How do you check for a pulse when you are giving rescue breathing to an adult?

Discuss the objectives for Session 3.

Spinal Injury (35 minutes—including a 25-minute video)
EWS, pp. 24–32; S&D, pp. 302–312

Review with participants how to evaluate a situation and ask participants to think about the situations that could lead to a spinal injury. Review with participants the signs and symptoms of a possible spinal injury.

Explain and discuss the general procedures for handling the victim of a suspected spinal injury in the water. This information can be found in *Swimming and Diving,* page 304.

Optional Audiovisual

American Red Cross *Spinal Injury Management*

BREAK (15 minutes)

Participants change into swimsuits.

WATER ACTIVITIES PRACTICE

SPINAL INJURY MANAGEMENT
(60 minutes)
EWS, pp. 33–44; S&D, pp. 304–312

Hip and Shoulder Support

Explain that this technique is used only in calm,
shallow water for a face-up victim of suspected
spinal injury when no help is immediately available to assist in boarding (placing the victim on a
backboard).
- Demonstrate hip and shoulder support in
  shallow water.
- Have participants practice with partners in
  shallow water.

Head Splint

Explain that this technique is for calm or choppy
water, deep or shallow, for a face-down victim.
Use the head splint to turn the victim face up.
- Explain and demonstrate the head splint.
- Have participants practice with partners in
  shallow water.

Head/Chin Support

Explain that this technique is used in any type or
condition of water for face-up or face-down
victims.
- Explain and demonstrate the head/chin support
  technique.
- Have participants practice the head/chin
  support technique in shallow water.

Boarding Procedures

Explain that these techniques are for moving a
victim onto a backboard after stabilization.
- Explain and demonstrate boarding procedures.
- Have participants practice this procedure with
  a minimum of four people, one at the head and
  three around the board.

Removal From Water

Demonstrate and explain the steps for removing
the backboard from the water to a pool deck or
dock.
- Remind participants that the rescuer at the
  victim's head gives directions.
- Have participants practice removing a boarded
  spinal injury victim from the water.

SKILLS TEST (35 minutes)

Explain the testing procedures. Remind participants that all skills must be performed satisfactorily for the participant to pass the test and the
course. Use the space provided under "Final
Tests" in the Emergency Water Safety Skills
Checklist in Appendix M to check off the test
skills as the participants satisfactorily complete
them.
    Participants must successfully perform all of
the skills listed below:
1. Stride jump to a passive victim in deep water.
   Using a single armpit tow, return the victim to
   the side or dock.
2. Ease into shallow water, swim to a passive
   victim, perform a wrist tow, return to
   shallow water, and position victim for
   rescue breathing.

3. Enter the water, perform a feet-first or a pike surface dive, retrieve brick in 6 to 8 feet of water, and bring it to the surface.
4. Perform the hip and shoulder support technique.

Written Test (20 minutes)

Hand out the written tests and answer sheets from Appendix N. Make sure you have made one copy of each for each participant.
■ Tell the participants not to use their texts or notes and not to talk to other participants when taking the test.
■ Give participants 20 minutes to complete the test.
■ Have them return the tests and answer sheets to you.
■ Correct the test using the answer key in the back of this manual.
■ While you are correcting the tests, have participants complete the Participant Evaluation Form found in Appendix E, or another evaluation used by your local Red Cross unit.

EVALUATION, ADMINISTRATION, AND WRAP-UP (10 minutes)

Review with participants the Emergency Water Safety course objectives and how they have been met. Encourage participants to continue their training by taking other American Red Cross Swimming and Water Safety courses.

Complete the *Course Record* (Form 6418) and return it to your local Red Cross unit with the participant evaluations. Remember when you teach this course the first and fourth times to fill out the Instructor Evaluation Form (Appendix F) and send it to the Red Cross national headquarters.

Issue or mail an *American Red Cross Emergency Water Safety Course Completion Certificate* to participants who scored 80 percent or better on the written test and who demonstrated proficiency in all the required skills.

OPTIONAL SESSION: MASK, FINS, AND SNORKEL (70 minutes)

Equipment

■ *Emergency Water Safety Textbook*, 1 per participant
■ Mask, fins, and snorkel, 1 set for every 1 to 3 participants
■ Optional audiovisual: *Snorkeling Skills and Rescue Techniques* (13 minutes)
■ Mask-defogging solution

Objectives

At the end of this session, participants should be able to—
■ Identify criteria for selecting mask, fins, and snorkel.
■ Put on mask, fins, and snorkel properly.
■ Clear snorkel and mask.
■ Enter water with mask and snorkel using a sit-in entry.
■ Enter water using a stride-jump entry wearing mask, fins, and snorkel.
■ Swim with mask, fins, and snorkel.

Optional audiovisual

Snorkeling Skills and Rescue Techniques

Show the video (13 minutes) or hold a discussion (15 minutes). Point out that mask, fins, and snorkel can be used for added swimming enjoyment, underwater exploration, rescue, and recovery.

Emphasize that swimming with this equipment requires knowledge of each piece of equipment, an understanding of safety guidelines, and plenty of practice. Point out that using the equipment properly and safely will add to swimming enjoyment and help prevent injury.

Discuss the advantage of using mask, fins, and snorkel in rescues:
■ Help in swimming
■ Speed in getting to victim
■ Conservation of energy
■ Additional power to tow victim or recover submerged victim

- Help in keeping suspected spinal injury victim horizontal in deep water
- Help in locating victim under water

Review the safety tips (pages 49–50 in *Emergency Water Safety*) for using mask, fins, and snorkel. Ask participants to explain why each one is important.

BREAK (10 minutes)

Participants change clothes and prepare for water activities.

> **Instructor's note:**
> See the water skills guide at the end of this chapter for the steps of each water skill to be taught and practiced in this session. Use the Emergency Water Safety Skills Checklist in Appendix M to keep a record of participants' progress.

MASK AND SNORKEL (10 minutes)
EWS, pp. 51–53, 56–57

Display a swim mask and point out its features. Note the importance of proper fit. Demonstrate how to test a mask for proper fit and have participants test theirs. Check each participant's mask to be sure of proper fit.

Demonstrate and have participants practice defogging and putting on a mask. In shallow water, demonstrate and have participants practice clearing a mask in an upright position or in a horizontal position.

Explain that mask and ear pressure can result from deep diving and can cause pain and possible injury. Demonstrate and have participants practice equalizing mask pressure.

Discuss the function and features of a snorkel, using one or more snorkels for illustration. Demonstrate and have participants practice putting on and breathing through a snorkel in chest-deep water. Explain that getting water in the snorkel is common, both from diving and from splashing at the surface.

Demonstrate and have participants practice flooding and emptying a snorkel in chest-deep water.

FINS (10 minutes)
EWS, pp. 53–55

Discuss types of fins and proper fit, using a pair of fins for illustration. Demonstrate and have participants practice putting on and walking backward with fins on land and in water.

Demonstrate and have participants practice a modified flutter kick with fins. Demonstrate and have participants practice the dolphin kick with fins. Tell them to keep fins under water to maximize propulsion.

WATER ENTRIES WITH EQUIPMENT (10 minutes)
EWS, pp. 57–59

Discuss how to enter the water wearing a mask, snorkel, and fins. Explain that the sit-in entry can be done safely from a height no greater than one foot above the water. Demonstrate without fins a sit-in entry from a low surface.

Explain and demonstrate the stride-jump entry. Have participants practice the sit-in entry without fins and the stride-jump entry with fins.

SWIMMING WITH EQUIPMENT (15 minutes)
EWS, pp. 58–59

Demonstrate swimming with equipment. Demonstrate a pike surface dive, swim, and resurface using mask, fins, and snorkel.

Have participants practice the following routine:
1. Enter water.
2. Swim to designated point.
3. Do pike surface dive.
4. Return to surface.
5. Swim back to starting point.

Using a weighted object as the victim, review, demonstrate, and have the participants practice the procedures for recovering a submerged victim by surface diving. Review tows and have participants practice towing a victim.

REVIEW

Review and summarize the key points of this session by asking some of the following questions:

- Why is it important to swim with companions?
- How can you check for proper fit of a mask?
- What is in a full set of equipment for diving in open water areas?
- What is the purpose of clearing a mask?
- What should you do if your snorkel floods?
- What precautions should you take before resurfacing?

Since this section is optional, you will not need to test participants on its content.

WATER SKILLS GUIDE

Clearing Mask

1. In shallow water, submerge and flood mask by briefly lifting an edge or pulling mask away from face.
2. From vertical position, place palms across top of mask and firmly apply pressure against forehead. Tilt head back and exhale forcefully through nose, forcing water out bottom of mask.
3. From face-down horizontal position, turn head to one side, apply firm pressure on high side of mask, exhale forcefully through nose, forcing water out bottom of mask.

Equalizing Pressure (Mask and Ear)

1. Mask pressure: Submerge and exhale through nose.
2. Ear pressure: Place thumb against bottom of mask, press mask against face, and exhale through nose. Swallow and move jaws.

Sit-In Entry

1. Stand at edge of pool with back toward water, heels at edge.
2. Hold mask and snorkel securely against face with one hand. Keep elbow against ribs, other arm extended down by side.
3. Tuck chin and bend into sitting position. Lean back and sit in water.

Stride-Jump Entry

1. Hold mask firmly in place with one hand covering faceplate and elbow close to chest, other arm extended at side.
2. Step out with a long stride over water leaning slightly forward.
3. When fins touch water, bring legs together with toes pointed.
4. Keep head and shoulders above water.

■ the water safety instructor aide course

training water safety instructor aides

28 the water safety instructor aide course

The purpose of the Water Safety Instructor Aide course is to provide training for individuals who wish to assist Water Safety Instructors in conducting American Red Cross Swimming and Water Safety courses. The Water Safety Instructor Aide course also provides an excellent opportunity for lifeguards who do not meet the minimum age requirement for the Water Safety Instructor course but who would like to further their water safety training.

Water Safety Instructor Aides receive credit for the volunteer hours they spend in Swimming and Water Safety courses. This information is included on the *Course Record* each time an aide assists with a course, and the local Red Cross unit keeps a record of the aide's contribution.

Do not limit yourself to recruiting only youths to be Water Safety Instructor Aides. Older adults can be very reliable and competent aides. Their lifelong experiences can contribute to the success of your Swimming and Water Safety program—especially with courses for adults.

Training Options

You can train Water Safety Instructor Aides in two ways. The Water Safety Instructor Aide course is designed for 6–10 aide candidates and is primarily for training Water Safety Instructor Aides for an upcoming season or for a specific program. The apprenticeship program can be used to train one or two aides at a time, as needed.

OBJECTIVES OF WATER SAFETY INSTRUCTOR AIDE TRAINING

Regardless of the method used, training should enable aide candidates to understand the roles and responsibilities of a Water Safety Instructor Aide. This includes an understanding of the clerical, instructional, supervisory, and maintenance duties of a Water Safety Instructor Aide.

ADMINISTRATIVE NOTES

The following points apply to the Water Safety Instructor Aide training:

Prerequisites

Individuals who are 10 years of age or older who exhibit a strong sense of maturity and responsibility are eligible to be trained as Water Safety Instructor Aides. In addition, aide candidates must be able to demonstrate all the skills listed as completion requirements for Level IV of the American Red Cross Learn to Swim program.

It is recommended that prospective aide candidates complete Level IV of the Learn to Swim program before they begin their training. You may allow aide candidates who do not meet Level IV proficiency to continue in the Water Safety Instructor Aide course. However, you should advise them that their responsibilities as aides will be limited. Such aide candidates may have more success in the apprenticeship program, which allows more individual counseling and flexibility.

Course Length

This course is designed to be taught in a minimum of 12 hours. The basic course content is presented in four sessions of 2½ hours each and a fifth session of 2 hours. These sessions cover material and skills found in Levels I–V of the Learn to Swim program. Two optional sessions of 2 hours each may also be taken by aide candidates who wish to assist in Level VI and Level VII courses. Each session includes a classroom discussion followed by a short break. You demonstrate and explain aquatic and safety skills or show a video and then aide candidates practice them.

Class Size

It is recommended that there be one instructor for every 10 aide candidates in the course. If the class has more than 10 aide candidates, there should be a co-instructor. Close supervision is required to ensure effective practice and the safety of participants. Furthermore, you can run a class more efficiently if you keep the class reasonably small, and you are less likely to exceed the allotted time periods for various activities. If you have fewer than six aide candidates, consider conducting an apprenticeship program.

Facilities

The course includes classroom activities requiring dry land space with a writing surface for each person and water activities requiring a swimming facility such as a pool or lake. For scheduling purposes, it may be necessary to rearrange the sequence of sessions or to devote an entire session to classroom activities and another to water activities. Breaks are short, so advise aide candidates to come to the sessions with their swimsuits on, so they are ready for the practice sessions.

Equipment and Supplies

In Appendix A is a list of required equipment and supplies. Make sure all the equipment is ready and in working order before you teach the course.

Evaluation

To complete the course successfully, aide candidates must—
■ Attend and participate enthusiastically in all sessions.
■ Be able to correctly demonstrate the swimming and safety skills. (Ideally, aide candidates will be able to demonstrate all the skills through Level V. If they are only able to demonstrate skills at a lower level, that should be noted on their *Aide Certificate.)*
■ Complete the Water Safety Instructor Aide test in Appendix Q. *(Note:* Aide candidates need

not score a certain grade on the test. It is offered as a review tool for the course.)

Apprenticeship Program

In an apprenticeship program, you cover the material appropriate for the course(s) in the American Red Cross Learn to Swim program with which the aides will be assisting. Apprenticeship training also includes a discussion of—
■ Course objectives, both content and skill
■ Course materials and their use
■ The role of the aide in assisting with practice sessions
■ Responsibilities of the instructor and aide

During the apprenticeship, you should plan time to help the aide candidates improve their skills. Provide opportunities for the aide candidates to observe successful Water Safety Instructors and other Water Safety Instructor Aides.

Certificates

Aide candidates who successfully complete the Water Safety Instructor Aide course or an apprenticeship program are eligible to receive an *Aide Certificate* (Cert. 3003). They may then assist Water Safety Instructors in conducting the courses for which they are trained. Aide candidates may also fulfill the course requirements for Level V of the Learn to Swim program. Those aide candidates are eligible to receive a certificate for Level V.

Complete the certificates accurately. Be sure to indicate the level(s) of the American Red Cross Learn to Swim program with which the aide may assist. Aides who wish to assist with Levels VI and VII of the Learn to Swim program must also demonstrate swimming proficiency at the corresponding level.

When the Water Safety Instructor Aides have finished their training, thank them for participating and urge them to take active roles in the American Red Cross Swimming and Water Safety program. Encourage them to participate in instructor courses when they are eligible.

Reporting

If you conducted a course, enter "Water Safety Instructor Aide" as the course name on the *Course Record* (Form 6418), then turn it in promptly to your local Red Cross unit. (For more information on awarding certificates, completing records, and conducting course evaluations, see Chapter 5.)

COURSE MATERIALS

Participant's Materials

Each aide candidate will need the following:
- *American Red Cross Swimming and Diving* (Stock No. 652000)
- Notebook and pencil
- Swimsuit and towel (for every session)
- Written test and answer sheet

Instructor's Materials and Equipment

- American Red Cross Identification
- *American Red Cross Swimming and Diving* (Stock No. 652000)
- This instructor's manual
- *American Red Cross Instructor Candidate Training Participant's Manual* (Stock No. 329741)
- *Course Record* (Form 6418)
- Water Safety Instructor Aide Candidate Evaluation Form, (Appendix O), one per participant
- The following American Red Cross videos are recommended:
  - *Swimming and Diving Skills* (Stock No. 652005)
  - *Selected Aquatics* (Stock No. 321895)
  - *Instructor Candidate Training* (Stock No. 329740) or *General Orientation* (Stock No. 321867)
  - *American Red Cross Adult CPR* (Stock No. 329130)
- Half-inch videocassette recorder (VCR) and monitor, if you show videos
- Shepherd's crook and/or reaching pole
- Ring buoys
- Rescue tubes
- Diving brick
- Coast Guard-approved life jackets of appropriate sizes
- *American Red Cross Aquatics* brochure, one per participant
- *Aide Certificates* (Cert. 3003), one per participant

ROLE AND RESPONSIBILITIES OF WATER SAFETY INSTRUCTOR AIDES

Be sure the aide candidates understand that they play a valuable role in the instructional process. They need to work cooperatively with the lead instructor to ensure that participants receive a positive and safe learning experience. Water Safety Instructor Aides have a responsibility to uphold the standards of the American Red Cross Learn to Swim program and to represent the American Red Cross in a positive manner at all times.

Water Safety Instructor Aides may assist Water Safety Instructors in several ways:
- **Clerical**. Aides can prepare class attendance rolls, call the roll at class time, check participants in and out of the facility, and update swimming skills checklists.
- **Supervisory**. Aides can help maintain order in dressing rooms, shower rooms, and while waiting for lessons to start. They can assign partners for practice sessions, assist with general class control, and act as safety monitors.
- **Instructional**. Because of their swimming ability and water safety training, aides can be especially helpful in assisting with courses by demonstrating skills, assisting participants who need individual assistance, and conducting many aspects of practice sessions under the supervision of the instructor.
- **Maintenance**. Aides can be helpful in distributing, collecting, and storing equipment and supplies. In addition, they can help minimize or remove hazards in and around the swimming areas.

Course Outlines

Water Safety Instructor Aide Course Outline

Session 1

Activity	Approximate Time	Method	Resources*
Introductions and registration	10 minutes	L	
Objectives of Water Safety Instructor Aide training	10 minutes	L/D	*IM*, p. 223
Duties and responsibilities of a Water Safety Instructor Aide	15 minutes	L/D	*IM*, p. 225
Overview of the American Red Cross Learn to Swim program	20 minutes	L/D	*IM*, pp. 1–15
Video: *Swimming and Diving Skills*	20 minutes	AV	Segments relevant to Levels I and II
Break	5 minutes		
Skills pretest (course requirements for Level IV)	20 minutes	T	*IM*, pp. 102–103
Demonstration of Level I and II skills	30 minutes	Demo	*IM*, pp. 96–99
Practice of Level I and II skills. Aide candidates practice teach. Instructor helps aide candidates learn to recognize common errors and to provide corrective feedback.	15 minutes	P	
Closing	5 minutes	L/D	
Session 1, Total Time	**2½ hours**		

*IM = Instructor's Manual AV = Audiovisual D = Discussion T = Test
L = Lecture P = Practice Demo = Demonstration

WATER SAFETY INSTRUCTOR AIDE COURSE OUTLINE

SESSION 2

Activity	Approximate Time	Method	Resources*
Review of Session 1	5 minutes	L	
Role of the Water Safety Instructor Aide and relationship to the Water Safety Instructor	5 minutes	L/D	*IM*, p. 225
Video: *Swimming and Diving Skills*	30 minutes	AV	Segments relevant to Levels III and IV
Break	5 minutes		
Demonstration of Level III skills	15 minutes	Demo	*IM*, pp. 100–101
Practice of Level III skills. Aide candidates practice teach. Instructor helps aide candidates learn to recognize common errors and to provide corrective feedback.	40 minutes	P	
Demonstration of Level IV skills	10 minutes	Demo	*IM*, pp. 102–103
Practice of Level IV skills. Aide candidates practice teach. Instructor helps aide candidates learn to recognize common errors and to provide corrective feedback.	35 minutes	P	
Closing	5 minutes	L/D	
SESSION 2, TOTAL TIME	**$2^1/_2$ HOURS**		

*IM = Instructor's Manual   AV = Audiovisual   D = Discussion
  L = Lecture   P = Practice   Demo = Demonstration

Water Safety Instructor Aide Course Outline

Session 3

Activity	Approximate Time	Method	Resources*
Review of Session 2	5 minutes	L	
Class formations and teaching progressions	20 minutes	L/D	*IM*, pp. 47–50, 117–133
Video: *Swimming and Diving Skills*	15 minutes	AV	Segments relevant to Level V
Break	5 minutes		
Demonstration of Level V skills	15 minutes	Demo	*IM*, p. 104–105
Practice of Level V skills. Aide candidates practice teach. Instructor helps aide candidates learn to recognize common errors and to provide corrective feedback.	45 minutes	P	
Evaluation of aide candidates' Level V skills. Remediation as needed	40 minutes	T	
Closing	5 minutes	L/D	
Session 3, Total Time	**2½ hours**		

*IM = *Instructor's Manual* AV = Audiovisual D = Discussion T = Test
L = Lecture P = Practice Demo = Demonstration

Water Safety Instructor Aide Course Outline

Session 4

Activity	Approximate Time	Method	Resources*
Review of Session 3	5 minutes	L	
Emergency action plans	10 minutes	L/D	*IM*, p. 12; *S&D*, p. 27
General safety rules and facility safety rules	15 minutes	L/D	*IM*, p. 12; *S&D*, p. 27, copy of local rules
Demonstration of rescue breathing or video on rescue breathing	15 minutes	Demo/ AV	*S&D*, pp. 300–301 Segment from *Adult CPR*
Practice of rescue breathing (without mouth-to-mouth contact)	25 minutes	P	
Video on nonswimming rescues	10 minutes	AV	Segment from *Selected Aquatics*
Break	5 minute		
Demonstration and practice of Level I–V safety skills	60 minutes	Demo/P	*IM*, pp. 96–105
Closing	5 minutes	L/D	
Session 4, Total Time	**$2^{1}/_{2}$ hours**		

IM = Instructor's Manual   AV = Audiovisual   D = Discussion   L = Lecture
S&D = Swimming and Diving   P = Practice   Demo = Demonstration

WATER SAFETY INSTRUCTOR AIDE COURSE OUTLINE

SESSION 5

Activity	Approximate Time	Method	Resources*
Review of Session 4	5 minutes	L	
Water games as teaching tool	10 minutes	L/D	*IM*, pp. 173–184
Demonstration and playing of several water games	35 minutes	Demo/P	*IM*, pp. 174–184
Break	5 minutes		
Review of role and responsibilities of a Water Safety Instructor Aide	10 minutes	L	*IM*, p. 225
Representing the American Red Cross	10 minutes	L/D	*IM*, pp. 4; 225; ICT*, pp. 101–104
Video: *"Behind the Headlines"*	10 minutes	AV	Segment from *Instructor Candidate Training* or *General Orientation*
Final test and review	20 minutes	T	Appendix Q
Discussion of other leadership opportunities in the Swimming and Water Safety Program	10 minutes	L/D	*IM*, pp. 4; 225
Certification and evaluation	5 minutes	L/D	*Aide Certificates*
SESSION 5, TOTAL TIME	**2 HOURS**		

IM = Instructor's Manual   AV = Audiovisual   D = Discussion   L = Lecture
ICT = Instructor Candidate   P = Practice   Demo = Demonstration   T = Test
     Training Participants
     Manual

WATER SAFETY INSTRUCTOR AIDE COURSE OUTLINE

OPTIONAL SESSION 6

Activity	Approximate Time	Method	Resources*
Review of Session 5 or introduction	5 minutes	L	
Purpose and objectives of Level VI	10 minutes	L/D	*IM*, p. 94
Video: *Swimming and Diving Skills*	25 minutes	AV	Segments relevant to Level VI
Break	5 minutes		
Demonstration of Level VI skills	15 minutes	Demo	*IM*, pp. 106–107
Practice of Level VI skills. Aide candidates practice teach. Instructor helps aide candidates learn to recognize common errors and to provide corrective feedback.	60 minutes	P	
Evaluation of aide candidates' Level VI skills. Remediation as needed.	25 minutes	T	
Certification and closing	5 minutes	L/D	*Aide Certificates*
SESSION 6, TOTAL TIME	**$2^{1}/_{2}$ HOURS**		

*IM = *Instructor's Manual* AV = Audiovisual D = Discussion T = Test
L = Lecture   P = Practice   Demo = Demonstration

WATER SAFETY INSTRUCTOR AIDE COURSE OUTLINE

OPTIONAL SESSION 7

Activity	Approximate Time	Method	Resources*
Review of Session 6 or introduction	5 minutes	L	
Purpose and objectives of Level VII	10 minutes	L/D	*IM*, p. 95
Video: *Swimming and Diving Skills*	15 minutes	AV	Segments relevant to Level VII
Break	15 minutes		
Demonstration of Level VII skills	15 minutes	Demo	*IM*, pp. 108–109
Practice of Level VII skills. Aide candidates practice teach. Instructor helps aide candidates learn to recognize common errors and to provide corrective feedback.	60 minutes	P	
Evaluation of aide candidates' Level VII skills. Remediation as needed.	25 minutes	T	
Certification and closing	5 minutes	L/D	*Aide Certificates*
SESSION 7, TOTAL TIME	$2\frac{1}{2}$ **HOURS**		

IM = Instructor's Manual   AV = Audiovisual   D = Discussion   T = Test
L = Lecture   P = Practice   Demo = Demonstration

appendixes

EQUIPMENT AND SUPPLIES CHECKLISTS

AMERICAN RED CROSS INFANT AND PRESCHOOL AQUATICS PROGRAM

Instructor Materials (applies to all three levels)

- ❏ *American Red Cross Swimming and Diving* (Stock No. 652000)
- ❏ Water Safety Instructor Course Evaluation (Appendix F)

Supplies Required for Participants

- ❏ Coast Guard-approved life jackets in good condition, one per participant (appropriately sized)
- ❏ Swimsuit and towel
- ❏ Parent Course Evaluation (Appendix E), one per parent
- ❏ Certificates (Cert. 3400), one per child

Recommended Materials for Parents

- ❏ *American Red Cross Infant and Preschool Aquatic Program Parent's Guide*
- ❏ *Waddles Presents AQUACKtic Safety*
- ❏ Appropriate facility handouts
- ❏ Ancillary materials
- ❏ American Red Cross Aquatics brochure

Recommended Video

- ❏ American Red Cross *Infant and Preschool Aquatic Program* video (Stock No. 329322), "A Good Beginning" segment
- ❏ Half-inch videocassette recorder (VCR) and monitor

AMERICAN RED CROSS LEARN TO SWIM PROGRAM

Instructor Materials

❒ *American Red Cross Swimming and Diving* (Stock No. 652000)
❒ *Swimming and Diving Skills* video (Stock No. 652005) (optional)
❒ VCR and monitor (optional)
❒ American Red Cross *Swimming and Diving Wall Charts* (Stock No. 652007) (optional)
❒ Participant Course Evaluation (Appendix E), one per participant
❒ Water Safety Instructor Course Evaluation (Appendix F)
❒ Certificates, one per participant
  ❒ Level I (Cert. 653431)
  ❒ Level II (Cert. 653432)
  ❒ Level III (Cert. 653433)
  ❒ Level IV (Cert. 653434)
  ❒ Level V (Cert. 653435)
  ❒ Level VI (Cert. 653436)
  ❒ Level VII (Cert. 653437)

Recommended Materials for Participants

Level I
❒ Coast Guard-approved life jackets, one per participant (appropriately sized)

Level II
❒ Coast Guard-approved life jackets, one per participant (appropriately sized)
❒ Shepherd's crook and/or reaching pole
❒ Kickboards or other flotation devices (optional)
❒ Optional videos (for rescue breathing segment)
  ❒ *American Red Cross First Aid—Responding to Emergencies*
  ❒ *American Red Cross Adult CPR*
  ❒ *American Red Cross CPR: Infant and Child*
  ❒ *American Red Cross Community CPR*
❒ VCR and monitor

Level III
❒ Coast Guard-approved life jackets, one per participant (appropriately sized)
❒ Kickboards or other flotation devices (optional)
❒ Manikins to teach rescue breathing (optional)

Level IV
❒ Kickboards or other flotation devices (optional)
❒ Manikins to teach rescue breathing (optional)
❒ Optional videos (for CPR segment)
  ❒ *American Red Cross First Aid—Responding to Emergencies*
  ❒ *American Red Cross Adult CPR*
  ❒ *American Red Cross CPR: Infant and Child*
  ❒ *American Red Cross Community CPR*
❒ VCR and monitor (optional)

Level V
❒ Kickboards or other flotation devices (optional)

Level VI
❒ Kickboards or other flotation devices (optional)
❒ Equipment for throwing rescues, such as rescue tubes, ring buoys, a heaving line, or a throw bag

Level VII
❒ Rescue tube or other device for in-water rescue
❒ Diving Brick
❒ Backboard
❒ Safety devices listed for the Basic Water Safety course (see page 237)

Basic Water Safety

Instructor Materials

- [ ] *American Red Cross Swimming and Diving* (Stock No. 652000)
- [ ] Enrollment and registration materials
- [ ] Basic Water Safety Skills Checklist (Appendix H)
- [ ] Chalkboard and chalk or flip chart and markers
- [ ] VCR and monitor
- [ ] 5 different types of lifejackets or PFDs for display
- [ ] Rescue tubes and ring buoys, 1 for every 3 to 4 participants
- [ ] Shepherd's crook or reaching pole
- [ ] Heaving line
- [ ] Throw bag
- [ ] Improvised reaching assist equipment
- [ ] Water Safety Instructor Course Evaluation (Appendix F)
- [ ] Recommended video
  - [ ] *Spinal Injury Management* (Stock No. 329328) 25 minutes
- [ ] Boating Safety Equipment
  - [ ] Sound-signaling device—whistle, horn, or bell
  - [ ] Visual distress signaling devices—flares or flags for daytime, flares or electric lights for nighttime
  - [ ] Anchor
  - [ ] Extra line
  - [ ] Throw bag
  - [ ] First aid kit
  - [ ] Bailing device
- [ ] Copies of federal, state, and local boating regulations
- [ ] One or more small craft (under 16 feet in length) such as a row boat or canoe (optional)
- [ ] Optional videos
  - [ ] *Selected Aquatics* (Stock No. 321895) 47 minutes—a compilation into a single video of the following five water safety films— *Snorkeling Skills and Rescue Techniques, Survival Swimming, Nonswimming Rescues* (also available as a separate video—7 minutes) (Stock No. 321650), *Preventive Lifeguarding,* and *Boating Safety and Rescues.*
  - [ ] *Water: The Deceptive Power* (Stock No. 329475) 30 minutes
  - [ ] *Home Pool Safety: It Only Takes a Minute* (Stock No. 329474) 20 minutes

Supplies Required for Participants

- [ ] *American Red Cross Basic Water Safety Textbook* (Stock No. 329312) or *American Red Cross Swimming and Diving* (Stock No. 652000)
- [ ] Well-fitting Coast Guard-approved life jackets, 1 per participant
- [ ] Clothing to wear in water: long-sleeved shirts and pants
- [ ] Notebook and pen or pencil
- [ ] Swimsuit and towel for every session
- [ ] Participant Course Evaluation (Appendix E), one per participant
- [ ] Basic Water Safety course participation certificate (Cert. 3411), one per participant

EMERGENCY WATER SAFETY

Instructor Materials

❏ *American Red Cross Swimming and Diving* (Stock No. 652000)
❏ Enrollment and registration materials
❏ Emergency Water Safety Skills Checklist (Appendix H)
❏ Chalkboard and chalk or flip chart and markers
❏ 5 different types of lifejackets or PFDs for display
❏ 10-pound diving brick
❏ Adult manikins, 1 for every 2 to 3 participants
❏ Extra manikin lungs if appropriate
❏ Manikin decontamination solution: one-quarter cup liquid household chlorine bleach per gallon of tap water. The solution must be made fresh just prior to each class and discarded after use.
❏ Clean gauze pads (4" x 4"), a baby bottle brush, soap and water, basins or buckets, nonsterile disposable gloves, and other supplies recommended by the manufacturer
❏ Backboard, 1 for every 5 participants
❏ Rigid cervical collar, 1 for every backboard
❏ Velcro straps, cravats, or ties for use with backboard
❏ Written tests and answer sheets, 1 per participant
❏ Mask, fins, and snorkel (optional), 1 set per every 2 to 3 participants
❏ Mask-defogging solution (optional)
❏ Water Safety Instructor Course Evaluation (Appendix F)
❏ Recommended videos
  ❏ "Rescue Breathing" segment of *American Red Cross Adult CPR* (Stock No. 329130) or of *American Red Cross Community CPR* (Stock No. 329371) 10 minutes
  ❏ *Spinal Injury Management* (Stock No. 329328) 25 minutes
❏ VCR and monitor
❏ Optional Videos
  ❏ *Selected Aquatics* (Stock No. 321895) 47 minutes— a compilation into a single video of the following five water safety films— *Snorkeling Skills and Rescue Techniques, Survival Swimming, Nonswimming Rescues* (also available as a separate video—7 minutes) (Stock No. 321650), *Preventive Lifeguarding*, and *Boating Safety and Rescues.*
  ❏ *Margin for Error* (Stock No. 321748) 21 minutes
  ❏ *Uncalculated Risk* (Stock No. 321752) 15 minutes

Supplies Required for Participants

❏ *American Red Cross Basic Water Safety Textbook* (Stock No. 329312), *American Red Cross Emergency Water Safety Textbook* (Stock No. 329313), and *American Red Cross Rescue Breathing and Choking Supplement* (Stock No. 329286)

or

❏ *American Red Cross Swimming and Diving* (Stock No. 652000)
❏ Notebook and pen or pencil
❏ Swimsuit and towel for every session
❏ Participant Course Evaluation (Appendix E), one per participant
❏ Emergency Water Safety course completion certificate (Cert. No. 3413), one per participant

Water Safety Instructor Aide Course

Instructor Materials

❏ American Red Cross Identification
❏ *American Red Cross Swimming and Diving* (Stock No. 652000)
❏ *American Red Cross Instructor Candidate Training Participant's Manual* (Stock No. 329741)
❏ Water Safety Instructor Course Evaluation (Appendix F)
❏ Water Safety Instructor Aide Candidate Evaluation Form (Appendix O), 1 per participant
❏ Recommended Videos
  ❏ *Swimming and Diving Skills* (Stock No. 652005)
  ❏ *Selected Aquatics* (Stock No. 321895) 47 minutes— a compilation into a single video of the following five water safety films— *Snorkeling Skills and Rescue Techniques, Survival Swimming, Nonswimming Rescues* (also available as a separate video—7 minutes) (Stock No. 321650), *Preventive Lifeguarding,* and *Boating Safety and Rescues.*

  ❏ *Instructor Candidate Training* (Stock No. 329740) or *General Orientation* (Stock No. 321867)
  ❏ *American Red Cross Adult CPR* (Stock No. 329130)
❏ VCR and Monitor, if you show videos
❏ Shepherd's crook and/or reaching pole
❏ Ring Buoys
❏ Rescue tubes
❏ Diving Brick
❏ Coast Guard-approved life jackets, one per participant (appropriately sized)
❏ American Red Cross Aquatics brochure, one per participant
❏ *Instructor Aide Certificates* (Cert No. 3003), one per participant

ADDITIONAL INSTRUCTOR REFERENCES

Depending on the course(s) you teach, you may also find it useful to consult the lists of audio-visuals and publications on page 7.

Also, consider the following:

On Drowning (1970) 17 minutes
The Reason People Drown (1988) 25 minutes

Available for purchase from:

Water Safety, Inc.
3 Boulder Brae Lane
Larchmont, New York 10538
(914) 834-7536

The Drowning Machine (1981) 20 minutes

Available for purchase from:

Hornbein Productions
106 Boalsburg Pike, P.O. Box 909
Lemont, PA 16851
(814) 234-7886

PERFORMANCE STANDARDS

The information in this appendix is provided for use by Red Cross instructors to evaluate student performances for each of the basic strokes and for each level in which the strokes appear.

Within the context of acceptable performance, instructors must consider the individual differences of students and are reminded that strokes are adapted to the individual.

In reference to the charts, a standard of performance for a skill that is acceptable at one level is acceptable for all lower levels unless otherwise stated.

The criteria are to be used for the following purposes.

1. To determine which course a student is prepared to take.
2. To evaluate the acceptability of performance of the strokes, and their components, in the course in which the students are enrolled.

FRONT CRAWL

Component	Level II	Level III	Level IV	Level V	Level VI
Body Position		Body inclined less than 45° Side-to-side motion acceptable	Body inclined less than 30° No side-to-side motion	Body inclined less than 15°	
Arms		Underwater recovery acceptable Catch may be inside or outside of shoulder Pull must extend to waist Straight arm pull acceptable	Straight arm recovery above water acceptable Catch must be in front of shoulder Pull extends past waist Bent arm pull required	Elbow high during recovery Hand enters index finger first Arm fully extended at finish of pull Arms pull in "S" pattern	Wrist and hand relaxed during recovery Arm fully extended at catch Hand accelerates at finish
Kick	Alternating up-and-down motion Any position of hips and knees	Bicycling action from knees not acceptable Knees bent on downbeat Feet break surface of water	Legs nearly straight during upbeat Feet slightly pigeon-toed	Emphasis on downbeat Relaxed feet with floppy ankles	Continuous fluid motion of hip, knee, and ankle
Breathing/Timing		Breathing as necessary Head lift during breathing acceptable Face in water Any timing of arms and legs	Exhale under water Breathe to side, occasional lift acceptable Arms alternate, but may hesitate during breathing	Head lift not acceptable during breathing Continuous arm motion in time with breathing	Rhythmic pattern relating arm stroke to kick

BACK CRAWL

Component	Level II	Level III	Level IV	Level V	Level VI
Body Position/Motion		Body inclined less than 45° Lack of body roll is acceptable	Body inclined less than 30° Body roll required Side-to-side movement of head acceptable	Body nearly horizontal No side-to-side movement of head	
Arms		Alternating arm recovery Hand enters water in line with head Straight arm pull acceptable	Bent arm recovery acceptable Hand enters water in line with shoulder Occasional straight arm pull acceptable	Straight arm recovery Hand enters water just outside shoulder Elbow bent during pull	Thumb exits water first Hand enters water, little finger first, just outside shoulder Hand sweeps in S-shaped pattern
Kick	Alternating up-and-down motion Any position of hips and knees	Bicycling action from knees not acceptable Feet break surface of water Knees bent on upbeat	Feet slightly pigeon-toed Legs nearly straight on downbeat	Relaxed feet with floppy ankles Emphasis on upbeat	Fluid motion of hip, knee, and ankle
Breathing/Timing			Any regular breathing pattern acceptable Arms may hesitate before recovery	Exhale during power phase, inhale during recovery of the same arm Opposition rhythm of arms	Rhythmic pattern of arm stroke to kick

ELEMENTARY BACKSTROKE

Component	Level III	Level IV	Level V	Level VI
Body Position		Chin tucked, ears may be out of water Body inclined less than 30°	Slight chin tuck, ears near or below the surface Legs may separate during glide	Chin up, ears in water Body streamlined during glide
Arms		"Winging" motion recovery acceptable Arms may extend below shoulder, elbows may be bent Pull finishes short of waist	Arms recover close to body to a position near armpits Arms extended at shoulder level, elbows may be bent Arms almost fully extended during glide	Recovery not to exceed armpits, fingertips lead arm extension Arms extend no further than top of head, arms nearly straight at beginning of power phase Arms extend along body and hands touch thighs during glide
Kick	Hips may bend up to 45° Knees may be outside feet during power phase Ankles flexed throughout power phase Occasional scissors kick acceptable	Hips may not bend beyond 30° Feet outside knees during power phase Scissors kick not acceptable		
Breathing and Timing		Breathing at any time Arms and legs may recover at same time Occasional deviation from symmetrical movements	Inhale during recovery, exhale anytime Arms begin recovery before legs Arms and legs pull simultaneously	Inhale during recovery, exhale during power phase Symmetrical movement throughout stroke

BREASTSTROKE

Component	Level IV	Level V	Level VI
Body Position/Motion		Body inclined less than 30° during glide Forehead may be out of water throughout stroke Arms/legs may be separated during glide	Body nearly horizontal during glide Forehead submerged during glide Body streamlined during glide Smooth rocking action
Arms		Elbows must bend during pull Elbows and hands may be at same level during pull Arms may pull past shoulders	Hands must be deeper than elbows during pull Arms may not pull past shoulders Elbows squeeze toward body at start of recovery
Kick	Knees may be outside feet during power phase Ankles flexed throughout power phase Occasional scissors kick	Feet outside knees during power phase Ankles rotated outward at start of power phase Scissors kick not acceptable	
Breathing/Timing		Breathing every stroke during arm pull Arm pull and kick must alternate	Breathing at end of arm stroke power phase Pull and breathe, kick and glide

SIDESTROKE

Component	Level IV	Level V	Level VI
Body Position/ Motion		Side-lying position Some rolling of hips Head position may vary Torso may bend	Body nearly parallel to surface Body roll not acceptable Lower ear remains in water Torso straight throughout stroke
Arms		Hands may break surface Elbow of trailing arm remains close to body throughout stroke Trailing arm recovers beyond shoulders Power phase of trailing arm might not end at hip Dropped elbow of leading arm acceptable Leading arm may pull past upper chest	Hands below surface Trailing arm recovers no higher than shoulder of leading arm Power phase of trailing arm ends at hip Dropped elbow of leading arm not acceptable during pull Leading arm pull ends at upper chest
Kick	Both knees bend during recovery Legs separate when the knees bend Occasional breaststroke kick acceptable Foot positions may vary	Knees and hips bend, pulling heels toward buttocks Legs separate after knees bend Lower leg may drop after recovery Inverted scissors kick acceptable Foot of back leg is pointed Ankle of forward leg is flexed	Both legs remain parallel to the surface during all movements Inverted scissors kick not acceptable Foot of bottom leg is pointed Ankle of top leg is flexed
Breathing/Timing		Any breathing pattern acceptable Arms must alternate Minimal glide acceptable	Inhale as legs recover, exhale during power phase Leading arm pulls while trailing arm and both legs recover Leading arm recovers as legs and trailing arm apply power Glide is maintained until momentum slows

BUTTERFLY

Component	Level V	Level VI	Level VII
Body Position/Motion	Body prone, hip flexion acceptable	Some wave-like motion	Wave-like motion throughout
Arms		Hands may enter inside or outside shoulders	Hands enter in front of or slightly outside shoulders
		Straight arm pull acceptable	Arms pull in keyhole pattern
		Arms may touch surface during recovery	Arms recover above the surface
		Occasional nonsymmetrical recovery acceptable	Arms recover simultaneously
		Elbows bend up to 90° during recovery	Arms straight or nearly straight and relaxed during recovery
Kick	Occasional flutter kick acceptable	Flutter kick not acceptable	Legs move together in the same horizontal plane
		Some vertical separation of legs	No vertical separation of legs
	Knees are bent throughout kick	Knees are bent slightly on downbeat	
		Occasional knee bend on upbeat	Legs straighten on upbeat
Breathing/Timing		Breathing as needed	Establish rhythmic breathing pattern
		Breathing anytime during arm stroke	Breathing at the end of arm stroke power phase
		One or more kicks per arm stroke acceptable	Two kicks per arm stroke

ADMINISTRATIVE TERMS AND PROCEDURES

For further information on the following terms and procedures, ask your instructor trainer or contact your local Red Cross unit.

Instructor—A member of a select group of individuals authorized to serve as agents of the Red Cross by teaching Red Cross basic courses and imparting knowledge and skills consistent with Red Cross policies, procedures, standards, and guidelines.

Red Cross Unit—Any Red Cross chapter, field service territory, or SAF station.

Certified—Receipt of a completion certificate when a participant has met all minimum requirements of a Red Cross course.

Authorized—To be accepted by a local Red Cross unit to teach a Red Cross course in that unit's jurisdiction. To become authorized, the *Health and Safety Instructor Certificate* (Form 5736) and the *Instructor Agreement* (Form 6574) must be signed by you and an official from your Red Cross unit of authorization.

Reauthorization—The act of being authorized again by teaching or co-teaching at least one Swimming and Water Safety course during your authorization period. You will receive a *Health Services Instructor Authorization* certificate (Cert. 3005) when you are reauthorized.

Extended Authorization—When you wish to teach on a temporary basis within another Red Cross unit's jurisdiction, you must contact that unit to get your instructor certificate endorsed for extended authorization. You must also notify that unit before any teaching activity and observe any procedures specific to that unit.

Transfer of Authorization—If you relocate for any reason, your authorization may be accepted by the Red Cross unit in your new jurisdiction. Contact your **new** Red Cross unit for further information on how the Red Cross can transfer your teaching records to your new location.

Suspension/Withdrawal of Authorization—The local Red Cross unit grants an instructor authorization to teach. It is also the Red Cross unit's responsibility to suspend or withdraw the instructor authorization for due cause. Due cause generally means that the instructor does not or will not abide by the standards, policies, or procedures of the Red Cross organization and its programs or in some way abuses the position of an authorized Red Cross instructor.

Teaching Records—Your Red Cross unit of authorization maintains your teaching and training records for the purpose of reauthorization, awards and recognition, etc.

Course of Record—A course for which a properly completed, duly signed *Course Record* (Form 6418) and, if necessary, a *Course Record Addendum* (Form 6418A) have been submitted to and accepted by a Red Cross unit in the jurisdiction in which the course was conducted.

Minimum Enrollment for Courses—Each course must have enough participants to provide them with sufficient skills practice to accomplish the course objectives. Therefore, you must obtain prior permission from your local Red Cross unit to conduct a Swimming and Water Safety course with fewer than six students. Courses must have a minimum of six students enrolled, not necessarily passing.

Co-teach—Sharing full or 100 percent participation in course leadership with one or more co-instructors. Also known as team teaching.

Water Safety Instructor Aide—An individual who successfully completes instructor aide training to help an instructor with a basic course.

Instructor Agreement (Form 6574)—A form signed by Red Cross instructors before being authorized to teach a Red Cross course. This form explains the rights and responsibilities of both the instructor and the Red Cross unit of authorization.

Uniform Code (Cert. 1824)—A certificate that is signed and issued to every authorized Red Cross instructor and that serves as a general agreement between the instructor and the Red Cross unit. It also provides an individual a means by which to display his or her sense of pride in being an American Red Cross instructor.

Authorized Provider Agreement (Form 6575)—An agreement between a Red Cross unit and a third-party provider of Red Cross courses that defines the responsibilities of each party.

DEALING WITH CULTURAL DIVERSITY

The word "culture" refers to the life patterns within a community. The community may be based on geography, race, health conditions, religion, socioeconomic status, or other factors. Life patterns may include language and communication styles, health beliefs and practices, and religious and spiritual practices, as well as formal and informal educational, family, and community systems.

Participants in the Swimming and Water Safety program come from many diverse cultures. Any given class may consist of children or adults from a culturally homogeneous group, or from a variety of cultures. In addition, your own background could be entirely different from that of some or even all of the participants. Regardless of the makeup of the class, today, more than ever, there is a compelling need to be sensitive to one's own cultural heritage and the differing backgrounds of participants.

As an American Red Cross Water Safety Instructor, it is important to remember that you have the potential to be a role model for participants and, as such, it is your job to set a climate in your courses that accepts differences, shows dignity, and respects and values others.

It may be difficult for you to work with culturally different participants to help them reach their potential. You may perceive yourself as having such a different background and lifestyle that you find it hard to relate comfortably to participants from different ethnic, cultural, or social groups. When there are obvious physical or language differences, the gaps may seem even greater.

One of the first things you can do to help yourself deal successfully with participants of diverse backgrounds is to learn to appreciate yourself. Pride in yourself can help you feel more comfortable in reaching out to others. You need to feel good about who you are and where you come from—your own ethnic and cultural background.

In attempting to understand and accept yourself, it is vital that you become aware of your own cultural norms and how they influence your beliefs, attitudes, practices, and teaching strategies. Such self-knowledge will help you remain alert to your own cultural biases and to be creative in presenting material in a culturally appropriate and effective manner. You may want to ask the local Red Cross unit to refer you to activities or courses in your community that are designed to increase awareness of your own cultural beliefs and practices. "Serving the Diverse Community", offered by some American Red Cross units, is one such course.

Once you can identify and begin to understand your own life patterns, you will be well on your way to understanding those of your participants and the meaning of these patterns for them. One way to help you and your participants understand and enjoy the multicultural experience is to learn about the backgrounds of your course participants through precourse interviews. If you find that you will be teaching a group whose cultural background is different from yours and think that special efforts are needed to make the course understandable and useful, you should learn all you can about the culture. Once the course has begun, you can get to know the participants better through informal conversation periods planned for each lesson. Contacting community leaders with your questions or visiting your participants at home are two more ways of learning about the culture of the participants.

Following are several categories of information that can help you begin to understand cultures that are different from your own. Each category is accompanied by some questions to ask and strategies to try. The information is not complete, but you can use it as a starting point when you need to adapt lesson plans to a specific cultural group.

1. Family relationships, roles, and social systems

- Is the family headed by two parents or only one?
- Are members of the extended family actively involved in the daily life of the family?
- Do members of other generations live in the home of the participants?
- What are the roles of males and females in the participant's cultural group?
- Are males and females permitted to fraternize with each other publicly?
- What are parental attitudes towards the children participating in aquatics programs?
- What cultural norms have influenced your participant's style of competition and play?

Strategies: Learn all you can about family life in the culture. If extended family members are involved in daily family life, encourage them to participate in the classes. Schedule class meetings at a time when extended family members can attend. If you have several single parents in a fitness course for example, arrangements for child care may be needed. The local Red Cross unit may be able to help by training or recruiting certified baby sitters. If the children in your classes come from largely single-parent households, you may be perceived as a significant male or female role model. You may need to offer children some of the support and encouragement that a single parent doesn't have the time or the energy to offer.

Some parents may be hesitant about letting their children participate in indoor aquatics programs during the winter because they are afraid the children will become ill when the weather turns colder. Others might not want their daughters to participate because they feel the swimming apparel is too revealing. Try to reassure parents that their children are safe, that they won't be stared at, and that swimming is good for their physical well-being.

Certain cultural differences influence the way children have learned to play various games. It is important that you understand that some participants strive to win as a team and some emphasize playing their personal best. For some, winning is more important than simply playing for fun.

2. Patterns of communication, decision making, and problem solving

- What languages are spoken in the community and what languages are understood?
- Are decisions made by the family as a group or by individuals?
- Is communication direct or indirect? Are there rules for how males and females may communicate with each other?
- What are some of the nonverbal and verbal communication patterns?

Strategies: The course should be presented in a language and communication style that the participants understand. Do not assume that non-English speakers cannot read English or vice versa. Get to know your participants and understand their unique mannerisms and informal slang, learn how to pronounce their names correctly, and make sure your participants understand your own terms and expressions. Most important, become an active listener.

Remember that some hearing-impaired people use American Sign Language and others use signed English. If you use an interpreter, it is important to know the skills of the interpreter.

If participants speak a language different than your own, decide if paraphrases are as satisfactory as more exact translations. It may be possible for some of the participants to translate material for others in the course.

Communicate with participants' parents from the beginning. Be open and honest with them and listen carefully so that you fully understand what they are trying to say. Establish trusting relationships with them before possible problems arise, so that they will know you are committed to their children and have the children's best interests at heart.

3. **Methods of learning and characteristics of teachers**
   - Do the participants learn more effectively by seeing, hearing, or doing?
   - What kind of learning is done formally? Informally?
   - What are the qualifications for teaching? Are teachers expected to act or talk in particular ways?
   - What are the participants' attitudes about personal space?

Strategies: Learn all you can about who the teachers are and how they teach. Find out if it is acceptable to touch a participant in order to demonstrate a skill. Use teaching methods and approaches the participants are familiar with. If you are not skilled in these approaches or if you are uncomfortable with certain styles, recruit an Instructor Aide who is able to present the material in the appropriate style. Initially, you and any aides should behave and teach according to the expectations that the participants have of teachers or leaders. Once the participants become comfortable with you, you can introduce and explore less familiar methods and strategies of learning.

SUMMARY

As a general rule, try to avoid interpreting actions and information from your personal cultural viewpoint. Meaning must be interpreted from within the participants' cultural framework. Community leaders or experts can help interpret the meaning of information within the community. Remember, however, that each person is an individual within his or her community and that the meaning of any specific cultural practice for that individual can only be explained by the individual. Most participants will explain the significance of their cultural beliefs and practices if you approach them with an open and accepting attitude.

As an American Red Cross Water Safety Instructor, you can significantly help culturally different participants by looking at things from their perspective, by showing that you care about their problems and concerns, and by conducting the course in a culturally appropriate way.

SWIMMING AND WATER SAFETY
PARTICIPANT AND PARENT COURSE EVALUATIONS

Included here are samples of participant course evaluations that you may photocopy and use to find out what participants thought of the course. There is also one that you may distribute to parents if you are teaching young children in an IPAP course or a Learn to Swim course.

By asking participants or parents to complete an evaluation, you can learn more about how well you teach and how well course materials are meeting the participants' and parents' needs. This evaluation also reminds participants and parents that the Red Cross is continually trying to improve its courses.

You should talk with health and safety personnel at your local Red Cross unit to find out if they want you to use this form or an alternative. Follow their instructions for returning the completed forms. If your local unit does not require an evaluation, you may want to use this form for your own information to help you improve your teaching. Please do not return it to National Headquarters.

How to Use the Participant/Parent Course Evaluation

Ask participants or parents to fill out the participant course evaluation at the end of the course. Tell participants or parents that they do not have to identify themselves on the evaluation. To make responses confidential, ask them to leave the completed evaluation in a box or envelope that you have placed nearby. Tell participants or parents that if they prefer to identify themselves on the evaluation, there is space on the form for them to do so.

AMERICAN RED CROSS SWIMMING AND WATER SAFETY
PARENT EVALUATION

We would like to know what you thought about this American Red Cross Swimming and Water Safety course. You can help maintain the high quality of the course by completing this evaluation.

About the Course

1. Which American Red Cross course did you or your child just finish? (Ask your instructor for the correct name.)

   _____

2. Who taught the course? (List all instructors' names.)

   _____

   _____

3. Tell us what you thought of the course. (Circle or check your choice; "N/A" means not applicable.)

Instructor	Strongly Agree	Agree	Not Sure	Disagree	Strongly Disagree	N/A
a. The instructor was well prepared.	1	2	3	4	5	❑
b. The instructor knew how to explain things.	1	2	3	4	5	❑
c. The instructor gave my child individual attention.	1	2	3	4	5	❑
d. The instructor answered questions clearly.	1	2	3	4	5	❑

Course						
e. I learned how to help my child in the water.	1	2	3	4	5	❑
f. I learned how to help my child with swimming readiness skills.	1	2	3	4	5	❑
g. I learned how to keep my child safe around water.	1	2	3	4	5	❑
h. My child learned what I expected him/her to learn.	1	2	3	4	5	❑
i. My child enjoyed the course.	1	2	3	4	5	❑
j. I would recommend this American Red Cross course to a friend.	1	2	3	4	5	❑

Time and Equipment

4. Was there enough time to practice? ❑ Yes ❑ No ❑ N/A

5. Was there enough space? ❑ Yes ❑ No ❑ N/A

6. Was there enough equipment for everyone?   ❑ Yes   ❑ No   ❑ N/A

7. Was the equipment in good condition?   ❑ Yes   ❑ No   ❑ N/A

8. Were the changing facilities adequate?   ❑ Yes   ❑ No   ❑ N/A

Some Information About You and Your Child

9. How old is your child? _____ years, _____ months

10. Is your child male or female?   ❑ Male   ❑ Female

11. Do you or any of your close friends or relatives own a pool?   ❑ Yes   ❑ No

12. Why did you enroll your child in this course?

_____

_____

Comments and Suggestions

13. If you have suggestions or comments, please write them below.

_____

_____

Thank you for answering these questions. We hope you enjoyed the course.

Optional: If you are willing to discuss your comments with use, please give us your name and a daytime telephone number. We would like to be able to call you if we have questions.

Name _____ Phone number ( ) _____

Your mailing address   City   State   Zip + 4

Name of your Red Cross unit _____
                               (if applicable)

American Red Cross Swimming and Water Safety Participant Course Evaluation

We would like to know what you thought about this American Red Cross Swimming and Water Safety course. You can help maintain the high quality of the course by completing this evaluation.

1. Which American Red Cross course did you or your child just finish? (Ask your instructor for the correct name.)

   _____

2. Who taught the course? (List all instructors' names.)

   _____

   _____

3. Tell us what you thought of the course. (Circle or check your choice; "N/A" means not applicable.)

		Strongly Agree	Agree	Not Sure	Disagree	Strongly Disagree	N/A
a.	The participant's materials explained things clearly.	1	2	3	4	5	❑
b.	The demonstrations and audiovisuals were clear and helpful.	1	2	3	4	5	❑
c.	I have confidence that I can perform the skills I learned.	1	2	3	4	5	❑
d.	I know when to use the safety skills I learned in this course.	1	2	3	4	5	❑
e.	The instructor was well prepared.	1	2	3	4	5	❑
f.	The instructor gave clear instructions on what to do.	1	2	3	4	5	❑
g.	The instructor answered questions clearly.	1	2	3	4	5	❑
h.	The instructor's guidance during the practice sessions was helpful.	1	2	3	4	5	❑
i.	I would recommend this course to a friend.	1	2	3	4	5	❑
j.	The course was well paced.	1	2	3	4	5	❑
k.	I had to work hard to pass this course.	1	2	3	4	5	❑

4. Was all the equipment in working order? ❑ Yes ❑ No ❑ N/A

5. Was the classroom clean and comfortable? ❑ Yes ❑ No ❑ N/A

6. Was the aquatic facility clean and well maintained? ❑ Yes ❑ No ❑ N/A

7. Did you have enough time to read assigned materials?   ❑ Yes   ❑ No   ❑ N/A

8. Did you have enough time to practice?   ❑ Yes   ❑ No   ❑ N/A

9. Did you take this course to fulfill a job or work requirement?   ❑ Yes   ❑ No   ❑ N/A

   If not, why did you take this course?

   _____

   _____

10. Did you learn what you wanted to learn?   ❑ Yes   ❑ No

    If yes, please specify: _____

    _____

    If no, what else did you want to learn? _____

    _____

11. What was your age at your last birthday?_____

12. Please check the highest level of education you have completed.

    ❑ Elementary school   ❑ Junior high school   ❑ High school

    ❑ Some college   ❑ College degree or beyond

13. How did you hear about this course?

    ❑ Newspaper   ❑ Television   ❑ Radio

    ❑ Other (please specify): _____

    _____

14. Are you: ❑ Male   ❑ Female

15. Do you have any other comments about this course or your instructor that you would like to share with us?

    _____

    _____

Thank you for answering these questions. We hope you enjoyed the course.

Optional: If you are willing to discuss your comments with use, please give us your name and a daytime telephone number. We would like to be able to call you if we have questions.

Name _____ Phone number ( )_____

Your mailing address _____ City _____ State ____ Zip + 4 ____

Name of your Red Cross unit _____

(if applicable)

AMERICAN RED CROSS WATER SAFETY INSTRUCTOR EVALUATION

To continue to improve the Water Safety Program, the American Red Cross needs your help. This appendix contains two instructor evaluation forms. Please complete an evaluation form the **FIRST** time you teach this course. Detach and return the completed evaluation (either as a self-fold-and-seal mailer, or by placing a copy in an envelope) to—

American Red Cross
National Headquarters
Health and Safety Course Evaluations
17th & D Streets, N.W.
Washington, D.C. 20006

We also invite you to share any observations that you may have about the course at any time by completing the second evaluation form or by writing to the above address.

American Red Cross Water Safety
Instructor Evaluation

Background

1. Course completion date ___ / ___ / ___

2. I taught a(n):
   - ❑ IPAP   ❑ WSI Aide
   - ❑ BWS   ❑ EWS
   - ❑ Learn To Swim Level ___

3. Is this your first time teaching this course?
   - ❑ Yes   ❑ No

   If no, how many times have you taught this course? ___

4. Total time required to teach was: ___ hours

5. Total number of participants:
   # passed ___   # incomplete ___

6. Number of sessions in this course: ___

7. How would you describe the participants in this course? Check relevant boxes.
   - ❑ Infant (6–18 months)
   - ❑ Toddler (18–36 months)
   - ❑ Preschool (3–5 years)
   - ❑ Mostly ages 6–12
   - ❑ Mostly ages 12–18
   - ❑ Mostly ages 18–40
   - ❑ Mostly ages 41–65
   - ❑ Mostly over age 65
   - ❑ Mixed ages

8. In what setting did you teach this course? (If at a pool, also check indoor or outdoor.)
   - ❑ Public school pool
   - ❑ College/university pool
   - ❑ Community pool
     - ❑ indoor   ❑ outdoor
   - ❑ Waterfront (lake)
   - ❑ Other (describe)

9. Is there a diving board at the facility where you taught?
   - ❑ Yes   ❑ No

   If yes, how deep is the water under the board? ___

10. How long have you been an American Red Cross Water Safety Instructor? ___

11. What type of instructor are you?
    - ❑ Agency /Organization paid instructor
    - ❑ American Red Cross volunteer instructor
    - ❑ American Red Cross paid instructor
    - ❑ Other (please specify) ___

12. When you taught this course, which of the following did you use?
    - ❑ *Swimming and Diving*
    - ❑ Instructor's Manual
    - ❑ Swimming and Diving Skills video
    - ❑ IPAP video, parents' segment
    - ❑ IPAP Parent's Guide
    - ❑ *Waddles*
    - ❑ Basic Water Safety textbook
    - ❑ Emergency Water Safety textbook
    - ❑ Other (describe)

13. Were the entry and exit skill requirements appropriate for the level you taught? Please explain.
    _____
    _____

14. Were there "stalling points" for your participants in the course? What were they?
    _____
    _____
    _____

over

Optional: If you are willing to discuss your comments with us, please give us your name and a daytime phone number. We would like to be able to call you if we have any questions.

Name _____ Phone number (_____) _____

_____   _____ _____ _____
Your mailing address   City   State   Zip + 4

Red Cross unit name _____
                            (if applicable)

If one is developed, would you like to receive a national newsletter for instructors?
If yes, please check box ❏

—Fold here first—

—Tape closed here after second fold—

15. List any questions about the course that are not answered in the instructor's manual.

_____

_____

_____

16. List any suggestions for improving the American Red Cross Water Safety Program.

_____

_____

_____

17. List any suggestions for improving the audiovisuals.

_____

_____

_____

Thank you for taking the time to answer these questions. If you have any additional comments about the course, please include them on a separate sheet and include it with this evaluation.

—Fold here second—

WSI IM
5/92

_____

_____

_____

Stamp

American Red Cross
National Headquarters
Health and Safety Course Evaluations
17th & D Streets, N.W.
Washington, DC 20006–5399

AMERICAN RED CROSS WATER SAFETY
INSTRUCTOR EVALUATION

BACKGROUND

1. Course completion date ___ / ___ / ___

2. I taught a(n):
   - ☐ IPAP   ☐ WSI Aide
   - ☐ BWS   ☐ EWS
   - ☐ Learn To Swim Level ___

3. Is this your first time teaching this course?
   - ☐ Yes   ☐ No

   If no, how many times have you taught this course? ___

4. Total time required to teach was:
   ___ hours

5. Total number of participants:
   # passed ___   # incomplete ___

6. Number of sessions in this course: ___

7. How would you describe the participants in this course? Check relevant boxes.
   - ☐ Infant (6–18 months)
   - ☐ Toddler (18–36 months)
   - ☐ Preschool (3–5 years)
   - ☐ Mostly ages 6–12
   - ☐ Mostly ages 12–18
   - ☐ Mostly ages 18–40
   - ☐ Mostly ages 41–65
   - ☐ Mostly over age 65
   - ☐ Mixed ages

8. In what setting did you teach this course? (If at a pool, also check indoor or outdoor.)
   - ☐ Public school pool
   - ☐ College/university pool
   - ☐ Community pool
     - ☐ indoor   ☐ outdoor
   - ☐ Waterfront (lake)
   - ☐ Other (describe) _____

9. Is there a diving board at the facility where you taught?
   - ☐ Yes   ☐ No

   If yes, how deep is the water under the board? _____

10. How long have you been an American Red Cross Water Safety Instructor? _____

11. What type of instructor are you?
   - ☐ Agency /Organization paid instructor
   - ☐ American Red Cross volunteer instructor
   - ☐ American Red Cross paid instructor
   - ☐ Other (please specify) _____

12. When you taught this course, which of the following did you use?
   - ☐ *Swimming and Diving*
   - ☐ Instructor's Manual
   - ☐ Swimming and Diving Skills video
   - ☐ IPAP video, parents' segment
   - ☐ IPAP Parent's Guide
   - ☐ *Waddles*
   - ☐ Basic Water Safety textbook
   - ☐ Emergency Water Safety textbook
   - ☐ Other (describe)

13. Were the entry and exit skill requirements appropriate for the level you taught? Please explain.
   _____
   _____
   _____

14. Were there "stalling points" for your participants in the course? What were they?
   _____
   _____
   _____

over

Optional: If you are willing to discuss your comments with us, please give us your name and a daytime phone number. We would like to be able to call you if we have any questions.

Name _____   Phone number (_____) _____

_____   _____   _____   _____
Your mailing address   City   State   Zip + 4

Red Cross unit name _____
(if applicable)

If one is developed, would you like to receive a national newsletter for instructors?
If yes, please check box ❑

—Fold here first—

—Tape closed here after second fold—

15. List any questions about the course that are not answered in the instructor's manual.

_____

_____

_____

16. List any suggestions for improving the American Red Cross Water Safety Program.

_____

_____

_____

17. List any suggestions for improving the audiovisuals.

_____

_____

_____

Thank you for taking the time to answer these questions. If you have any additional comments about the course, please include them on a separate sheet and include it with this evaluation.

—Fold here second—

WSI IM
5/92

_____

_____

_____

Stamp

American Red Cross
National Headquarters
Health and Safety Course Evaluations
17th & D Streets, N.W.
Washington, DC 20006–5399

WATER SAFETY INSTRUCTOR SELF-ASSESSMENT

Water Safety Instructors: Using the assessment categories (1, 2, 3, and 4) described below, rate yourself as well as you can on each of the following instructor skills.

> 1 — Fully successful
> 2 — Successful
> 3 — Adequate
> 4 — Needs improvement
> N/A — Not applicable

1	2	3	4	N/A	Instruction
					1. Planning and managing physical environment (safety, audiovisual aids, equipment, excess noise, distraction, etc.)
					2. Designing effective block plans and lesson plans.
					3. Adjusting block plans and/or lesson plans for the next class as necessary.
					4. Managing time—allowing enough time for practice, review and evaluation; beginning and ending class on time.
					5. Using appropriate opening and closing activities.
					6. Explaining and presenting material from *Swimming and Diving* or other American Red Cross books.
					7. Conducting effective practice sessions.
					8. Assessing participant's progress and skill proficiency.
					9. Keeping participants actively involved throughout the lessons.
					10. Conducting effective discussions.
					11. Being sensitive to cultural diversity and individuals with disabilities and other conditions.
					12. Bridging effectively—moving from one topic or skill practice to another.
					13. Utilizing other instructors and instructor aides effectively.
					14. Being aware of your personal image—qualities that add or detract from your other instructor skills.

MATERIALS FOR PLANNING COURSES

Block Plan
Lesson Plan
Skills Checklist

BLOCK PLAN

Instructor _____ Course Level _____

# of Students _____ # of Days _____ Length of Lesson _____

Dates _____ Aides _____

Safety Topic:	Date
Equipment:	
Review Skills New Skills	

Safety Topic:	Date
Equipment:	
Review Skills New Skills	

Safety Topic:	Date
Equipment:	
Review Skills New Skills	

Safety Topic:	Date
Equipment:	
Review Skills New Skills	

Safety Topic:	Date
Equipment:	
Review Skills New Skills	

Safety Topic:	Date
Equipment:	
Review Skills New Skills	

Safety Topic:	Date
Equipment:	
Review Skills New Skills	

Safety Topic:	Date
Equipment:	
Review Skills New Skills	

Safety Topic:	Date
Equipment:	
Review Skills New Skills	

Safety Topic:	Date
Equipment:	
Review Skills New Skills	

Safety Topic:	Date
Equipment:	
Review Skills New Skills	

Safety Topic:	Date
Equipment:	
Review Skills New Skills	

LESSON PLAN

Instructor		Level	Lesson #	Date	Day	Time

Safety Topics:	Equipment:

Assignment:

Time	Activity/Topic	Key words/ Phrases	Practice Method	Pattern of Organization
	Opening:			
	Closing:			

American Red Cross

American Red Cross

SWIMMING COURSES SKILLS CHECKLIST

Name of Course	Group										Date Started								Date Completed								Instructor or Aide					
• Skills for courses are listed in Chapter 16 of the Water Safety Instructor's Manual • Record activity on Course Record (Form 6418)	Skills																														Grade Pass (P) Fail (F) Incomplete (Inc)	
PARTICIPANT'S NAME	1	2	3	4	5	6	7	8	9	10	11	12	13	14	15	16	17	18	19	20	21	22	23	24	25	26	27					

Checklists are not to be sent to chapter. Retain for own use.

AQUATIC ACTIVITY PROGRAMS FOR CHILDREN UNDER THE AGE OF THREE (COUNCIL FOR NATIONAL COOPERATION IN AQUATICS)

1. AQUATIC PROGRAMS FOR CHILDREN UNDER THE AGE OF THREE YEARS, MOST APPROPRIATELY, SHOULD BE PROMOTED, DESCRIBED, AND CONDUCTED AS WATER "ADJUSTMENT," "ORIENTATION," OR "FAMILIARIZATION" PROGRAMS. EMPHASIS SHOULD BE PLACED UPON THE NEED FOR YOUNG CHILDREN TO EXPLORE THE AQUATIC ENVIRONMENT IN ENJOYABLE, NON-STRESSFUL SITUATIONS THAT PROVIDE A WIDE VARIETY OF GAMES AND EXPERIENCES.

RATIONALE: Other terms, such as "drownproofing," "waterproofing," and "water safe," often can suggest to parents and the general public that children can be safe in and around the water without careful supervision. In addition, the developmental literature supports the primary role of play activities and movement exploration in the acquisition of movement competence by young children.

2. WATER EXPERIENCE/ORIENTATION PROGRAMS SHOULD HAVE THE IN-WATER PARTICIPATION OF A PARENT, GUARDIAN, OR OTHER PERSON WHO IS RESPONSIBLE FOR AND TRUSTED BY THE CHILD.

RATIONALE: The parent is the first and primary teacher of the young child. As such, the parent must assume actual responsibility for the supervision and learning of the child. Aquatic programs, when properly structured, can provide an excellent type of parent-child learning environment. Programs conducted without parents in the water should be limited in size, and make every consideration for the safety and psychological comfort of the child.

3. THE PARTICIPATING PARENT, GUARDIAN, OR OTHER RESPONSIBLE ADULT ASSUMES PRIMARY RESPONSIBILITY FOR MONITORING THE CHILD'S HEALTH BEFORE, DURING, AND AFTER PARTICIPATION IN AQUATIC PROGRAMS. ALL CHILDREN, ESPECIALLY THOSE WITH KNOWN MEDICAL PROBLEMS, SHOULD RECEIVE CLEARANCE FROM THEIR PHYSICIAN PRIOR TO PARTICIPATION IN THE AQUATIC PROGRAM.

RATIONALE: The child's parent and physician are the persons who can best judge the child's medical and developmental readiness for exposure to a public swimming pool at an early age. There is disagreement among professionals about the benefits and detriments of the child's early exposure to the aquatic environment. The potential benefits of enhanced movement, socialization, and parent-child interaction must be weighed against problems such as possible increased susceptibility to eye, ear, respiratory, and bacterial infections. More definitive research evidence is needed to assist parents and physicians in evaluating the child's readiness.

4. PERSONNEL DIRECTING AND OPERATING AQUATIC PROGRAMS FOR CHILDREN UNDER THREE YEARS OF AGE SHOULD HAVE TRAINING IN CHILD DEVELOPMENT AND PARENTING AS WELL AS AQUATICS, OR HAVE CONSULTANTS WHO HAVE BEEN TRAINED IN THESE AREAS. FULLY TRAINED AND QUALIFIED LIFEGUARDS MUST BE ON DUTY AT ALL TIMES DURING PROGRAMS.

RATIONALE: Because of the developmental differences in cognitive, psychomotor, and affective domains between the young child and older children, the directors and teachers of these programs must have a well-founded understanding of child development. Because the programs usually involve both the parents and the children, a further understanding of parenting principles also is necessary. Finally, in spite of the presence of parents in the pool, it must be recognized that the instructor cannot assume lifeguarding responsibilities while teaching. A certified lifeguard in addition to the instructor is needed.

5. PARTICIPATION IN AQUATIC PROGRAMS BY NEONATES AND BY YOUNG CHILDREN LACKING PRONE HEAD CONTROL SHOULD BE LIMITED.

RATIONALE: While there is general disagreement among professionals and practitioners regarding the youngest age at which children should begin water experiences, there is some evidence suggesting that until the child can voluntarily control the head by lifting it 90 degrees when prone, they probably will gain little from the water experience, and may be more at risk of accidentally submerging or swallowing water. Certain aquatic skills can successfully be introduced when the child demonstrates rolling over, crawling, and creeping. Due to individual differences among young children, behavioral, rather than strict age, criteria are usually the most valid way to evaluate children for program participation.

6. CERTAIN TEACHING TECHNIQUES, SUCH AS DROPPING A CHILD FROM A HEIGHT, SHOULD BE STRICTLY PROHIBITED. OTHER PROCEDURES SUCH AS FACE SUBMERSIONS, ESPECIALLY THOSE WHICH ARE CONTROLLED BY AN ADULT, MUST BE LIMITED BOTH IN DURATION AND IN NUMBER FOR THE YOUNG CHILD.

RATIONALE: Dropping a child from any height is unnecessary and serves no reasonable purpose. In fact, it is extremely dangerous, as it may produce head, neck, or organ damage to a young child, as well as introduce water and bacteria into the nose, ears, and sinuses. There is also potential for psychological trauma in such an activity.

A growing number of recent clinical reports have implicated the practice of repeated submersions during aquatic programs in producing hyponatremia, or "water intoxication" in young children. Hyponatremia is a condition in which an electrolyte (especially sodium) imbalance results from the loss of electrolytes or rapid ingestion of fluids or both. The symptoms include such "soft" signs as irritability, crying, and fussing, as well as more serious signs of vomiting, convulsions, and coma. Despite claims that a young child has a "breathholding" or epiglottal reflex, both children and adults can swallow significant amounts of water while learning to swim. Due to the small body size and large skin area to body weight ratio of most children under 18 months of age, water ingestion can produce symptoms of hyponatremia, some of which may be going unnoticed by parents and teachers. Therefore, submersions by young children must be brief (one to five seconds), and few in number (less than six per lesson) while the child is initially learning. Once the child can initiate the submersions AND can demonstrate competent breath control, submersions can become longer and more frequent. However, the parents and teachers still must be alert to bloated stomachs and "soft" signs that may indicate excessive water ingestion and incipient problems.

The condition of hyponatremia must be the focus of a concerted research effort to discover the extent and scope of its presence in infant swimming classes. Clinical and empirical evidence should be the basis for subsequent amendments to this guidelines.

7. MAXIMUM IN-WATER CLASS TIME FOR INFANTS AND VERY YOUNG CHILDREN MUST NOT EXCEED 30 MINUTES.

RATIONALE: Most children benefit from shorter, but more frequent, learning experiences. Limiting in-water time to less than 30 minutes should maximize the learning and enjoyment of children while avoiding fatigue, hypothermia and possible hyponatremia. One of the constant factors discovered in each clinical hyponatremia case was that children had been in the water far in excess of 30 minutes. Apparently, fatigue, chilling, and excessive submersions all may contribute to hyponatremia.

8. WATER AND AIR TEMPERATURE MUST BE MAINTAINED AT SUFFICIENT LEVELS AND IN PROPER PROPORTION TO ONE ANOTHER TO GUARANTEE THE COMFORT OF YOUNG CHILDREN.

RATIONALE: Young children can become chilled more easily than adults and may have immature thermal regulatory systems. They also cannot enjoy the experience or learn optimally if chilled. There is no general agreement as to the proper level of water temperature in indoor pools. However, experience suggests that water temperature should be a MINIMUM of 82 degrees Fahrenheit (86 is preferable) and that air temperature should be at least three degrees higher than the water temperature. Locker and changing room temperatures also should be maintained at warm levels. Failure to achieve these minimum standards should be a strong factor in cancelling or shortening classes.

9. ALL LAWS AND REGULATIONS PERTAINING TO WATER PURITY, POOL CARE, AND SANITATION MUST BE CAREFULLY FOLLOWED.

RATIONALE: Young children are extremely susceptible to diseases. Utmost care in maintaining facilities in accord with bathing codes and water purity standards can prevent unnecessary outbreaks of disease and infections. Locker rooms and pool decks must be clean and free of clutter. Slippery surfaces and impeded walkways can be very dangerous to beginning and inexperienced walkers. Proper facilities for the changing and disposal of diapers and soiled clothing must be provided.

10. APPROPRIATE, BUT NOT EXCESSIVE CLOTHING SHOULD BE WORN BY YOUNG CHILDREN TO MINIMIZE THE SPREAD OF BODY WASTES INTO THE WATER.

RATIONALE: Fecal matter is aesthetically unattractive and potentially hazardous to other swimmers. Children should wear some type of tight-fitting but lightweight apparel, perhaps covered by rubber pants. Heavier diapers can be both a health and safety hazard and should not be worn. Parents and instructors should monitor young children and remove them from the water if a bowel movement is apparent.

Printed with permission of the Council for National Cooperation in Aquatics, 901 West New York St., Indianapolis, IN 46223

SAMPLE LETTER TO PARENTS OF IPAP PARTICIPANTS (INFANT AND TODDLER LEVELS)

On the following pages is a sample letter which can be used to confirm registration and to give parents and/or guardians of IPAP participants important information about the course. There are blanks for you to fill in and tailor for your particular class and facility.

Dear Parent or Guardian,

The _____ is pleased to have you participate in the American Red Cross Infant and Preschool Aquatic Program. You and your child will have an opportunity to experience water play and water safety. The following information will help create a safe, positive experience for you and your child.

Before the First Class

There are many things you can do even before the first lesson to prepare your child for his or her first aquatic experience. Depending on his or her age and ability, begin talking to your child about swimming lessons, perhaps during bath time. Take your child into the tub or shower or with you. Dribble water on each other in a non-threatening manner with a sponge and sing "It's raining, it's pouring." If possible, arrange to bring him or her to the facility one or two days before classes begin, especially if he or she has never been in a swimming pool before. You can also obtain the book, *Waddles Presents AQUACKtic Safety,* to help familiarize your child with some of the safety rules in a fun way, and help him or her about his or her concerns regarding water. Check with your local Red Cross unit for availability.

Parent's Role During the Lesson

- Children copy parental attitudes. What you say, do, and your facial expressions will influence your child.
- Praise your child. Reinforce all skills you want your child to repeat. Reward effort as well as accomplishments.
- Be positive. Ignore or minimize negative reactions such as crying and temper tantrums.
- Have patience. Children progress at their own rate in swimming readiness, just as in all other areas of development.

Class Schedule

- _____

- _____

- _____

Please be on time for class. Allow plenty of time before and after class for showering and dressing. Attend every class, as frequency is the key to learning.

Related Courses

The following is a list of recommended American Red Cross Health and Safety courses you may be interested in. Check with your local Red Cross unit for course availability.

American Red Cross CPR: Infant and Child
American Red Cross Standard First Aid
American Red Cross Basic Water Safety
American Red Cross Learn to Swim Program

Facility Rules and Regulations

■ _____

_____

_____

- No shoes are allowed on the pool deck.
- No drinks, food, or gum is allowed in the pool or locker room.
- Diapers should be properly disposed of in the locker room.
- Use plastic bottles or containers in showers.
- Do not use electrical appliances in the locker room.
- No one is allowed to go into the pool area until one of the class instructors is on deck.

Clothing
- Jewelry should be removed prior to class.
- Corrective lenses should be worn when necessary.
- Your child must wear cloth diapers and plastic pants with tight-fitting legs, if he or she is not toilet-trained.
- Bring two towels for your child—one for the pool area and one for after showering.
- Try to leave valuables at home, but check with the pool facility to see if you can bring a padlock from home or rent one from the facility for a small fee.

Health
- Please tell your instructor if you and/or your child have any medical problems or disabilities.
- Food or drink, especially citrus products, should not be consumed for at least one hour before class.
- If your child becomes chilled or tired, take your child out of the water, wrap him or her up warmly, and observe the remainder of the class.

PARENTS ARE RESPONSIBLE AT ALL TIMES FOR THE SAFETY OF THEIR CHILDREN.
We know that this will be a fun and rewarding time for each of you. Do not hesitate to talk to the instructors at any time throughout the program.

Sincerely,

Water Safety Instructor

MANIKIN USE AND DECONTAMINATION

Because preventing the spread of infectious disease through manikin use is of vital importance, the following health measures should be followed:

Acute Infections

Participants and instructors should postpone mouth-to-mouth training on a manikin if they:

- Have any cuts or sores that cannot be adequately covered, such as on the lips or in the mouth.
- Have any respiratory infections, such as a cold or a sore throat.
- Have recently been exposed to or are showing symptoms of any infectious disease.

Chronic Infections

Chronic infections such as HBV (hepatitis B virus) and HIV (human immunodeficiency virus, the virus that causes AIDS) persist over an extended period and can be transmitted through breaks in the skin or mucosa. While acute infections run their natural course and therefore eventually allow participants to take part in mouth-to-mouth training on a manikin, this is not the case for chronic infections.

If an instructor wishes to train an individual with a chronic infection or if the instructor has a chronic infection, precautions should be taken to protect all participants. This is best accomplished by providing the infected individual with a separate manikin that is not used by anyone else until it has been cleaned according to recommended end-of-class decontamination procedures. Requests for individual manikins should be honored, within reason. Equitable accommodations for all participants in training programs are encouraged. Participants are not required to disclose the reason for their request.

Because of the theoretical risk of contracting even the common cold from a contaminated manikin, which could worsen the present infected person's condition (AIDS, for instance), an individual who has a chronic infection should not participate in mouth-to-mouth training on a manikin until his or her own personal physician has reviewed the circumstances carefully and indicated whether participation is appropriate.

To minimize the risk of disease transmission during mouth-to-mouth training on a manikin, all participants should:

- Wash their hands thoroughly before working with the manikin.
- Not eat or drink during manikin use.
- Use their own face shield, if one is provided, each time they practice on the manikin.
- Properly clean the manikin between uses.

Before each class, inspect the manikins for cracks or rips in the face that make it difficult or impossible to clean the manikin properly. Do not use any manikin that has cracks or rips in the face.

Manikin Decontamination During Practice Sessions

Before using the manikin, and between its use by the students, vigorously wipe the entire face of the manikin and the inside of the mouth with a clean gauze pad (4 inches by 4 inches), soaked with a disinfecting solution. Let the surfaces remain wet for at least 30 seconds before wiping them dry with another gauze pad.

The recommended solution for decontamination is 1/4 cup of liquid household chlorine bleach per gallon of tap water. This solution must be made fresh just before each class and discarded after use. Since bleach may be objectionable to some people, an alternative is 70 percent alcohol (isopropanol or ethanol). Although alcohols can kill many bacteria and viruses, there are some that they cannot kill. However, if the manikin's face is scrubbed vigorously with 70 percent alcohol and a clean gauze pad, it is unlikely that any infectious disease will be transmitted.

Manikin Decontamination After Class

To decontaminate the manikins after class, you will need, besides the decontamination solution and gauze pads, a bottle brush, soap and water, basins or buckets, immunodeficiency disposable gloves, and any other supplies recommended by the manikin manufacturer.

As soon as possible after the end of each practice session, the manikin's head and airway passages must be cleaned and decontaminated as follows:

1. Wash with warm soapy water.
2. Rinse with clean water.
3. Decontaminate by soaking in the bleach solution for 10 minutes.
4. Rinse with fresh water.
5. Dry all internal and external surfaces; rinsing with alcohol will aid drying on internal surfaces.

Vigorous scrubbing with soap and water is as important as soaking in the bleach solution. Protective gloves should be worn throughout the disassembling, cleaning, and decontaminating procedures.

SWIMMING AND DIVING SKILLS VIDEO CALIBRATION CHART

Because there is no standard "counter" on VCR equipment, and because machines can vary slightly in playing speed, instructors may find it useful to fill out this chart prior to class. It will allow the instructor and participants to locate specific segments of the video for reviewing.

INSTRUCTIONS (PRIOR TO CLASS):
1. Use the same VCR you will use during class.
2. Make sure the tape is completely rewound.
3. Set the VCR counter to zero. (The button to set the counter to zero is often called "Reset.")
4. Set the VCR in the play mode.
5. Enter the counter number at the start of each segment in the space provided below.

---

1. Introduction .... _____

2. Front Crawl .... _____

3. Back Crawl .... _____

4. Breaststroke .... _____

5. Butterfly .... _____

6. Elementary Backstroke .... _____

7. Sidestroke .... _____

8. Grab Start .... _____

9. Backstroke Start .... _____

10. Front Flip Turn .... _____

11. Backstroke Flip Turn .... _____

12. Backstroke Spin Turn .... _____

13. Breaststroke Turn .... _____

14. Butterfly Turn .... _____

15. Diving Progressions .... _____

WATER SAFETY SKILLS CHECKLISTS

Basic Water Safety Skills Checklist
Emergency Water Safety Skills Checklist

American Red Cross

Basic Water Safety
Skills Checklist

		Names																
Level of Participation	Observer (O)																	
	Life jacket Wearer																	
	Swimmer (S)																	
Sudden Immersion Skills	Survival Floating																	
	Back Float with Winging and Kick																	
	Treading Water																	
	Bobbing																	
	Cramp Release																	
	Clothing—Swimming																	
	Clothing—Inflating																	
Spinal Injury	Hip and Shoulder Support																	
Assists	Reaching—Out-of-Water																	
	Reaching—In-Water																	
	Throwing																	
	Wading																	
Life-jackets	H.E.L.P.																	
	Huddle Position																	
Rescue Breathing	Opening Airway—on Land																	
	Opening Airway—in Shallow Water																	
Boating Safety	Trimming																	
	Change Positions																	
	Use Overturned Boat for Flotation																	
	Reenter and Paddle Swamped Boat																	
	Assists																	

Checklists are not to be sent to chapter. Retain for own use.

American Red Cross

EMERGENCY WATER SAFETY SKILLS CHECKLIST

	Names															
Assist	Human Chain															
Entries	Stride Jump															
	Feetfirst Jump															
Tows	Positioning															
	Rescue Tube															
	Wrist															
	Armpit															
	Collar															
	Changing Positions															
Recovery of Submerged Victim	Feetfirst Surface Dive															
	Pike Surface Dive															
	Underwater Swimming															
	Recovery															
Escapes	Block															
	Front Head-Hold															
	Rear Head-Hold															
	Wrist/Arm															

Checklists are not to be sent to chapter. Retain for own use.

over

American Red Cross
EMERGENCY WATER SAFETY
SKILLS CHECKLIST

	Names																	
Removal From Water	Shallow Water Assist																	
	Drag																	
	Lift																	
Spinal Injury Management	Hip and Shoulder Support																	
	Head Splint																	
	Head/Chin Support																	
	Boarding Procedures																	
	Removal From Water																	
Rescue Breathing	Shallow Water																	
	Deep Water																	
Mask, Fins, Snorkel	Clearing and Relieving Pressure																	
	Sit-in Entry																	
	Stride-Jump Entry																	
	Swimming																	
Final Tests	Written																	
	Skill 1																	
	Skill 2																	
	Skill 3																	
	Skill 4																	

Checklists are not to be sent to chapter. Retain for own use.

EMERGENCY WATER SAFETY
WRITTEN TEST

Written Test

Answer Sheet

Note: The answer key is bound on the last page of this manual.

AMERICAN RED CROSS
EMERGENCY WATER SAFETY

IMPORTANT: Read all instructions before beginning this test.

INSTRUCTIONS: Mark all answers in pencil on the separate answer sheet. Do not write on this test. The questions on this test are multiple choice. Read each question slowly and carefully. Then choose the best answer and fill in that circle on the answer sheet. If you wish to change an answer, erase your first answer completely. Return this test to your instructor when you are finished.

1. A useful skill for water rescue is:
   a. Water skiing.
   b. Treading water.
   c. Bobbing.
   d. Butterfly stroke.

2. The difference between an active drowning victim and a passive drowning victim is:
   a. An active victim is quiet, and a passive victim shouts for help.
   b. An active victim floats on his or her back, and a passive victim treads water.
   c. An active victim struggles, and a passive victim slips under water with little or no warning.
   d. An active victim slips underwater with little or no warning, and a passive victim struggles.

3. A human chain is designed to:
   a. Be used in fast moving water.
   b. Be used in water more than waist deep.
   c. Count swimmers at a facility.
   d. Assist someone who is having difficulty in water not above chest depth.

4. When entering water where the depth and bottom conditions are not known, the rescuer should use the:
   a. Stride jump entry.
   b. Compact jump entry.
   c. Feet-first entry.
   d. Ease-in entry.

5. The safest way to rescue a swimmer in deep water 10 feet away is to:
   a. Make a throwing assist.
   b. Make a reaching assist with with your leg.
   c. Swim to the victim.
   d. Make a wading assist.

6. The technique of stabilizing a victim's spine is known as:
   a. Neck stabilization.
   b. Arm/head stabilization.
   c. In-line stabilization.
   d. Shoulder/head stabilization.

7. Approximately 95 percent of diving injuries occur in water that is:
   a. Over 10 feet deep.
   b. Less that 10 feet deep.
   c. Over 5 feet deep.
   d. Less than 5 feet deep.

8. Which of the following factors should influence a rescuer's actions when attempting a rescue?
   a. The location of the victim
   b. The temperature of the water
   c. Strong currents
   d. All of the above

9. Signs and symptoms of possible spinal injury include:
   a. Tingling or numbness in the extremities.
   b. Unconsciousness.
   c. Distortion of the neck.
   d. All of the above.

10. The correct sequence of rescue procedures for a victim of a suspected spinal injury is:
    a. Check for breathing, stabilization of the spine, and removal from the water.
    b. Activate the facility emergency plan, approach the victim carefully, and reduce any movement of the victim's spine.
    c. Approach the victim carefully, remove victim from the water, and check for breathing.
    d. Secure victim to a backboard, check for breathing, and keep victim warm.

11. When no immediate help is available, the simplest support in shallow water for a faceup victim of a suspected spinal injury is:
    a. Hip and foot support.
    b. Hip and shoulder support.
    c. Head and chin support.
    d. Head splint technique.

12. Use of the head/chin support technique requires the rescuer to apply pressure to the chest and spine with his or her:
    a. Hands.
    b. Wrists.
    c. Forearms.
    d. Shoulders.

13. When assessing a victim's injuries, in which situation would you suspect a spinal injury?
    a. Any fall from a height greater than the victim's height
    b. Any person found unconscious or submerged in shallow water for unknown reasons
    c. Any victim with significant head trauma
    d. All of the above

14. A properly performed wrist tow can be used:
    a. On both active and passive victims.
    b. Only on active victims.
    c. Only on passive victims.
    d. Only when a surface dive is used.

15. When lifting a victim from deep water, you should:
    a. Take care to protect the victim's head.
    b. Always maintain contact with the victim.
    c. Lift with your legs, not your back.
    d. All of the above.

16. If a distressed swimmer suddenly tries to grab you, your first reaction would be to use the:
    a. Front head hold escape.
    b. Rear head hold escape.
    c. Block.
    d. Wrist/arm escape.

17. If a victim grasps you firmly by the upper arm, you should:
    a. Submerge and try to swim away.
    b. Allow the victim to hang on until you get tired.
    c. Use the backstroke to swim to safety.
    d. Block the victim and submerge until the victim lets go.

18. The first thing you should do if you are grabbed around the head by a distressed swimmer is to:
    a. Tuck and turn your chin.
    b. Take a breath.
    c. Try to shake free.
    d. Submerge.

19. When entering deep water from a height of more than 5 feet, use the:
    a. Compact jump.
    b. Stride jump.
    c. Ease-in entry.
    d. Feet-first entry.

20. A ladder, flat-bottomed boat, plank, and spare car tire without a rim:
    a. Can be used to make an ice rescue.
    b. Are poor examples of ice rescue equipment.
    c. Should be used to assist a victim with possible spinal injury.
    d. Should not be used in water rescues.

21. What is the best way to open the airway of an unconscious victim?
    a. Tilt the head back and lift the chin.
    b. Tilt the head back and lift the neck.
    c. Tilt the head back and push down on the chin.
    d. Do a finger sweep followed by 6 to 10 abdominal thrusts.

22. A victim is not breathing, You give two breaths and the chest rises. What should you do next?
    a. Give two more breaths.
    b. Begin CPR.
    c. Check for a pulse.
    d. Remove water from the victim's mouth.

23. While boating, you spot a swimmer in distress. You should:
    a. Circle the victim twice before attempting a rescue.
    b. Use a reaching or throwing assist.
    c. Get to shore quickly and seek help.
    d. Leave your boat and swim to the victim.

24. The feet-first surface dive should be used in:
    a. Murky water.
    b. Thick, grassy bottom areas.
    c. Water of unknown depth and bottom conditions.
    d. All of the above.

25. If you see a victim go under water as you are approaching:
    a. Surface dive in the vicinity where you last saw the victim.
    b. Go back to safety and call for help.
    c. Wait for a team of scuba divers to help.
    d. None of the above.

Name _____ Date _____

DIRECTIONS: Fill in the correct answer for each question.

1. (a) (b) (c) (d)   16. (a) (b) (c) (d)

2. (a) (b) (c) (d)   17. (a) (b) (c) (d)

3. (a) (b) (c) (d)   18. (a) (b) (c) (d)

4. (a) (b) (c) (d)   19. (a) (b) (c) (d)

5. (a) (b) (c) (d)   20. (a) (b) (c) (d)

6. (a) (b) (c) (d)   21. (a) (b) (c) (d)

7. (a) (b) (c) (d)   22. (a) (b) (c) (d)

8. (a) (b) (c) (d)   23. (a) (b) (c) (d)

9. (a) (b) (c) (d)   24. (a) (b) (c) (d)

10. (a) (b) (c) (d)   25. (a) (b) (c) (d)

11. (a) (b) (c) (d)

12. (a) (b) (c) (d)

13. (a) (b) (c) (d)

14. (a) (b) (c) (d)

15. (a) (b) (c) (d)

You may wish to go back and check your answers to be sure that you matched the right answer with the right question.

Water Safety Instructor Aide Candidate Evaluation Form

Instructor _____

Course Date(s) and Time(s) _____

Location _____

Water Safety Aide Candidate _____

For each of the following areas, circle "S" (satisfactory), "NI" (needs improvement), or "U" (unsatisfactory). A Water Safety Instructor Aide Candidate must be rated as Satisfactory in order to be certified as an American Red Cross Water Safety Instructor Aide.

Pretest Skills

Level IV Skills   S   NI   UN   _____

Water Safety Skills

Level I   S   NI   UN   _____

Level II   S   NI   UN   _____

Level III   S   NI   UN   _____

Level IV   S   NI   UN   _____

Level V   S   NI   UN   _____

Level VI (Optional)   S   NI   UN   _____

Level VII (Optional)   S   NI   UN   _____

Water Safety Aide Skills

Demonstrating skills correctly   S   NI   UN   _____

Providing corrective feedback   S   NI   UN   _____

Exhibiting enthusiasm   S   NI   UN   _____

Using instructional aids   S   NI   UN   _____

Carrying out instructions in a
    positive manner   S   NI   UN   _____

Final Evaluation

Written test   S   NI   UN   _____

WATER SAFETY INSTRUCTOR AIDE SELF-ASSESSMENT

Water Safety Instructor Aide: Using the assessment categories (1, 2, 3, and 4) described below, rate yourself as well as you can on each of the following water safety aide skills.

```
1 — Fully successful
2 — Successful
3 — Adequate
4 — Needs improvement
N/A — Not applicable
```

1	2	3	4	N/A	Instruction
					1. Possessing knowledge of the American Red Cross Swimming and Water Safety program.
					2. Being able to assist in identifying, removing, and/or minimizing hazards in or around the swimming areas.
					3. Assisting with registration and record keeping.
					4. Assisting with setting up and storing equipment as necessary.
					5. Providing accurate demonstrations of the swimming strokes, skills, and safety techniques when needed.
					6. Observing and noting participant errors.
					7. Providing corrective feedback to participants.
					8. Being able to understand and explain the facility's safety rules and regulations.
					9. Demonstrating the use of various instructional swimming aids.
					10. Using and leading games and water activities in the water effectively.
					11. Encouraging student participation.
					12. Being aware of my personal image—qualities that add or detract from my other Water Safety Instructor Aide Skills.

WATER SAFETY INSTRUCTOR AIDE
WRITTEN TEST

Written Test
Answer Key

Name _____

IMPORTANT: Read all instructions before beginning this test.

INSTRUCTIONS: Mark all answers in pencil on this sheet. The questions on this test are multiple choice. Read each question slowly and carefully, then fill in the blank with the letter of your answer. If you wish to change an answer, erase your first answer completely. Return this test to your instructor when you are finished.

1. _____ The minimum age required to enroll in an American Red Cross Learn to Swim course is—
   A. 10 years of age.
   B. 16 years of age.
   C. None, **except** for Infant and Preschool Aquatics.
   D. Any age, as long as the student has finished the seventh grade.

2. _____ The best reason for everyone to be aware of safe diving rules is to—
   A. Prevent possible spinal injury.
   B. Avoid legal problems.
   C. Prevent double drowning.
   D. Encourage participation in competitive diving.

3. _____ A Water Safety Instructor Aide can issue student—
   A. Certificates.
   B. Diplomas.
   C. Authorizations.
   D. None of the above.

4. _____ The role and responsibilities of a Water Safety Instructor Aide include all of the following **except**—
   A. Providing clerical assistance to the instructor.
   B. Providing medical assistance to the instructor.
   C. Providing supervisory assistance to the instructor.
   D. Providing teaching assistance to the instructor.

5. _____ Appropriate water adjustment activities for children include all of the following **except**—

    A. Blowing floatable toys across the water.

    B. Squeezing a sponge full of water over their parent's head.

    C. Playing games.

    D. Being forced into the water.

6. _____ To perform a reaching assist in a drowning situation, an appropriate item to use is—

    A. A ring buoy.

    B. An oar.

    C. A towel.

    D. All of the above.

7. _____ The minimum age required to enroll in an American Red Cross Water Safety Instructor course is—

    A. 5 years of age.

    B. 17 years of age.

    C. Any age, as long as the participant can swim well.

    D. No age requirement.

8. _____ To increase buoyancy while learning a skill, a student may use—

    A. A Coast Guard-approved life jacket.

    B. Inflatable arm bands.

    C. A kickboard.

    D. All of the above.

9. _____ A Water Safety Instructor Aide can assist an instructor in all of the following ways **except**—

    A. Preparing equipment.

    B. Giving demonstrations.

    C. Providing participants with corrective feedback.

    D. Accepting sole responsibility for the participants.

10. _____ A Water Safety Instructor Aide is responsible for following a facility's Emergency Action Plan (EAP). An EAP includes all of the following **except**—

    A. Having posted procedures on how to call 911.

    B. Having safety equipment and a well-stocked first aid kit readily available.

    C. Having an emergency signal.

    D. Knowing how to perform emergency medical techniques.

1. **C**   The minimum age required to enroll in an American Red Cross Learn to Swim course is—
   A. 10 years of age.
   B. 16 years of age.
   C. None, **except** for Infant and Preschool Aquatics.
   D. Any age, as long as the student has finished the seventh grade.

2. **A**   The best reason for everyone to be aware of safe diving rules is to—
   A. Prevent possible spinal injury.
   B. Avoid legal problems.
   C. Prevent double drowning.
   D. Encourage participation in competitive diving.

3. **D**   A Water Safety Instructor Aide can issue student—
   A. Certificates.
   B. Diplomas.
   C. Authorizations.
   D. None of the above.

4. **B**   The role and responsibilities of a Water Safety Instructor Aide include all of the following **except**—
   A. Providing clerical assistance to the instructor.
   B. Providing medical assistance to the instructor.
   C. Providing supervisory assistance to the instructor.
   D. Providing teaching assistance to the instructor.

5. **D**   Appropriate water adjustment activities for children include all of the following **except**—
   A. Blowing floatable toys across the water.
   B. Squeezing a sponge full of water over their parent's head.
   C. Playing games.
   D. Being forced into the water.

6. __D__   To perform a reaching assist in a drowning situation, an appropriate item to use is—

     A. A ring buoy.

     B. An oar.

     C. A towel.

     D. All of the above.

7. __B__   The minimum age required to enroll in an American Red Cross Water Safety Instructor course is—

     A. 5 years of age.

     B. 17 years of age.

     C. Any age, as long as the participant can swim well.

     D. No age requirement.

8. __D__   To increase buoyancy while learning a skill, a student may use—

     A. A Coast Guard-approved life jacket.

     B. Inflatable arm bands.

     C. A kickboard.

     D. All of the above.

9. __D__   A Water Safety Instructor Aide can assist an instructor in all of the following ways **except**—

     A. Preparing equipment.

     B. Giving demonstrations.

     C. Providing participants with corrective feedback.

     D. Accepting sole responsibility for the participants.

10. __D__   A Water Safety Instructor Aide is responsible for following a facility's Emergency Action Plan (EAP). An EAP includes all of the following **except**—

     A. Having posted procedures on how to call 911.

     B. Having safety equipment and a well-stocked first aid kit readily available.

     C. Having an emergency signal.

     D. Knowing how to perform emergency medical techniques.

SOURCES FOR WATER SAFETY INSTRUCTOR'S MANUAL

Adams, J. A. "A Closed-Loop Theory of Motor Learning." *Journal of Motor Behavior,* 3(1971):111-150.

The American National Red Cross. *Adapted Aquatics: Swimming for Persons with Physical or Mental Impairments.* Garden City, New York: Doubleday & Co., Inc., 1977.

The American National Red Cross. *Guide for Training Instructors: Adapted Aquatics Programs.* Washington, D.C.: The American National Red Cross, 1980.

The American National Red Cross. *Methods in Adapted Aquatics: A Manual for the Instructor.* Washington, D.C.: The American National Red Cross, 1980.

Anshel, M.H. "Cognitive Strategies to Teach Motor Skills to Elderly Learners in Nursing Homes." Paper presented to American Alliance for Physical Education, Recreation and Dance, 17-21 April 1985, in Atlanta, Georgia.

Arthur, M. & Ackroyd-Stoland, S. *A Resource Manual on Canoeing for Disabled People.* Toronto: Canadian Recreational Canoeing Association., (n.d.)

Brancazio, P. *Sport Sciences.* New York: Simon & Schuster, 1984.

British Sports Association for the Disabled. *Water Sports for the Disabled.* Woking, England: Royal Yachting Association Seamanship Foundation, 1983.

Bruya, L.D. & Langendorfer, S.J. "Decrease Liability Risks with Proper Documentation." *Aquatics* 1 (1989):21-24.

Canadian Red Cross *Manual on Teaching Swimming for the Disabled.* Toronto: Canadian Red Cross Society., (n.d.)

Colwin, C. *Swimming into the Twenty-first Century.* Champaign, Illinois: Human Kinetics Publishers, 1991.

Councilman: J.E. *The Science of Swimming.* Englewood Cliffs, New Jersey: Prentice Hall, 1968.

Fitts, P. M. "Factors in Complex Skill Training." In R. Glasser (Ed.), *Training Research and Education.* New York: John Wiley, 1965.

_____. "Perceptual-Motor Skill Learning." In A.W. Melton (Ed.), *Categories of Human Learning,* New York: Academic Press, 1964.

_____. *Human Performance.* Belmont, California: Brooks/Cole Publishing, 1967. Gentile, A.M. "A Working Model of Skill Acquisition with Application to Teaching." *Quest,* 17(1972):3-23.

_____. The Structure of Motor Tasks. *Mouvement.* Actes du 7e Symposium en Apprentissage Psycho-moteur et Psychologie due Sport. Quebec City, Canada: 1975.

Grosse, S.J. "It's a Wet and Wonderful World." *Palaestra* 2 (1985):14f.

_____. "Use and Misuse of Flotation Devices in Adapted Aquatics." *Palaestra* 4 (1987):31f.

Harrod, D.L. & Langendorfer, S.J. "A Scalogram Analysis of the American Red Cross Beginner Skill Order." *National Aquatic Journal* 6: (1990) 12-16.

Hay, J.G. & Reid, J.G. *The Anatomical and Biomechanical Basis for Human Motion.* Englewood Cliffs, New Jersey: Prentice Hall, 1982.

Haywood, K.M. *Lifespan Motor Development.* Champaign, Illinois: Human Kinetics Publishers, 1986.

Heckathorn, J. *Strokes and Strokes.* Reston, Virginia: American Alliance for Health, Physical Education, Recreation and Dance, 1980.

Hedley, E. *Boating for the Handicapped.* Albertson, New York: Human Resources Center, 1980.

Jackson, E. "Cultural Diversity: Attracting Minority Staff, Participants, Requires Understanding and Perseverance" Aquatics *International,* November/December 1991:14-18.

Johnson, R. & Nelson, J. *Measurement and Evaluation in Physical Education.* 3rd Ed. Minneapolis: Burgess, 1986.

Langendorfer, S. J. "Aquatic Movement Patterns: Developmental and Environmental Perspectives." *Children and Water,* Special Issue of *Children's Environments Quarterly,* 1987.

_____. "Aquatics for the Young Child: Facts and Myths." Journal of Physical Education, Recreation, and Dance, 57 (1986):63-69.

_____. "Early Childhood Aquatics: Risks and Benefits." *Pediatric Exercise Science* 1 (1989)3:30-43.

Langendorfer, S.J., Bruya, L.D., & Reid, A. "Facilitating Aquatic Motor Development: A Review of Developmental and Environmental Variables." In J.H. Humphrey & J.E. Clark (Eds.), *Advances in Motor Development Research,* Vol. 2, AMS Press, 1987.

Langendorfer, S.J., Harrod, D.L., & Bruya, L.D. "Prescriptive Aquatic Instruction." *National Aquatics Journal* 5 (1989):10,12.

Langendorfer, S. J. "Separating Fact from Fiction in Preschool Aquatics." *National Aquatics Journal,* 3 (1987):1.

Langendorfer, S.J., Roberts, M., & Ropka, C.R. "Aquatic Readiness: A Developmental Test." *National Aquatics Journal* 3(1987):9-12.

Langendorfer, S.J. "Aquatics for Young Children with Handicapping Conditions." *Palaestra,* Spring 1989:17-19, 37-40.

Langendorfer, S.J. & Bruya, L.D. "Developmental Aquatics: Water Experiences for Preschool Children." *Future Focus,* Winter 1989, G-9.

Langendorfer, S.J., German, E.W., & Kral, D. "Aquatics Games and Gimmicks for Young Children." *National Aquatics Journal* 4 (1988):14-16.

Langendorfer, S.J., Gray, D.P., & Bruya, L.D. "Children's Aquatics: Managing the Risks." *Parks and Recreation* February, 1989:20-24.

Magill, R.A. *Motor Learning: Concepts and Applications.* Dubuque: W.C. Brown, 1989.

Maglisho, E. *Swimming Faster.* Palo Alto, California: Mayfield, 1984.

Newman, J. *Swimming for Children with Physical and Sensory Impairments.* Springfield, Illinois: Charles Thomas, 1976.

Priest, L. "Diving for the Disabled." *National Aquatics Journal,* 1 (1985):14.

_____. "Lifeguarding the Disabled." *National Aquatics Journal* 5 (1989):17.

Roberton, M. A. & Halverson, L.E. *Developing Children—Their Changing Movement.* Philadelphia: Lea & Febiger, 1984.

_____. *Developing Children—Their Changing Movement:* Philadelphia Lea & Febiger, 1984.

Robinson, J., & Fox, A.D. *Diving with Disabilities.* Champaign, Illinois: Leisure Press, 1986.

Safrit, M.J. *Introduction to Measurement in Exercise and Sport,* St. Louis: Mosby Yearbook, 1989.

Sage, G.H. *Motor Learning and Control: A Neuropsychological Approach.* Dubuque: W.C. Brown, 1984.

Schmidt, R.A. "A Schema Theory of Discrete Motor Skill Learning," *Psychological Review* 82 (1975):225-260.

_____. *Motor Control and Learning.* Champaign, Illinois: Human Kinetics, 1982.

Smith, D.W.; Bierman, E.L.; and Robinson, N.M. *The Biologic Ages of Man from Conception through Old Age.* Philadelphia: W.B. Saunders Co., 1978.

Smith, E.L.; and Serfass, R.C. "Exercise and Aging." Papers presented at the ACSM annual meeting, 28-30 May 1991, in Las Vegas, Nevada.

Smith, Y. R. "Issues and Strategies for Working with Multicultural Athletes." *Journal of Physical Education, and Dance,* March 1991:39-44.

Whitbourne, S.K. *Physiological Changes and Psychological Consequences.* New York: Springer-Verlag New York Inc., 1985.

YMCA of the USA. *Aquatics for Special Populations.* Champaign, Illinois: Human Kinetics, 1987.